THE ALLIANCE FOR YOUNG ARTISTS & WRITERS PRESENTS

THE BEST TEEN WRITING OF 2009

FOREWORD BY

LEE PFAEHLER
Portfolio Gold Medalist

GENERAL WRITING PORTFOLIO	SHORT STORY	HUMOR	NOVEL	SELECTED NATIONAL AWARD WINNERS FROM THE SCHOLASTIC ART & WRITING AWARDS
		PERSONAL ESSAY/ MEMOIR	DRAMATIC SCRIPT	
		NONFICTION PORTFOLIO	JOURNALISM	SCIENCE FICTION/ FANTASY / POETRY

THE SCHOLASTIC ART & WRITING AWARDS

Alliance for Young Artists & Writers

For information or permission contact:
Alliance for Young Artists & Writers
557 Broadway
New York, NY 10012
212-343-6493
www.artandwriting.org

Anthology printing, September 2009
ISBN-13: 978-0-545-23153-4
ISBN-10: 0-545-23153-1

The Best Teen Writing of 2009 is dedicated to
Lisa Feder-Feitel, the most generous, intelligent,
compassionate, passionate, patient volunteer ever to serve
the Alliance for Young Artists & Writers. Lisa's contribution to
the lives of countless creative teenagers is immeasurable, and the
Alliance is deeply grateful for her tireless commitment to the
future innovators, visionaries, and paradigm-shifters who
will one day reshape America.

ABOUT THE BEST TEEN WRITING OF 2009

The works featured in *The Best Teen Writing of 2009* are selected from The Scholastic Art & Writing Awards, a national program presented by the Alliance for Young Artists & Writers, which recognizes talented teenagers in the visual and literary arts. The Awards were founded in 1923 to celebrate the accomplishments of creative students and extend to them the same opportunities for recognition that their athletic and academic classmates enjoy.

In 2009, more than 140,000 artworks and manuscripts were submitted to 81 regional affiliates. Professional artists, authors, educators, and creative industry leaders reviewed the works without knowledge of the students' identities and with no restrictions on the content, looking for excellence in three criteria: technical skill, originality, and the emergence of a personal voice.

Approximately 30,000 students were recognized on the local level. Of those students, 1,000 received national awards. These young artists and writers have joined the ranks of artists and authors including Richard Avedon, Truman Capote, Bernard Malamud, Carolyn Forché, Philip Pearlstein, Sylvia Plath, Joyce Carol Oates, Joyce Maynard, Andy Warhol, and countless others who won awards when they were teenagers.

This year, 385 young writers received national recognition through The Awards. Forty-eight were chosen for *The Best Teen Writing of 2009*. The writing selected represents the diversity of the national award winners, including age and grade, gender, genre, geography, and subject matter. A complete listing of national award winners and a broader selection of works from The Awards can be found on our website at **www.artandwriting.org**.

To learn how to submit writing to The Scholastic Art & Writing Awards visit **www.artandwriting.org**.

NATIONAL JURORS

Student works are juried by an impressive roster of creative professionals—artists, authors, educators and industry leaders—some of whom are past Scholastic Award recipients. Notable jurors have included Philip Pearlstein, Robert Frost, Judy Blume, Chuck Palahniuk, Faith Ringgold, and Billy Collins. Panelists look for works that exemplify originality, technical skill and the emergence of a personal voice and vision. All work is judged blindly, without any knowledge of the student's gender, age, or hometown.

We are grateful the 2009 jurors for their commitment to finding compelling young voices:

GENERAL WRITING PORTFOLIO
Francine Prose
Mirtha Ojito
Nancy Bass Wyden

DRAMATIC SCRIPT
Stew
Deborah Forte
Liz Swados

HUMOR
Carmelita Tropicana
Marga Gomez
Sarah MacLean
Will Durst

JOURNALISM
Andrea Barnet
Moira Bailey
Steve Silberman

PERSONAL ESSAY/MEMOIR
Esther Allen
Karrie Jacobs
Richard Gehr

POETRY
Alice Quinn
Thomas Ellis
Patricia Smith

NONFICTION WRITING PORTFOLIO
David Shenk
Lauren Keane
Thane Rosenbaum

SCIENCE FICTION/FANTASY
Alan Dean Foster
Paul Giamatti
Elizabeth Devereaux

SHORT STORY
Rick Moody
Judy Goldberg
Sarah Darer Littman

SHORT SHORT STORY
Kathryn Harrison
Jill Eisenstadt
Francisco Goldman

AMERICAN VOICES
Sarah Lazin
Mary Beth Barber
Gersh Kuntzman

CONTENTS

PORTFOLIO GOLD MEDALS

Graduating high school seniors may submit a portfolio of 3 to 8
works for review by authors, educators, and literary professionals.
Winners of the General Writing Portfolio and Nonfiction Portfolio
Gold Medals receive a $10,000 scholarship.

SELECTIONS FROM THE GOLD, SILVER, & AMERICAN VOICES MEDALS

Students in grades 7–12 submit work in 11 writing categories. This year, more than 20,000 writing submissions were reviewed by authors, educators, and literary professionals. Gold, Silver, and American Voices Medals were awarded to works that demonstrated originality, technical skill, and emergence of a personal voice.

Poetry

Personal Essay/Memoir

Science Fiction/Fantasy

Dramatic Script

Journalism

Short Story

Humor

Short Short Story

EDITOR'S INTRODUCTION

Twenty-one pounds of literature squatted on my front porch: muddy cardboard, dubious FedEx man, barking dogs, and all. After lugging it up into my small corner room, I glared at the box. How dare those not-for-profit New Yorkers charge me with this duty? Best Teen Writing indeed! I was 19, back at home, and still in my pajamas at noon. Who in their right mind would entrust this to me?

I opened the box. It was the thought of actually having to read that struck me as daunting. I had no doubts that the writing would be above-par. Judging was going to be the hardest part. I read several cubic ounces of humor, plumbed poetry from stacks the width of my spread palm, gleaned meaning from each personal essay.

As much as our generation strives to unveil its personality, it is in seeking universal truths that we excel. Writers choose to grapple with pen and paper, dragging words from the corners of our minds and pinning them into a form or molding a shape from captured diction. The writing in this collection brings together essays on how to cope with a parent's death and how to lead yourself out of silence; poetry pining for lost innocence and celebrating dietary diversity; humorous looks at the SAT and female images in the media; dramatic scripts that pluck emotion from the most immutable hearts.

All of the writers and artists who submitted their work to The Scholastic Art & Writing Awards willingly put their work in front of professionals. While reading through 21 pounds of winning submissions, one word flitted through my mind: brave. Each writer put their heart in the piece and their piece on the line. Anyone who has the courage to make a move as gutsy as taking something they fully believe in and saying, "Look, you should believe too," has won my admiration. If later they profess that they didn't believe in it at all—that the piece was a happy accident born of strife—then I am even more astounded.

Though The Scholastic Art & Writing Awards remains a prestigious contest, winning should not be the goal. Submitting as many works as you can is fine. But if you find yourself catering to that rumored Scholastic Art & Writing Awards ideal, you must stop. You must put down pen and paper, retreat from your computer, and find something adventurous to read. Or go outside and experience something new. Do anything that will free yourself from self-limitation.

The moral: Winning is not the end-all-be-all. The point is to keep writing. If you stop, you'll never get anywhere. Don't just write what you know. Write what you think others know, how you think cars will work in the future, why loons sound so sad. Write what you feel. Write what you think. Write what you believe in!

Remember to also thank those who helped you along the way. I wouldn't have been able to even find my way to the office if it weren't for the entire Alliance staff. Special thanks go to Lisa Feder-Feitel (for providing a wonderful place to stay), Alex Tapnio (for keeping me on task), and Matt Boyd (for being so patient with each of my thousand questions). I must award my parents, my stepfather, and my little brother special gratitude for making my life thus far so positive and thought-provoking. Lastly, I have to thank the people who most influenced this wonderful experience: Jeffrey, Victoria, Zan, Rachael, Lucy, Tristan, Amanda, Kaitelyn, Harry, Katherine, Blake, Maddie, Logan, Kevin, and Rene Bufo Miles.

—Virginia Lee Pfaehler

Virginia Lee Pfaehler received the General Writing Portfolio Gold Medal and a $10,000 scholarship from the Alliance for Young Artists & Writers in 2008. She painstakingly selected all of the works in this anthology. Virginia is also the author of a poetry collection, Weighted Friction. *In 2009, she will be a college sophomore in Charleston, South Carolina.*

A MESSAGE FROM THE NATIONAL WRITING PROJECT

Pablo Picasso said, "All children are artists. The problem is how to remain an artist once one grows up." In this anthology, we see the work of young adults perched between childhood and adulthood, who have learned, or are in the process of learning, how to remain artists as they grow up. We are thankful to the Alliance for Young Artists & Writers for its dedication to fostering a lifelong commitment to the art of writing in the best young writers of today. We know, in part from the legacy of Scholastic Award winners, that these student writers will shape the literary landscape of the United States in the future.

The Best Teen Writing of 2009 anthologizes works selected from the winners of The Scholastic Art & Writing Awards. The pieces represent a wide range of the very best writing by teens from around the country.

The young people whose pieces are anthologized here represent students from rural and urban places, and from many different racial and ethnic cultural backgrounds. The National Writing Project appreciates The Alliance's commitment to value and seek diversity. We believe this anthology is strengthened by the vast array of cultures and experiences that the young authors bring to their writing.

The National Writing Project strives to focus the knowledge, expertise, and leadership of our nation's educators on sustained efforts to improve writing and learning for all young people. We know that learning to write well is one of the most challenging tasks for anyone, regardless of age. It takes time, practice, and lots of encouragement. We are pleased to celebrate the talent and the diligence of the authors represented in this book. We also recognize and salute the work of the adults—parents, teachers, and out-of-school mentors—who supported, nurtured, and helped to develop the skills and practices that produced these pieces.

—Dr. Sharon J. Washington, Ph.D.
Executive Director,
National Writing Project

YOUNG WRITERS

Like you, I began writing as a teenager. First, at home, far away, in the Carpathian Mountains. I wrote thoughts and commentaries on the Bible. Then, in various children's homes in France. Actually, I cannot remember myself without pen and paper–except when I was over there.

By now, I am sure you already know that there is something magically painful and exulting in putting words together. In a way, it is like bringing two people together. Their encounter is always fruitful, for it creates meaning.

The curiosity before a blank page, the anguish in trying to discover the right word, the joy in finding it: Obviously, you have already experienced it. Now you must continue. Invent your own myths, draw from your fantasy. Your worries, your aspirations. Impressions of your teachers, nostalgic memories of wanderings, the awakening of desire. There is more in your adolescence than you think; you will never run out of themes.

But remember, writers are and must be readers. He or she who thinks otherwise lives to regret it. The more books you read, the more pages you write. You absorb images and feelings invented by others; subconsciously, they help you communicate your own.

Naturally, you are neither Shakespeare nor Faulkner; but nor were they when they were young.

Good luck.

—Elie Wiesel

Elie Wiesel has written numerous novels, poetry collections, and essays on the Jewish religion. He is best known for his trilogy of memoirs Night, Dawn, *and* Day. *He was awarded the Nobel Peace Prize in 1986, the same year he established the Elie Wiesel Foundation for Humanity.*

PORTFOLIO GOLD MEDALS

GRADUATING HIGH SCHOOL SENIORS MAY SUBMIT A PORTFOLIO OF 3–8 WORKS FOR REVIEW BY AUTHORS, EDUCATORS, AND LITERARY PROFESSIONALS. WINNERS OF THE GENERAL WRITING PORTFOLIO AND NONFICTION PORTFOLIO GOLD MEDALS RECEIVE A $10,000 SCHOLARSHIP.

SUMMER
LAUREN YOUNGSMITH, 18

COLORADO ACADEMY
DENVER, CO
TEACHER: BETSEY COLEMAN

On days of quiet
when those who pray to traditions kneel with their knees
making warm circles in the wood
I can watch my mother mowing squares into our backyard
and imagine the explosions going on between each
pillow of grey matter inside her skull,
flickering, kicking off chains of electricity that take turns
tugging each rope of muscle, moving her like a tough little doll
around mulch, haltingly, with frightening strength.
I can watch two mossy brown pools, hooded with lashes,
opening and closing in my sister's face while
she eats a bowl of ramen with red plastic chopsticks
and ask her if she's heard the woodpeckers
in her bedroom wall, and nod, and nothing more.
I can look twice at the softly cooing sheaves of empty watercolor paper
slouching as if with their arms draped around the back of the easel
and wonder what might perhaps bloom across them
in a week's time, in black strings of ink,
from the corner up, when the paper's paling cheeks
and the inevitable screech of arthritis
swoops down too many times through the explosions in my head.
I can fold my hands around paperback and toothbrushes
and the wrists of trees, but the cups of my palms plucking at pockets of air
feels louder and bigger than bars of soap or kitchen counters
I can retreat to bed, my face just warm with the
evening's oil, wearing the same plaid pj's I woke up in,
understand nothing more than the opening and closing of another,
the last summer Sunday.

MY DAD'S MOTHER LIVES IN A PLACE WHERE
LAUREN YOUNGSMITH

My dad's mother lives in a place where Jesus' eyes
hang from every wall, framed with sleepless greens
from hallways full of the sounds of shuffling
feet wrapped in paper, release forms, like insects rubbing dry wing against wing
through the smell of disinfectant she plods on all fours, front legs chrome bones
and curled little cloven tennis ball paws
that make her walk like there's no need to be heard.
Her room is full of pictures of family members: ten children, their children,
their wives and their husbands, for pointing themselves out when they visit,
as if photographs speak louder than flesh
in a memory blurred by stroke.
The other inmates huddle around the birdcage like tired clouds
remembering yellow, knees that bend and straighten, things that sing.

She used to lead us out into the courtyard, decked out in florals,
slip me the peppermints my dad loved
and pass the evergreen—as tall as me—that began growing
the year he died, her knuckles pulled tight
by Jesus and war, a dead husband, wheelchair rubber, and
the dirt of a farm where he caught a turkey for Thanksgiving bare-handed.
The picture of my family—pairs of eyes that don't match the rest—
I am wearing a pink sweatshirt I don't remember owning.
My mother, as if she's conducting an experiment,
asks her if she remembers my dad, and she replies that
he hasn't been here since last week.

DEMONS CAN'T JUMP
LAUREN YOUNGSMITH

"Demons can't jump," says my grandmother, and then shakes her head, her jowls moving along with it. "Not where I grow up."

My grandmother, Popo, sits cross-legged on the sunken couch like a frog, folding the laundry, eternally 12 and 70 at the same time. She grew up in a village in southern China where nobody had any doors to keep closed. Popo says there was an old blind woman who spent all her days sitting with a cat in her lap, just within sight of anyone standing outside her front door. Popo straightens the creases in the folded clothing the way she does when she makes paper cranes. "We sit and sit and watch her," she says, "just sitting there, and then we take turns and one of my friends ruuun-run-run up and touch her, like dat! And then we ruuun-run-run back, and she yell and try chase us, but she trip over the doorstep because she blind, and we laaaaugh-laugh-laugh." She laughs now, her eyes folded into soft pillows of flesh. She explains to me that in her village, although nobody had doors, they all had a bar of earth or bricks that rose a foot from the ground to separate the inside of the house from the outside. "And so well, we can get in, but the demons can't," she says, "because in China, the demon, he can't jump." When she finishes, she has the bright look of someone who just stumbled upon something they'd long decided was lost. She laughs again, now softer, and says, "You know, I feel bad for dat lady."

Popo always asks a week ahead of time what kind of food my sisters and I want to eat when we get to Hawaii, but we always ask for the same things. She never called the year her sister died. But the table was still set when we got there, laden with bowls of boiled red peanuts, edemame, sashimi, mangoes, poke, and sliced papayas. My Popo ushered us in saying, "Popo know what you girls like," her hands moving like two thin brown moths.

She sits, nibbling on peanuts and telling us about her child self like she was still the same little girl, plucking the wings off of dragonflies and teasing blind women. She remembers the ship that brought her from China to America, and how her sisters just told her now that pirates had boarded the ship while she was asleep.

"My sisters call me Baby," she says, "and all my life, everybody call me Baby." Popo still lives up to that nickname at 76, four-foot-eleven, with an incredible love for what small things she can laugh at. The only thing about Popo that ever grows is her purse. "I got everything but da kitchen sink," she says. When we take her to the dim sum restaurant on the outskirts of Honolulu's Chinatown, I put my arm in hers and walk her across the street. I like to touch the soft skin on her arm where most people grow fatty flaps as they get older. Sometimes I wonder if she notices. She walks like a toddler, stumping along and laughing.

The space and time between Popo as a child and Popo now are something I only know about through fragments and hasty stories my mother divulges in a voice that means to say, "You aren't big enough to know this, but I'll tell you anyway."

Somehow I think her sense of humor now is much the same as it was when she was a girl in China. I look at her and try to imagine the translation of Old-World Popo to the hot, bright, steamy, big-screen-reclining-chair-Today-World Popo. In my mind I see her suddenly waking up to realize that she was in this new place and time, a world where all the walls are white. I see her realizing that she was already too late to keep up with it, and then settling down inside her own little sweet-smelling kitchen full of jars, perfectly content to fill the sink with soap bubbles in her bare feet, toes painted red. Sometimes I catch her looking out the windows at Pearl Harbor, holding her heaviest pair of binoculars. She is allergic to the sun, so we always bring umbrellas when we go to the beach—Popo calls them "um-blellas"—but she always spots the rainbows first when each rainshower ends. Her favorite kinds are the double rainbows, one arc spreading a little higher than the other.

Sometimes, when she's being thoughtful, Popo gives me a skeleton—a sad memory. She gets a look in her eyes like they ache—difficult to imagine beneath the childlike drawl, and the careless little black bun perched at the top of her head. She gives me a skeleton, a memory, a girl from her village who had sex before she was married. "They take her and put her in big cage," she says, "Big enough to put the pig. And they drown her in the well." There are skeletons hidden behind my grandfather in his slippers and the belt he used to teach Popo lessons when my mother went to college. However, Popo's liveliest skeleton belongs to her son—a skeleton that lives in the basement, just below the white-carpeted floors of the square house on the hill. My Uncle Wesley lives there with his 7-year-old son Marcus, but for me, "Wesley" is just a voice outside packing Marcus into the car or a name spit from my mother's mouth like watermelon seeds. For several years now, my mother has banned him from coming upstairs when we are around. I knew nothing but assumed my mother had her reasons, as she always does. I can imagine my Popo protesting quietly, deriding herself for having somehow raised two children who could hate.

My mother told me the whole story, sitting over mashed potatoes in a diner in Anchorage last summer. Wesley assaulted his step-daughter, Rachel, who I met only twice and traded Beanie Babies with. His wife had been in bed with them. He lost his medical license, was put under house arrest, and the story was publicly broadcasted in Honolulu. "Popo didn't leave the house for two years," my mother said, her jaw clenching, "she refused to talk to any of her family, she was so ashamed. All of her hair fell out." I can't imagine my Popo, shut alone in her little white house, bald, a wounded baby owl—ashamed in a way only the Old World could have prepared her to be. I think of all the plastic hair clips she has in her bathroom drawers that look like little colored alligators. Jesus, Wesley, I think—Uncle Wesley, with his thin, nasal voice and horn-rimmed glasses—he used to call me "princess."

I know enough about my culture to know that my Popo was raised to obey. I can see it every day I'm with her. She never said a word to my grandfather, drunk and full of heavy, red rage; and she never says a word now. But my grandfather, Keong Keong, is too old to drink too much. He is too tired to get mad over nothing. Now the two just heckle each other like chickens. I flinch to hear Keong Keong snap: "Shut up, Mommy." She blinks several times, her eyes big beneath her glasses, and shuts up like she's used to it. Later, when I ask him something and he doesn't reply, Popo will giggle and say, "He can't hear you, Ro-ren," as she pantomimes a deaf person. I asked my mother why they fight so much, whether they truly didn't like each other, and she was stunned. "Not at all," she laughs, "Popo and Keong Keong have always been that way! That's the only way they know how to love."

A few years ago we bought my grandparents a framed portrait from their wedding as an anniversary gift. It was a hologram that morphed into a current picture of them standing together in the same exact position but weathered, a little shrunken. Keong Keong holds his arm around her just as he had on their wedding, grinning toothlessly. They look full in every way. Popo wears a tie-dyed t-shirt and jeans. I asked my mother what it was like, growing up, trying to get a better sense of that porcelain army-wife Popo from the wedding. She smiled in a way I hardly ever see my mother smile; the way she smiles when she looks at pictures of my sisters and me, chubby babies sleeping against each other on Popo and Keong Keong's porch. "My childhood was like the Cleavers'," she explained. "The mother stayed home, watched the kids and cooked, the father came home and played with the kids, and the kids played and never got into any trouble."

This is the most normal thing I've ever heard about anyone's life in my family. I was about to ask whether she wasn't severely mistaken, but I couldn't get over that smile. Her eyes fold back into the creases the way my grandmother's do. My mom still has scars behind her ears, where the doctors borrowed skin to create an extra crease in her eyelid. "I want two creases like you," she said, "Your Popo gave those to you."

I think my grandmother knows better than anyone else how demons move in America. Not only can they jump, but they can climb through windows and pick locks. And if they still can't get in, they might ply their trade at the doorstep of your basement, slipping in by some more sympathetic means and entering the house from below. Having grown up in a household without demons, she had the kind of childhood she wanted to give my mother—a white one, the kind with wide-open windows, the best of the Old World tucked inside the new. Apparently, she succeeded in those bright Cleaver years, but somehow that story is the least real to me—beautiful, maybe, but completely foreign. Instead, I feel more comfortable wading through my family's skeletons, building my own history as they turn up. It's the tragedies that make a family: the felonies, offenses, the mistakes and the missteps, the diseases and the deaths. It's not in moving on but in taking root, marrying yourself to the tragedies of your own people and culture. Popo may have raised my mom upon her one sublime slice of childhood, but that wasn't enough to escape tragedy. Nor was it enough for my own mother. Sometimes people tell me I am strong, and I'd like to say, "No, my family is just unlucky." Somehow it's the same thing. That strength is maybe the one thing my Popo never meant to give, something that grew inside her when she crossed the ocean in a boat full of pirates and woke up in America. Bad luck or strength, it's something my family will always have after Popo. We will fling our doors open and welcome the demons.

CYANOCITTA CRISTATA
CHELLI RIDDIOUGH, 18
WEST HIGH SCHOOL
MADISON, WI
TEACHER: TIMOTHY STORM

Sometimes the name they give you is all wrong. As if they really knew who you were, kicking your way out of the womb. As if any purple-faced baby, bald and blurry-eyed, looked different from the one across the hospital's hall. But they claimed you were special, that your bawls sounded less like suffering and more like singing. And your eyes, they used to say with wonder, were the most splendid shade of bright blue. So your parents called you Jay, like the bird. Like the bird with the obnoxious call that wakes you up at 5:00 a.m. most days of your childhood.

The thing is, when you're six months old, your eyes turn brown. A lot of human babies, like kittens, are born blue-eyed. Once the melanin branched through your little skull, your eyes deepened to the color of dirt after a storm. Dark, sticky brown, more like a sparrow than a jay. But that would have been a pretty stupid name, too. Your sister got the easy way out. They named her Grace, which wasn't wrong for her at all. She is a ballerina, as graceful as a little bird swooping through the air.

When you're 13 your English teacher makes everyone write a report about their name so you go to the library and check out every book about North American birds. You pick one up and turn to page 84: the blue jay. *Cyanocitta Cristata.* You frown as you read the list of characteristics. The blue jay, says the book, is noisy and bold. A scavenger and garbage-eater. A handsome and conspicuous flirt. A common, cruel bully. Everything you're not.

After you print your report, you look in the mirror. No, not very bird-like. Well, your nose is sort of beakish. But your tan hair, wild and spiraled, looks more like a lion's mane than the preened feathers of a jay. Look at your square jaw and sharp teeth. You could have been a Leo, you want to tell your parents. But they wouldn't understand. They don't know you at all, they just think they do. They don't know you any better than the day you came out of the womb, little hands balled into fists. They owned you, so they named you. Just like all their little goldfish and Barnaby, the dog.

One January morning, your senior year in high school, you're taking out the trash, and when you open the garage door, you find a little dead blue jay curled on the floor. Its talons clutch air; its tiny eyes are clenched shut. Its beak is open but no sound comes out. You put your bags of trash in the can, pick up the dead bird, and place it on top of the pile. Then you close the bin, close the garage, walk up to your house, and close the door. You wash your hands in the sink, take a shower, and put on clean clothes. Your name dies that day.

By the time summer rolls around, you've changed your name to Leo and moved to Manhattan. New York's state bird, you note with an ironic smile, is the bluebird. You like the city because it's a jungle, full of all kinds of animals and all sorts of names. You're not common there. You get an apartment in a tall building and look out the window. Good, you think. Not a bird in sight.

Your parents and sister stay in the Midwest. They're afraid to leave their comfortable little nest. You fly back there a couple of times a year before stopping. Life should be like birds, you think. You raise your kids and let them go and fly your separate ways. Just let me go, you want to tell them. But they won't, you know they won't. So you let them go.

The phone rings one day, deep into your life as Leo, and you pick it up.

"Hello?" you say.

"Jay?" says the voice. It's your sister Grace. Your sister with the plain name but the voice so whispery and full of needles that you'd recognize it anywhere, hidden among the calls of a hundred birds, or channeled through a telephone receiver eight states away and two years apart.

"Grace," you say.

"Mom and Dad are dead," she says.

Always plain with her words, Grace was. She never lied; she never pretended to know things she didn't. She never tried to own you or give you a label. You don't know what to say so you don't say anything. You can't name these emotions, so you don't try. You would just be calling them by names that aren't quite right. Your insides feel as cold as a January morning, and your heart starts to feel small and curled up, like a little dead blue jay lying on the floor of a garage.

"Jay?" she asks. "Jay? Are you there?"

Your name rattles empty inside your ears. Of course. Of course you're Jay, and they knew it all along. You were their son. Who are you to say they didn't know who you were? In fact, they probably knew you better than you know yourself. When you start to cry, it even sounds like singing.

MAYFLY
CHELLI RIDDIOUGH

When I was 11 and Jake Koeppel was 10, we decided to put a mayfly down an anthill. Every summer, our camp had a different insect invasion. One year, moths beat dust around our heads; another, yellow jackets terrorized the cabins. That summer, we'd look down to see mayflies meditating on our arms and legs, and we'd pick them up by their wings and release them into the air. Some of the boys liked to pull them apart, while others cracked them between their fingers like pieces of caramel corn. I didn't have the stomach to do either, so when Jake suggested we feed one to the red ants, I found this passive enough to nod yes.

I had met Jake two days earlier, during our Nature program. His crooked teeth, mischievous smile, and mohawk that curved into a widow's peak above his dark slits of eyes drew me to him like ants to a piece of rotting peach. I trace my chronic attraction to bad boys straight back to that mohawk. Obsessed with this prepubescent rebel, I introduced myself to him in the mud pit. Walking circles in the gray clay, we discussed adventures and Gary Paulson novels. We shared the juvenile dream of living in the wilderness, common among the idealistic kids in our woodsy YMCA camp.

The two of us befriended another camper, who I nicknamed "Ugly Boy." I called Jake "Mohawk" or "Mohawk Man," even though he was a year my junior. As the two boys set out to find a mayfly, I sat on the dirt and supervised the anthill. They brought a mayfly back pinched at the wings, its slim body curling back and forth. With a giggle, Mohawk placed the mayfly at the peak of the anthill and released its wings. He scrambled back and sat down next to me. The three of us watched with silent eyes, our knees pulled up to our chins.

The mayfly tried to crawl away at first, but its feet caught in the damp sand. It didn't take long for the ants to attack it. Piece by tiny piece, they dismembered the mayfly and carried it into the earth, sucking it down until the tips of its wings vanished into the anthill. I could not believe that something so huge, so alive, could be funneled into a pinhole. Neither Mohawk nor Ugly Boy said anything. One by one, we stood up, dusted off our shorts, and walked away.

I saw Jake again two summers later, in his hometown of Mishawaka, Indiana. I barely recognized him: dressed all in black, spikes around his wrist, a moody frown tugging at his mouth. The mohawk was gone, replaced by a forest of black curls. His eyes, though, had not changed: dark, narrow, serpentine. And when I finally coaxed a smile out of him, his lips curled back over familiar crooked teeth. He had ADHD, he told me, and bipolar syndrome. When I ran my fingertips over his smooth white wrists, they snagged on scabs of self-mutilation. I couldn't distinguish his pain from his melodrama. I left confused by this gothic boy, this angry boy. He lost his virginity and started smoking that year. He was twelve.

He seemed happier when I saw him the following summer. His hair had honey streaks from the sun, he wore brown instead of black, he took me to a movie and smiled the whole day. Then we went back to his house. He lived in a tiny, one-story ranch in a seedy section of Mishawaka. Trash and baby toys littered the floors, and the smell of animal urine emanated from the dirty rugs. His mother shouted; his baby brother sat on the floor and wailed; his little sister threw her hairbrush at Jake's head. I cried when I went home because I could do nothing for him. We lived in different universes. But we remained friends.

Jake seemed even better the following summer. His short but curly hair strayed into one eye, which reminded me of his mohawk days. He hugged me and told me he loved me, told me he missed me so much. Then he told me he had tried cocaine, screwed some girls, got drunk every night, and was once again expelled.

"What for?" I asked, concealing my shock.

"I set this black chick's weave on fire while riding the school bus."

If I had heard this on TV I might have laughed, but this was his life. When my mother drove me back home, I thought he was doing okay. I speculated his medication was serving him well, but he would always have some shadows in his heart. When I returned to Indiana for Christmas break, I was reminded that I should never think Jake is "okay."

We sat in his basement for four hours with his friend Anthony. A foot-deep layer of clothes coated the cement floor, concealing bottles of booze, knives, and a boombox. I perched on the couch, which stank of cat piss and watched Jake and Anthony smoke four bowls of weed, and then a fifth from a traffic cone hookah. When his girlfriend called him, Jake told her he had to go because he was busy having sex with me. He hung up cackling and started hitting me with a foam sword. Anthony told us we fought like an old married couple and I frowned, knowing Jake would one day turn into his own deadbeat dad. I knew this as sure as I knew he would turn into a "bad kid." As sure as I know he'll get worse, and worse, and I'll be one of the few people who never leaves him. When he reached over to prod me, I grabbed his wrist, but the milky scars had faded into skin.

Between rounds of weed, Jake helped himself to cigarettes. He closed his eyes and inhaled the smoke, but when I reached over to take a drag he jerked his hand away from mine.

"What are you doing?" he asked.

"Let me get some of that," I said. He looked at me and shook his head.

"That's not the path you're going to take," he told me.

"It's the path you're taking," I said, annoyed.

"Exactly." He took a deep breath of smoke and let it drift over his face.

The cloudy air hurt my eyes and my brain, so I walked upstairs and sat on the living room couch. Karla, his mom, sat down next to me. She wore sweatpants pulled high, a tie-dyed tanktop (no bra), and a light-blue bathrobe. She knew me well by then and regarded me warmly. She also treated me as an enigma among her son's line of slacker guy friends and skanky girlfriends. On the other side of me sat Jake's sister, Caitlyn, 12 years old. Chad, his little brother, was a toddler by then and madly in love with me. He sat on my lap, and together we all talked.

"So Jake takes after his dad?" I asked Karla. I was hesitant to ask this but I'd pried Jake for details about his father for years. His story had stayed the same: I look like him, I hate him, I want to kill him. I'll die before I become him.

"Yeah, he does," said Karla. "Especially as he gets older."

"Do you have any pictures of him?" I asked. She looked at me and for a second I was afraid she would get mad, but then a small, rueful smile crept over her mouth.

"I got pictures," she said, and walked upstairs. She returned a minute later, pulled a flimsy pile of photos from her bathrobe, and plopped down on the saggy couch. On either side of me, Caitlyn and Chad were chewing on miracle-whip-and-fried-baloney sandwiches.

"This is when Jacob was born," she said, and lifted the top picture. I stopped breathing for a moment.

Jake had his father's eyes. Dark, moody, a clear contrast to the mouth twisted into a smile below. The same ridge of his eyebrows, the same hawk nose. When I looked closer at his father's grin, I spotted crooked teeth between the thin lips. The man in the picture had a mullet. His hair was fraught with curls, like Jacob's when it grows out. He was standing with his arms slanted, so you could see the infant in his arms. Jake, I thought.

"This is later," she said. The man had a buzz cut in this photo and was standing outside. Thin, muscled arms stretched over his head. He looked triumphant, crazed.

"This is near the end," she said. He stood by a pool table. He looked angry, weary. I knew that look. I'd seen it on many occasions. I saw it every time I told Jake not to smoke pot. Not to get drunk. Not to have sex. I saw it every time I told him he was turning into his dad.

When I had to leave, I stood at Jake's door and hugged him for a long time. I finally pulled away but reached up and grabbed his face with my hands, holding him in front of me. For the first time in years I studied his skinny eyes and found them the same as the summer I had met him: deep, sticky swamps of molasses, framed with long eyelashes. My mother sat waiting for me in the car, but still I stared at my friend. Between the mirrors of our eyes, I saw the mayfly we had killed and forgotten, struggling at the top of the anthill, slowly being dragged to its death.

ALMONDS
PAULINE HOLDSWORTH, 17
STATE COLLEGE HIGH SCHOOL NORTH
STATE COLLEGE, PA
TEACHER: SANDRA WYNGAARD

I used to have this feeling that you were watching me, though I never caught you at it. Almond eyes feel prickly on my skin—blue ones either make me shiver or make my skin melt, depending on how dark they are. And I didn't know anyone else with eyes the color of dusty nuts or sesame tahini, so I knew it was you right away. You, with the boarded-up eyes and the smile, unpredictable, swinging like on old sign in the wind. Your hair I could never decide on. I used to think maybe wood starting to smoke. Brown with hints of something bursting out underneath, smoldering a bit where it knows it can wait for now.

I've never touched a boy's hair. The closest I ever got was when the shortest boy in my gym class tripped during a football game and hit his head on my knee. I'll admit I was tempted to reach out and just touch the very tips of his hair with the pads of my fingers, but that's not the kind of thing you do in front of people—and shouldn't the first time you touch a boy's hair be special? I didn't know anything about him except that he drank chocolate milk every day and that his last name started with a Z. And I'm twelve now—too old to get away with things like that.

So I still don't know whether sandy hair really leaves phantom grains and bits of salt under your fingernails, or if muddy hair squelches even though it's completely dry. Mud—that was the color of his hair. The boy I almost touched. I haven't really made up my mind about mud. My parents yell at me because they say it never comes out of the bottoms of my jeans, but I think it's one of those things that life would be a little too straight-edged without.

But everybody's felt someone's eyes on them before, so I can tell when yours are stuck to the corner of my right ear during Revolutionary War lessons. I guess I should be a little worried that you're not paying attention, but in case your daydreams have anything to do with me, I'm not going to say a word. Your eyes are sharp at the edges and have that little bite of lemon. Like the grated zest my mother uses to make goulash. It leaps out from the smooth pools that would otherwise be too well-stirred for me to read, in the glances I get when you're looking out the window at the crows arguing on the swing set and not at my ear.

Occasionally I get so worried thinking about how my eyes aren't dark or sweet enough to be chocolate. They're more like grainy wood, the kind you find in furniture from IKEA. Functional enough, but they're not going to compete with the storm clouds gathering in Sarah Miller's eyes. Hers are always threatening lightning, but always hanging on to a little bit of blue, so you think you're safe. Blue is supposed to be the prettiest color of eyes for girls, but Kayla has blue eyes and you couldn't pay me to swap with her. They're a little too easy not to notice.

Getting noticed isn't something I'm good at. Since I don't have flaming hair that makes my cheeks glow like embers, I would need Sarah's storm-cloud eyes. Or maybe eyes almost dark enough to be cracked pepper. People are afraid of Sarah, but they wouldn't be if she had boring dinner-table eyes like me, or hair as straight as the backs of the chairs at my grandmother's house. I don't want to have a wood-colored personality. You can't mix wood with Middle Eastern food or nuts that could have come from miles away. It just makes a mess. Spice mixes with spice and makes it even better. Wood has to be nailed to anything to make it stick. I wonder if you always know when I'm staring at you, because it's like getting a splinter. Or like bumping into a table and just forgetting about it.

But you, with the almond-flavored eyes and the hair that might singe my fingers or smear soot on my palms—you don't know it, but

I know where you live. It's in that plum house on the side of town that is farthest from mine. All your neighbors have dogs that bark too much at passing cars and girls on bicycles. I don't know if you have a dog or not; I didn't hear one barking behind your door (faded white—I thought I could smell the raindrops that left all those streaks on it from your sidewalk. I don't think it rains that much on my side of town), but there were so many different kinds of barks coming from so many different directions that maybe I just got confused. I think that if you do have a dog, it might be some strange quintuple breed, with one ear that stands up and one that flops over, and fur of no color other than dark. I'm not sure what flavor his eyes are, but I can imagine you resting your head on his tender belly and falling asleep reading *The Wind in the Willows*. Of course, he'd never bite.

I haven't been over there for weeks. Well, I haven't ever been over to your house in the sense that you invited me, and I came over after school, took my shoes off and stood there while your mother tried to serve me milk and we each asked the other what we wanted to do.

I haven't been over there for weeks because my mother found too many twigs in the spokes of my bicycle, and where we live all our neighbors rake the sidewalks every time the wind blows. I'm not allowed to ride my bike that far away from home. But I guess I don't really mind. What if you saw me pausing in front of your house (looking up from *The Wind in the Willows* to see if all the tree leaves—burnt sugar, all the artificial flavorings and dyes melting out—had fallen yet) and you came out and asked me what I was doing? What would I say?

"Hi, I was just wondering if you actually like almonds?" And also— I didn't like your neighbor, or at least the one I saw. Maybe your other neighbors are nice, but she looked at me with eyes that reminded me of being stuck in a tunnel and not being able to feel your way out.

There's a tunnel you can walk through and end up in the dried-out riverbed over near that part of town—I mean the part of town you live in; I guess "that part" could mean lots of parts, even mine, though when my mother says "that part" I think she's always talking about yours. It's more of a pipe, actually. It makes echoing sounds as you step. The memory of your passage booms out to get trapped and recorded for future adventurers in the metal above your head. The stones in the riverbed are sharp, because there hasn't been a river to wash the edges away since the summer I was 4, and my mother took me to a picnic with her book club. But the summer I was 7—that's almost five years ago—I ran the whole way down, wincing and trying to laugh. Partly because we were having so much fun and partly because I wanted to have the memory of cutting my feet open playing with my best friend and not minding. But really, I did mind, and really, it was because that best friend was Sarah Miller and her eyes were just starting to flash. I probably wouldn't have done it if they hadn't turned into storm clouds yet, but I could taste the tension of electricity starting to build up in her system when I brushed up against her. Maybe my eyes were beginning to dull into wood and that's another reason why I had to listen. I can't remember. When you're little, your eyes are constantly flitting back and forth, melting in and out of flavors. Somehow I imagine yours were always almond.

I wonder if you can tell my eyes are just wood, like the handles on dresser drawers. Do you ever look at my eyes? Maybe my ear is more interesting. I don't think I've ever really looked at ears, but maybe that's what you do. Maybe you judge people by the curve of their ears and how much space is between the side of the neck and where the ear starts. Maybe you don't think eyes have flavors at all. I could tell you mine are chocolate and you wouldn't question it at all, though I don't know how you bring that up in a conversation. But maybe if you liked my ears, you'd like my eyes and I could make up a new flavor. It wouldn't have to be chocolate. Too many people like chocolate and you can buy Hershey's chocolate bars for 55 cents in the vending machine next to the lunch line. Everything else costs 65 cents.

I never realized that until yesterday afternoon. You were three people behind me in the lunch line, and I'm pretty sure you were staring at the choices on the board instead of at my ear, because I couldn't feel anything prickling the back of my neck. But I guess that almonds go with chocolate. You can buy Hershey bars with almonds, but maybe you don't like that kind of almonds. I think that the kind of almonds your eyes remind me of come from somewhere far away. I'm not good with geography, but I imagine a whole bunch of them rattling and spilling about, in some dusty crate at the bottom of the ship. They wouldn't be coated with salt from the air, because they'd be in the hold (or whatever you call that part of a ship...only I shouldn't have called it that, because now I'm thinking about how maybe you want to hold Sarah's hand.)

Almonds. I have to concentrate.

They would all be different sizes and different shapes. I could take hours sorting them, and I still don't think I could find the one that tasted exactly like your eyes on my ear during history class. I've actually never tasted an almond at all. I think that's a problem. Maybe I could get my mother to buy me some at the supermarket when she's off shopping for pie crusts and cherries to fill them with. But I've never asked for almonds, or even pecans or peanuts, before, so I think she would think that was strange. I think I never thought about almonds till the first day of school, when I felt that strange prickling sensation on my neck and turned around. I think that maybe sometimes I think too much.

GHOSTING
PAULINE HOLDSWORTH

Smudges on car windows are one of the few things that never go away. You take the thing through the car wash. You wipe the windows down yourself, at home. And you stand back, satisfied in the knowledge that you've done your job, that you've done the impossible and turned back the clock. You've peeled away the years and the rainstorms and the salt from melted snow—almost like plucking off the hardened petals on an artichoke, one by one, to reveal the beating heart within.

But every time it rains, those traces of fingerprints come sneaking back. Your breath gets trapped in the cold window and shows you all the times you accidentally let your hand rest on the car window, or wrote your name out in the fog—backward so people in passing cars could read it. Raindrops cut through the haze, but it always closes back again, like the way the ocean slowly sews itself back up after a ship strains through, leaving scars behind, always getting closer to catching up with that receding horizon.

The ghosts start coming back—first slowly, then all at once. A tic-tac-toe game that no one won on the window farthest away from me; an inelegantly drawn heart a little above my left ear. And fingerprints, scattered about by a hand reaching reverently out to the closest thing wide eyes would get to the other world. The world outside, where mountains get swallowed up by mist-ships and where trees slowly give in and bow to the road, pulled into admiration by the weight of glass skins slowly forming on their half-bare branches.

I imagine how it would have looked to her. The world outside fading out as we flew through the clouds. I wonder if she heard the hum of the highway slip away as well, and thought we had actually left the ground. She couldn't feel, as I did, the brief unhinging of reality as we skidded over one of the delicately forming pools of ice, our wheels momentarily disconnected from the pavement. She couldn't see the glances we exchanged in the front seat and hadn't watched the news that morning and seen the warnings about wintry conditions and freezing rain. Face lifted, she waited for the world to come back.

I imagine that when the highway dipped and the car slid smoothly into the valley, it felt like slipping—"not closer and closer to the median" but through the clouds and into fairyland.

Everything sprinkled with sunlight. I once heard cathedrals described as frozen music, but I think it would be more accurate to say that ice storms are frozen music and cathedrals can only try to copy them. I heard the faint click of her seatbelt loosening and falling away as she leaned in and wrote her name on the cloudy window: Gracie. She peered out in the fresh, clean spaces the letters of her name had left behind. I wonder if she was straining to hear the music caught mid-chord outside, dangling, ready to break off in curious hands. The brittle twinkling of a music box. I always imagined the voices of angels, but maybe that's just me being sentimental. Inside the car it was as silent as the grave. It was one of those rare moments when you think even breathing, even swallowing, will break the spell, whatever the spell is. For better or worse, you always want to stay there, ghosting through wonderland, not leaving anything but the whisper of an exhausted car's exhale behind.

Today, it's raining again, and I'm only looking straight ahead, as I do these days. I've learned to keep my eyes on the road. When I remember to check behind me, looking for the crisscrossing lights of other cars trailing me through the needle-sharp bursts of rain, I notice that the glass has already pooled over, and I reach out, ready to wipe it all away.

I could see the messy arcs of fingerprints where I had done the same thing so many times before. Your fingers leave secret oils on glass, oils you don't even know are there that you can't ever wash away. I pause. How many times had I traced out fresh windows, never realizing that down the road I would only make it harder for myself to see? I look behind me—the two back windows are even worse. Little girls can never keep their hands to themselves. There's a layered map of crushes that were supposed to be secret and the memories of hands and hearts and eyes held wide, held there till they burst and—in the bottom corner, where I suppose it had been waiting for me all along—her name.

The crisscrossing lights are suddenly all around me and the horn blares across my line of consciousness. I realize I'm drifting, just following the rain. I have clear enough vision, even now, to know when to pull off the road. I have always been the one who kept her head. Last year, when the flashing lights came and all the people in their cars slowed to stare, it was I who stood alone in the haze of rain freezing at my feet and watched as they carried my 8-year-old daughter away, her eyes still wider than they were at birth, staring out at a whole new world. A bit of a smile was still stuck across her face.

Looking back, I can't resist the urge to connect it all and call it frozen music. My husband couldn't watch. He stayed in the car, his face pressed to the dashboard. His hands didn't touch the steering wheel at all that trip—not even once—so he did not feel, as I did, the way the car jerked away and spun out of fairyland. Still, it was I who stood and watched, as the rain froze in layers and layers around me, not quite splintering, not yet, freezing the sound of the sirens mid-wail.

But today, I can't watch anymore. I can only feel the squeezing ache of old and new tears mixing together and pressing their way up my throat, ready to explode into the silent air. I turn the engine off. I know I should drive on. It's getting late, and I have things to finish tonight. All I can do is notice, distantly, the way you can only see the sun dance during an ice storm.

The backseat is messy on one half of the car, but cuts off sharply, into the bare space a child could sit in. The invisible line is perfectly straight, but I never drew it deliberately, and I'm sure my husband didn't either. Call it unconscious superstition. Call it whatever you like. I know that in our culture no one comes back, but we still carve out spaces for them, in the hopes that ghosts can slip through whatever gaps time can't fill or heal.

I step out of the car. The rain stings my face, and I shield my eyes with my arm. I forget to shut the side door gently as I get in the back and slam it out of habit. I want the seat my daughter died in to feel different—special, like hallowed ground—but my body is trying to tell me that leather never changes.

I look out the back window at the world outside. The rain is easing up, and I wonder if it's going to snow. The sun, which starts its slow descent around 4:30 these days, is glinting off the icy branches and throwing the light straight in my eyes. I lean forward, rest my head so I can see through the letters of her name, and try, before the light fades and the rain eases into the blissful forgetfulness of snow, to see what she would have seen: the shining promise of a world just born.

THE IMPOSSIBLE FATE OF WILLIAM MINNAFEE

CELIA BELL, 17
BRYN MAWR SCHOOL
BALTIMORE, MD
TEACHER: WILLIAM WATERS

I

The pumpkins in Mrs. Jenkins's backyard were rotting. We split them open and scooped up the seeds and left the broken orange flesh to cave in and pucker with black mold. That was the night that Will streaked through the field behind the old Carter place wearing only a plastic Halloween mask and disappeared into the woods with pumpkin pulp draped across his shoulders and stray seeds stuck to his ankles. He never came back out.

The moon crept across the sky while we waited for him, but in the end there was a search with dogs and cops in reflective jackets, heavy flashlights, a big cop cruiser pulled up to the edge of the trees with the lights flashing and growing pallid against the slowly brightening sky—this after those endless hours of waiting for Will to reappear from some stand of trees with a howl like a troll and a laugh at his own trick; after we swallowed our fear and went into the woods after him, calling his name, first softly, then louder, until Janet Tillman's nerves broke and she screamed until she was hoarse. No one answered.

One of the cops who came later was Will's own uncle. It was that small a town. Mrs. Jenkins never scolded us about the wreckage of her prize pumpkins, and none of us had the heart to clean them up.

Today is a Wednesday, and no one is talking about Will. Not saying his name is kind of an unspoken agreement among those of us who were there. We move in a group, and if anyone asks, we just look away. Sometimes I wonder if our silence isn't about to devour us, but amongst ourselves we scarcely talk at all.

We each have our ways of being silent, of thinking of Will. Benjamin flicks his pocketknife open and closed, again and again, carving little slivers of wood from the table where we sit. James Angleford bites at the skin around his nails until sometimes you can see blood. Marion fidgets, folds her fingers together, taps one foot on the ground so impossibly fast so her movements are scarcely movements, just vibration—a tension you feel but can't see. Sometimes she throws her head back and stares at the sky like she wishes she could break it. Arthur Bradshaw is stony. And Janet—quieter than all of us—tugs her long, red hair over her shoulder and stares at whatever's before her, looking like she wants to lose herself in the unmown stand of grass outside the school, in the movement of Ben's knife, in the cold sky.

I don't know what it is I do when I think of him. Maybe that's why I'm the one who breaks the silence and asks why we don't drive back to the woods behind the old Carter place. Rightly, it should be Marion who says this, or Ben. Marion was full of crazy energy, the one who planned things. And Ben was always the first to follow Will's lead.

"Andrew, are you fucking crazy?" Marion asks.

Their eyes watch me blankly, like I'm an outsider, like I'm one more of those people who just wants a good ghost story.

"I need to see it."

Marion presses her lips together in a shadow of what her crazy smile used to look like.

"There is nothing to see."

And then the bell for the end of lunch is ringing, and they are all walking away and leaving me. Except Janet, who seems so much smaller and so much paler that sometimes I think she must be in danger of dissolving into air. When she touches my arm, I jump.

"Let's go," she says. "Let's go now."

The white paint is peeling in strips off the house where the Carters used to live, giving it the look of a snake shedding its skin. It's alone and derelict on a back road that no one ever drives down except kids looking for a place to drink in the enclosing hilly forest. A sign at the head of the road says that Sunshine Developments will soon be building 50 quality homes on this land. The sign is faded and overgrown with Virginia creeper.

Janet sits with her feet drawn up on the passenger seat as I drive, and I wonder if the hum of the car's engine sounds as lost to her under the November sky as it does to me.

I park the car in the long brittle grass.

"What do we do now?" Janet asks.

I take a breath. "I'm going into the woods."

Janet bends her head so that her hair falls over her face like rain. "I'll wait for you."

I look back once as I walk across the field. Janet looks impossibly small in the gray world, her bright auburn hair lost in the stirring wind.

The woods are quiet, and there's a kind of waiting stillness, a cessation of birds and wind and rustling leaves. I feel I'm not walking, that the trees are running away beneath my feet and on either side of me, and I'm held in suspension, waiting, waiting. It is growing dark. The shadows of the trees stretch and pool, and when I stop I see that the second hand of my watch is jammed, twitching feebly in one place like a moth pinned to cardboard. It is as if I have stopped breathing, and without any shock at all I look up to where Will's Halloween mask is hanging empty from the branch of an old oak tree, like a discarded skin, mouth open in a silent shout.

Its eyes are empty holes, and through them I see Will's eyes as clear and gray as they shone in the beam of our headlights that night, foreign as a bird's eyes; I see the lone red of Janet's hair under the blank sky; I see a flock of jackdaws rising over the trees. I see the pumpkins caved in and black in Mrs. Jenkins's yard—everything wavering, changing, too fast to comprehend.

II

A chill, fidgeting wind was blowing through Washington Square, and it caught at the sleeves of Janet's jacket and the fringes of her scarf, and ruffled the pages of her book as she held it open on her lap, so that finally she laid a hand over it and looked up across the square to where a middle-aged man in a red sweatshirt was playing the saxophone, fingers moving like the continuous sweep of a dancer's legs, and cheeks blown out with effort.

It was not a cold wind, but it was insistent, and Janet pulled her jacket a little closer around her. The book in her lap was Dostoevsky's *Adolescent.* She chafed her hands together and thought about leaving, for coffee or for her apartment, where she could read in quiet without the murmur of the wind or the saxophone's silky weeping.

She had always loved these moments of solitude in the city, when she was still and suspended in the pulsing movement of those around her, still amid the threads of so many lives. It was in these moments that her heart went out to the country, where she'd been raised, when the stillness of those hills and the stillness in her heart seemed inseparable. She knew that she would always carry in her this distance, this vast still sky bound together with saxophone notes, when the patternless bustle of the city moved in spirals like some celestially-decreed dance. Only in these moments did she believe in fate.

She held the book open without looking at its pages. Across the path from her, a man with a gray cap pulled down across his brow tapped on the shoulder of a sleeper who sat with his head fallen on his chest and the matted cloud of his red hair obscuring his face—red, almost, as a cardinal's wings, berry-red, not the no-color gray-brown of the streets, of the winter.

"Hey, man. Anyone home? Is anyone home?"

The sleeper raised his head, and Janet saw (she was looking, now not with the sidelong glance of the city—the look that follows its object from the corner of the eye, watching carefully, cataloging, taking notes—

she was watching him now with her chin raised and her eyes open and not even pretending to be reading the book in her lap)—she saw he was young beneath the weight of his hair, that his face was unlined and he was maybe no more than 17, for the way his eyes stared into some distant faraway place. He raised a hand without his eyes ever focusing to say to the man standing over him, "Fine. Fine."

Janet closed the book and stood, turning her back on the disquiet seething beneath her rib cage (the city dweller's fear that she'd been caught staring, that his blank eyes had, when they opened, looked at her and through her and seen. . . something). And she started away from the saxophone and toward the street.

"Janet. Hey, Janet—Janet Tillman, wait!"

She turned. The red-haired boy was behind her—he reached a hand toward her, nails dark with dirt. She pulled away.

"Sorry. I'm sorry. I wanted to—" he stopped, breathing as if he'd been running, as if he had trouble meeting her eyes. "I wanted to talk to you."

"How did you know my name?"

He looked at her, his eyes still and brown as honey, deep as the rings of age on the hewn trunk of a tree.

"You don't know me?"

Janet shook her head. "I'm sorry. I've never seen you before."

He shrugged, tucked his hands into his sleeves, awkward, gawky.

"It's alright. Everyone I used to know is gone. I tried looking. It took me a long time to find even you. Everyone else disappeared—my parents, everyone. Like I never existed. And after I came, after I left the woods, I wasn't ready to live in the real world."

She stepped back, a step, two, preparing to walk away, realizing that the dark side of the globe of silence she carried with her was that none of the city people would look twice at this scene. "I'm sorry. I don't know what you're talking about."

"Don't you remember Will Minnafee?" He held a hand

outstretched, and she faltered, reeled back like a trout upon a fishhook.

"Will? You know Will?"

"I knew him."

She breathed, feeling the wind go chill in her lungs, dry fire in her throat, her eyes. "Is he dead, then?"

"No. Maybe. I don't know."

There was something alien in him, some shadow too old for his face. He bowed his head and ran his fingers through his hair, nymph-like, like some wild creature caught out of its element.

"Are you hungry? I could buy you something to eat."

"Thank you."

"You never told me your name."

III

They were sitting in an Indian restaurant in the West Village at a table in the back, while before them the city passed outside the glass windows and the open door. He had eaten the food in front of him so quickly that she had given him most of her lunch as well, and now he neatly wiped the last of the spiced sauce from his plate with a piece of naan.

"It's Andrew."

"How did you know Will?"

His face froze into one of those still expressions, as when he'd first woken—the look of a deer surprised in the woods in the moment before it first springs away.

"I went to school with him. With you." He breathed and stumbled on, before she could object, before she could deny anything.

"You think I'm crazy. Remember, though, the night he disappeared, how it was Halloween and we went behind the houses and smashed Mrs. Jenkins' pumpkins, how she called out her bedroom window after us with curlers still in her hair, and all through the ride out to the woods Ben was threatening what he'd do if we ground the pumpkin pulp into the seats of his car? You had—your hair was long then. You've cut it now, but then it was long and almost pumpkin-colored, and you had some pumpkin seeds caught in it that night and you were laughing. We were all pretty drunk, remember? And Will put on this mask and disappeared into the woods howling like the devil himself was behind him. And he never came out.

"I," he stammered, "I went into the woods after him. And when I came out everything had changed. Do you remember?"

Janet sighed and bent her head toward the table, toward the empty dishes, laced her fingers together beneath her chin like a net to catch thoughts in.

"It didn't happen quite like that."

She looked up at Andrew, scarcely 17.

"I've been in the city seven years now. The disappearance, the way they wrote it in the newspaper… When I first came here, I kept expecting to see him. He always swore, you know, that when he left he'd come to Greenwich Village. God, I knew he was going to leave, we were all dying to get out of the country, and Will never believed he was smart enough to be anything. He was so afraid of being trapped. I could see the way something shut down behind his eyes every time he thought of it. I saw him closing down. I wanted to leave, but it was so much worse for him."

She took a breath, creased and uncreased the orange napkin in her lap. "I was the only one who knew that he was gay. His parents—he thought his dad would have disowned him. It was like that, that whole town, they all loved him as long as he was willing to pretend. That town was a hellhole. I knew he was going to leave, I helped him plan it, but he never told me when. I thought maybe he'd write me when he got to New York, just a note, something. But I guess he wanted to stay a legend after he left, a ghost story: 'This is how people disappear.'"

"Like that?" Andrew's eyes were still, far away. "I remember that night? You called the loudest."

"Did I?" Janet looked away from him, swiped the back of her hands across her eyes. "Is that what he told you?'

"It's what I remember." He crossed his arms over his chest, set his jaw grimly. "You loved him, didn't you?"

Janet blinked, passed her hand over her eyes again. The room was swimming, and she felt—now just an echo of what she'd felt, that night, when she realized he was gone forever. Still, how like drowning, after all this time.

"I guess I did, in a way. In a sick kind of way. Because I knew something about him that no one else did. Even though I knew he would never feel the same way about me. But he was good at making people fall in love with him."

She'd thought she was beyond being hurt by those memories.

"I thought he'd remember me, you know? If he'd sent even one postcard, even a blank one, I'd have known it was him, I'd have known he was still alive. But there was nothing. He forgot."

Andrew reached one hand across the table to her, drew back before they touched, as if shocked. "There wasn't anyone there, then, like me? No one with my name, no one with my face?"

"I'm sorry," said Janet.

He leaned forward intently. "What about Marion? Ben? James and Arthur? Were they there?"

"I don't know who you're talking about."

He sighed, looking away so that his hair hid his face. "So you're the only one. Everyone I knew is gone."

"I'm sorry."

The feet of the chair scraped back against the floor as he stood. "Thanks for the meal."

Janet stood too, followed him out of the restaurant, fumbling at her purse.

"Wait," she said, and he stopped as she caught his arm. "Can I give you something? I don't know, enough to buy dinner?"

He looked at her, and she wondered for a moment if perhaps she wasn't the one who'd lost her past. "No. S' fine. I can't take your money.

But thank you… for stopping."

Then he leaned forward and pressed his dry lips to her cheek—an awkward, teenage kiss—and before she could stop him, he was gone down the street, and the city was already closing around the hole where he'd been, like fate, like the arms of a friend, leaving her the one still figure in the autumn afternoon.

IV

That wasn't the way it happened.

Janet was sure of it. She'd spent only three short months in New York City before she came back to the country with her tail between her legs, humiliated, knowing that over coffee the women of the town were whispering to each other about how the Tillman girl had gone to the big city with such visions of being a star, an actress, a socialite, while they knew better. How much better it was that she should stay where she'd been born, for they were country folks, it ran in their blood: Fate itself decreed that Janet Tillman would never make it in the big city. It was another world.

And it shamed her. A full 55 years later, a widow at 73, it shamed her to remember how at 18 she had run from the city. How she had arrived, that first day at Hunter College, and had seen Will's face on every street corner, had felt the weight of so many people jostling her, rushing in the streets, the cabs, the noise. In three short months, it had destroyed her, and she had returned home in defeat. The children told stories, now, of how the old Carter place was haunted, how if you went into the woods on Halloween, the goblins ate you. But Janet knew better. At 18, she knew it was not the woods that were haunted, but the rest of the world.

She'd turned into one of the old women of the town, the ones who gossiped with each other in the grocery store. Her limbs had grown stout, her waist heavy, her red hair iron-gray. Her son was now the town exterminator, going to people's houses and spraying for cockroaches, termites—all the things that people imagine are eating away at the foundation of things. Her husband was dead, a heart attack at 63—a shock, no one had seen it coming. And her daughter lived two towns over, married her high school boyfriend, and sometimes now, Janet forgot and absently called her granddaughter by her daughter's name.

Day by day, she was beginning to forget things, small things at first, whether she'd moved the laundry from washer to dryer, whether she'd taken the pill that was supposed to keep her cholesterol down. There were the remarks that people made, the way she found herself asking the same question over again, two, three times. She blamed it on business. Wasn't it funny how she just couldn't keep the little things in her mind anymore?

Then there was the day she walked home from the grocery with her arms full of groceries and a store-bought cake, and went through the house calling her husband's name, passing from room to room calling, until she reached the bedroom which was awash in autumn sunlight, and only then did she remember that her husband had been dead for some ten years. And though she knew it well, still it seemed that if she only turned around, she would see him as he had been at 20, waiting to laugh at her silliness in believing in the passage of time, waiting to take her into his arms.

She didn't know how long she could conceal it, this strangeness in the passage of time. There were always ghosts around her now, but they no longer frightened her. It was a pleasure when Will Minnafee came to stand over her bed at night, and she spoke to him at length, asked him what was it like in the woods, what was it like to be stolen by goblins? Or did she mean New York still, for now in her old age she could no longer remember what the life she led had been. And hadn't she, indeed, met her husband one day when he was playing the saxophone in Washington Square Park? Hadn't they lived together in Brooklyn and been happy? And, one night before they married hadn't she had told him, at length, about her life in the country, how William

Minnafee was stolen away one Halloween. How she herself had gone away to live in the enchanted city? How, one day, she had met a boy like a sprite himself, like a lost spirit, who had borrowed her past? And which, in the end, was true?

Which life had she lived?

Day by day, she was forgetting things, and one day she saw herself on the street, young, but only 18 and with the reddest hair, and she called aloud, "Janet! Janet!" because she wanted to tell herself that she didn't have to live her mother's life, that she could live a hundred lives—she would live a hundred lives—and only in her old age would she understand, only at 73 would she look back and see how many people she had been. Fate, or chance.

But as the girl with the red hair turned, she saw that it was her granddaughter, her living ghost, and she was too young to understand that she would be everything, that the earth would have to spread immeasurably to encompass her, that the merest nutshell would become a galaxy. Her granddaughter only looked at her with shock, saying, "What is it, Grandma? What is it?"

And the old woman was lost for words, would not see a doctor, insisting she needed no one. And one night she woke to find her gnarled hands straightened, her gray hair turned red again, and knocking on her bedroom window was a boy—a wood-sprite, only 17—with his hair like a bird's nest around his face, and she followed him out onto the snowy ground, knowing that in the morning they would find her body empty on the bed like a snake's discarded skin, grown dull and fragile with age, and they would carry her out and put her in the ground, and she would become one more ghost with the rest of them, laughing over everything she'd lost.

V

Sometimes I don't know who I am. Because here the world ends only at the limits of my mind. I may still be the boy who walked into the forest in search of William Minnafee, or I may never have been him. Perhaps I only heard the story, one night sitting around a fire under the Williamsburg Bridge, where I was just one tramp out of the circle, warming my hands against the night when some bearded man, aged beyond the 24 years he'd lived, stretched out his voice and began to talk of the boy he used to be. Or perhaps I was never human, perhaps I never existed except as a sprite, a shade. Maybe I was only ever the threat of a ghost in the woods that keeps the children safe and in the sunlight, borne on an old woman's lips and carried with her to her death.

You choose. I've run out my voice trying to tell you, trying to make you see how the world is like a closed fan, how out of all that bright expanse of folded paper we see only the uppermost edges of the creases, nothing of the chasms we walk over every day. I lied when I let you believe you had a storyteller: My only art is to build illusions over the fragile world, then knock them down.

Sometimes I don't know who I am.

You choose.

VI

It was a windy day, the day of the funeral. The lilies over Janet Tillman's casket waved stiffly, and a few flakes of snow fluttered in the air, and the loose black skirt of Janet's daughter's dress belled out and beat about her legs as if it were trying to get free.

The old woman had wanted to be cremated, and her daughter clutched at her skirt against the wind and felt vaguely guilty as the coffin was lowered into the grave. But she couldn't quite bear to think of her mother's ashes blowing about in the hills behind her hometown, turning to silt and dust about the shell of a haunted house. Even before she had begun to wander in time, to see ghosts and mutter to herself in the supermarket, there had been something abstracted in her, something prone to vanishing. Her daughter remembered how—when she was a child—her mother used to forget to turn the lights on as the sun set, how she would come upon her mother with a book open in her lap and the light dying around her, not reading, but staring at the blank pages as if through a window. How when she tiptoed up on her child's feet to flick the light switch on, her mother would sometimes look up at her as startled as if she had forgotten that she did not live all alone. And how when her daughter asked what she had been thinking she would only say, "Nothing, nothing," and kiss her daughter's forehead, and offer to tell her some story while she cooked dinner.

She was never where she was looked for; she was always somewhere else—around the corner, across the road. And even folded into herself in death she was not contained; the waxen face and her bent hands were only a veil over something else, so that her daughter had a terrifying vision of those eyelids opening beneath the earth, as if she had only been lost in some reverie. She had wanted, for once, to be able to put a place to her mother, a grave, a headstone.

The coffin struck the earth with a thud. The dirt was muddy with melted snow, and it stained the hands of each member of the funeral party who threw a handful onto the shining lid of the coffin, leaving streaks on black skirts and black ties, turning them clay-colored— blood-colored—as the wind blew into a frenzy and the snow came down in thick, lacy flakes. And if there was any movement in the grave-yard after the funeral party made its way between the headstones and left, it might have been only the flash of a cardinal's wings in the snow.

FICTIONS
CELIA BELL

She is the woman who sits alone on the park bench throwing bread-crumbs for the sparrows and stealing morsels of thought from passersby. She is quiet. She sits in the sunlight with her skin like brown paper bags and in the rain with her bent umbrella opened over her head. Her bones creak like trees in the wind. She cannot tell you her age: she was born on a day when the sun was high and cold and the women wore long colored dresses with skirts that danced in the wind. She was born in a house by the sea far far before boats tore the ocean and disgorged men upon the shores. She was washed up on the shore like a Venus of weathered driftwood. She was born at night in the snow, beneath the rising northern lights that never fade in winter.

Perhaps these are not her memories but simply the musings of passing strangers, whose minds she inhabits for moments at a time, sharing loves and losses. She is the woman in the printed scarf who misses her lover but will not call him. She is the blue-eyed old man plucking at his sleeves at the bus stop, his mind returning to the son who, years ago now, plowed his car into a streetlamp on a deserted highway and died alone. She is the young girl chasing butterflies on legs that can run but not walk, and who is scarcely thinking at all.

Sometimes she suspects in herself an anomaly: she is not sure who she is, beyond the whirling crowd of voices that inhabit her mind, the riot of small lives. If you asked her name, she could not answer. There are summer days when she culls a banquet of voices from those who pass. There are days when she does not eat but she feasts. There are days when she sits empty and alone in the rain, stripped of her history.

On cold days, her hands scab and scale.

If you listen, she will tell you stories of angels and trolls. She will tell you of the fountain city, whose image wavers where the water falls, and how the people who walk its streets have skin as clear as glass, through which you can see their goldfish thoughts moving in the stream of their blood. She will tell you of the newspaper moths that fly in the night wind, delivering tales of fire and floods, and how—if you let them light on your face—you will see visions of faraway countries in their beating wings. She will tell you how to find the compass rose that grows only in the rain-washed footprints of those who have long ago lost their way.

But if you want to know these things, you will have to give her something in return: the memory, for instance, of the way you felt on the day that you woke to find that Hugo had left the apartment in the night, leaving only a note saying that he would be back, in a day or so, to collect his things. How you were entirely calm, relieved even, until you realized that, going about your morning routine, you had by accident made enough coffee for two, and how it was only when you were pouring the bitter excess down the kitchen sink that you burst into tears.

Perhaps you would prefer to forget these things anyway, and so giving them up to her is only too easy. She is an indiscriminate eater of stories and will not mind the bitterness: Like coffee, it will keep her warm on days when the wind blows cold, something to sip and savor when she is left alone.

And if you're left wondering, later, how you felt that day, when you felt the worst you will ever feel (or so you believe), you will have to go back and ask her: She knows. She can describe it better than you ever could.

STATEMENT OF PURPOSE
JARED DUMMITT, 17

STUYVESANT HIGH SCHOOL
NEW YORK, NY
TEACHER: ERIC GROSSMAN

I remember one day, in the middle of the fifth grade, when my English teacher asked everyone in my class to produce a book. It did not have to be too long, just ten pieces of loose-leaf, but it still seemed daunting at the time. How could I fill up so much space?

I nervously asked my teacher a question to that effect, and he told me simply, "Write what you know." I was immediately wary. Why should I write about the things around me, when they seemed mundane and boring? In a small, but seemingly important, rebellion, I rejected my teacher's advice and wrote a story about a golden aardvark. The story went all the way to the final line of the tenth page.

Throughout my middle school years, I read and wrote science fiction exclusively, with great satisfaction. What could be more exciting than leaving the world that I knew, abandoning the everyday people, and finding the fantastic? But as time went on, I began to realize something unsettling about my favorite genre. At the core of every great book that I had read, whether it was Frank Herbert's *Dune* or Robert A. Heinlein's *Stranger in a Strange Land,* there was a human struggle that would have been just as convincing on Earth as it had been on a foreign planet. The people in the stories were the part that interested me the most, no matter how strange or beautiful the worlds they inhabited might be. Thus disillusioned, I moved out of the confines of science fiction and began to read more broadly.

With this history in mind, I come back to my teacher's advice: "Write what you know." The people who populate all of the stories in this portfolio are, at face, quite mundane. I picked "How Pearl Harbor

Caused My Grandfather All Sorts of Trouble" because it represents how the people we often overlook—soldiers, faceless people in the street—have had experiences that are as dramatic as those experienced by even the most important of statesmen. The next piece, "One Might Think That It Was All Possible," is included because it tells the story of a man torn between two different cultures. The protagonist, Adrian Bowman, is based on my older sister, and his life largely mirrors hers. The last piece, "Parsing Our Sameness," is the most important to me. It is a factual account of my life, growing up with an identical twin brother.

None of the stories were chosen because anything remarkable happens in any of them. All three are based on family members, and most of the events in all of them have happened, in one form or another. What I have realized is that the events that are the most real are the most remarkable. By writing about the ordinary people and places that I know, I hope to find a grain of truth and share it with my readers.

HOW PEARL HARBOR CAUSED MY GRANDFATHER ALL SORTS OF TROUBLE

JARED DUMMITT

In April 1943, Arthur came across a concentration camp.

Weak sunlight bathed the flat, grassy plains. It was too hot for Arthur to wear his greatcoat comfortably, but without it he shivered when the wind whipped up around him. In the end he decided to wear it anyway, so he spent the journey soaked in greasy perspiration and cursing—like a sailor, one might say—under his breath.

"The hell is that?" said Alex Crenshaw, an infantryman who was Arthur's friend.

"What?" Arthur said. He could hear out of his right ear, but just barely.

"*That*," repeated Alex.

He pointed. Far off in the foothills, a column of black smoke rose into the sky.

"Don't know," said Arthur. The long caravan of jeeps was heading straight toward it.

"Uh, Sir?" said Alex, looking at the lieutenant of their group, Josh Harding. "What's that?"

"I don't know," said Josh.

"Fighting, Sir?" Arthur asked.

"No," replied Josh. "There haven't been any reports. But we're supposed to head towards it. That's orders, from the top."

"You're sure there hasn't been any combat, Sir?"

"Not that I know of," said Josh, and he added, "*Private*."

So on they went. The smoke became thicker and thicker, until it obscured the sky overhead. The soldiers were jabbering. Some were afraid. Most were just curious.

"That smell, what is that *smell*?" someone said when the smoke was only a few miles away.

Arthur inhaled. The thinnest trail of smoke rose into his nostrils and he gagged. It went beyond such phrases as "rotten eggs" and "dirty socks" that are often used to describe smells. The first thing that came to his mind was a time when his mother had left a chicken in the refrigerator when the family had gone on a two-week-long vacation, and the whole house had reeked of rancid meat for weeks. But not even that was close.

A few of the men leaned back, eyeballs rolling into their skulls. Arthur struggled for breath.

"Damn it, why are we slowing down? This is not a time to slow down..." said Alex, who was struggling to keep the bile from his mouth.

But the caravan was indeed coming to a halt.

"Roll out, move, move, *move*!" shouted the commanding officer of the group, a gray-haired Evangelist from Arkansas who carried a Bible in his breast pocket. He put it there because he believed that the 200 pages of the book, along with Jesus' blessing, would save him from being shot through the heart. One day he would find himself in a shootout in Kiev, and he would find that the book was printed on too-thin paper and that Jesus was not, in fact, there for him, and he would not live. But that was all in the misty future.

Arthur hopped over the edge of the jeep. His boots crashed into the dirt road, muddy with melted snow. He lined up with the others.

"Men!" shouted the Bible-toting officer. "We are approaching a German-manned post. It has been marked a 'special zone.' It is abandoned of combat personnel. There will be civilians. Take care when we arrive. This is a rescue situation."

"Sir, what is the status of the civilians, sir?" shouted a soldier.

"I'm afraid they will—they will—I'm afraid I don't know. Back in the jeeps!"

As Arthur hurled himself into his hard metal seat, he realized that he had never heard the Bible-toting officer stutter before.

*   *   *

When Arthur arrived at the camp, he could hardly focus on anything but the stench. He held his stomach. Some of the soldiers did not.

They cut their way through the barbed wire and walked among the rows of barracks and dormitories. They had been built with slabs of concrete; drab, low, and dull. Completely without character. The infantry ran into the guardhouses but they had been abandoned in anticipation of the approaching American column.

It looked like a little city to Arthur. It had houses and farms and hospitals and administrative buildings. At first it seemed to be empty; as things turned out, it was not. When they entered the third dormitory, they found beds filled with men who were thin—so thin that you could almost see through them. They were dirty and sick, but most of all, they were thin. They were all naked. They were less "men" than bands of flesh that tenaciously gripped at their bones so tightly that they were painful to look upon. They shrank away in fear at first, but then they clambered out of their bunks slowly and deliberately so that they would not exhaust themselves, for they had eaten nothing but a few bread crusts in the last week.

"They're Jews, they're all *Jews*," said Alex. "Uh, sorry," he said, and looked sheepishly away from Arthur, who was staring at the prisoners, too numb to be disgusted or horrified or upset.

"Who—who are you?" one of them asked.

Arthur understood him, but all of the other soldiers looked on uncomprehending. The man was speaking Yiddish.

"Am-Amer-i-cans?" he said haltingly, in English. Arthur stepped forward, feeling the weight of all of their eyes.

"We are from America," he said in Yiddish that was halting because he did not really speak the language but had merely picked up words here and there. "You are safe now."

He was not sure what else to say.

"Tell them to come with us," said the commanding officer.

"What the hell is going on here?" Arthur said. He had forgotten to call him "Sir" but he did not care.

"Excuse me, Private?"

"Who are these people? What are they doing here, and—oh, God—why are they so *thin*?" Arthur said.

"I don't know," said the commanding officer. "Private."

Arthur did not press the point. He translated mechanically as the starved Jews were brought out of the barracks and loaded into trucks. He helped get them food, although most of their stomachs had shrunk so that they could eat very little.

Three hours later, he found himself walking along in the interior of the camp. The source of the smoke column was in the very center of it, and soldiers had grouped themselves around it, staring and not speaking. Arthur, too tired and numb to do much of anything else, went over to investigate.

He had thought that he had become used to the wretched stink of the camp, and to some extent, he had. He was able, at least, to force it into a corner of his brain where it did not bother him so much. But when he reached the base of the smoke column the smell redoubled in strength, and he almost vomited.

"Arthur, you don't—you won't want to see—" said a soldier, but it was too late.

The smoke was pouring from a deep pit in the ground that was still smoldering. It was filled with bodies. There were hundreds of them; perhaps thousands. Most of the flesh and blood had been burned away, so that there was nothing but a pile of blackened bones that stretched deep into the charred earth.

Arthur looked down and stared into the eye sockets of a skull. It was not an adult's. In life, it's owner might have been Joe's age. He might have been Lester's.

That was when Arthur did vomit. He took a few steps away, his mind reeling, thoughts and images flying, *Lester dead dead bodies oh God so many so thin like skeletons skeletons buried in the ground mass grave lick the Japs oh God no.* He had intended to go back to the jeeps as fast as his legs would carry him, but he did not make it. He stopped and regurgitated the contents of his stomach in the dusty dirt that stank of burning corpses, heaving and heaving, until there was nothing more to bring up, but even then, he did not stop.

Years later he would learn that the German prison guards, fearing that their crimes would be discovered in the form of the corpses of the Jews who had died from malnutrition or poison gas, had set fire to the bodies. They had not realized that the bones would survive the burning. They had not realized that the Americans would arrive so soon.

Arthur Blumberg could not stand the stench nor the sight any longer. He wanted to be dead, dead so that he would no longer have to touch the world that would allow so many people to die like animals with their dignity gone like the tide that has left the shore, never to return. He did not want to see the emaciated Jews ever again. He did not want to live in a world where there was no Lester to see, no Japs to kill, and nothing that he could do about any of it, but just waves of vomit that wracked his body even though his stomach had long been empty.

He fell to the ground and felt nothing more.

*   *   *

Arthur came to in an army jeep. In his sleep he had had dreams that had not really been dreams because he had not really been asleep but unconscious.

When he awoke, his mind was filled with strange thoughts. He had never seriously considered his religion, which he had been born with and always practiced in a fairly automatic manner: bar mitzvah, synagogue on Saturdays, no pork, no shellfish, mezuzah on the frame of the door, et cetera, et cetera. He had always done it because his parents had done it, not because he had rationally or religiously found meaning in Judaism. The religion was comforting, regular; part of the fabric of his life, but not the center. For no matter how many times he had said the Shema or read in Hebrew, he had never seen the precise moral wrong of eating a hot dog, nor had he ever glimpsed the clock-work-like inner workings of the world through the lens of an omnipresent God.

But he was still a Jew. He knew that he was a Jew and he would be a Jew until the day he died, and nothing could change that.

PARSING OUR SAMENESS
JARED DUMMITT

"I sought my soul, but my soul I could not see. I sought my God, but my God eluded me. I sought my brother and I found all three."

Dr. Martin Luther King, Jr.

Rote Exchange
"Round here, we're carving out our names,
Round here, we all look the same."

Counting Crows, "Round Here"

Have you ever had the experience that, midway through some mundane task, an exact body-double of yourself walks into the room and strikes up a conversation?

It happens to me almost every day. From time to time, someone will walk in on us.

"Wait a second," the confounded third party will say. His eyes will narrow beneath bunched eyebrows, sending creases across his forehead like narrow, spidery fingers. Considering how it appears that the fundamental laws of physics have been mercilessly breached, it's a relatively mild reaction. His head will list, and then stabilize.

"Yes?" one of us will respond.

"There are two of you…"

"Yeah," I will say, trying to keep the weariness out of my voice. "There are two of us."

These exchanges all play out in the same way. It's almost as though there were a script out there, or an instruction manual: *How to Realize You're Talking to an Identical Twin in Ten Easy Steps.* After the initial shock has been overcome, I'll go on to explain how Morgan and I can be told apart.

This is where the rote exchange ends, and I have a bit of choice: will I mention my extra inch-and-a-quarter of height? My ever-so-slightly broader facial features? The numbness in my right heel, memento of my worst Tae Kwon Do mishap? Perhaps the elusive freckle that, for whatever reason, appears on my left earlobe but not my brother's? The list goes on and on, a lengthy compilation of differences that seem almost absurdly subtle. As I rattle off our distinguishing features, I feel a bit like I'm giving a birdwatcher tips on how to differentiate between two different species of parakeets. It's an occupational hazard, I suppose, of sharing another person's DNA.

Identity
"Sameness is the mother of disgust…"
Petrarch

When I think about who I am, I find myself thinking about who we are. I find myself thinking back to the beginning.

Common first memories: a crib, a highchair, climbing over shoes and milk cartons and other household items that present serious obstacles to the average baby. Not for me. Two little boys with blond hair sit in front of a mirror. Their hair is just like their father's was. . . won't stay that way for long, or so Mother says. One is dressed in red. That one is Jared; the last three letters of his name are the same as the color of his overalls to make it easy to tell who he is. Neither one has much of a personality yet, so color-coding will have to suffice. They squint with skepticism accessible even to 4-year-olds, because when they look in a mirror there are four of them, two who can be touched and two who can only be seen, and they can't tell which corresponds to which. And "Oh,

God," they would think, if they knew who God was, "It's a hell of a thing to see yourself but not know who you are." And, if they could wonder that, they might wonder why Morgan is dressed up in blue, when the two words don't share any letters at all. But, for now, they are all glazed eyes and quickly fading blonde hair and all they do is sit and stare and stare and stare.

Maybe this is where it all began, the years of confusion. When I was young, my twinship seemed to cause more grief than good. There is something very important about being an individual. We are told that we each bring something of our own to the table, that we are the best at being ourselves. I found it difficult to take these slogans to heart. A strange sense of lost ownership comes with knowing that you share everything that you are with another person; that you are no more unique than a half-clamshell that is bound forever to its mate. How could I make a name for myself, a life and identity for myself, if everything that I had was not quite mine?

This confusion ultimately led to competition, and most of my recollection of my younger years involves constant struggles for identity in areas that, in hindsight, were almost universally inconsequential. The search to be better at something, anything, never ended.

"Come on," I say as we lean over our dining room table, crayons splayed out across it like the wreckage of a spray-painted forest, splintered and twisted. "Stop it. I'm good at drawing. Don't—" Morgan glances over at my paper. Then, liking it, he picks up a Burnt Sienna and begins scribbling away. And there it goes, another opportunity to do something that he couldn't. I try not to show it, but it's hard for a 7-year-old to hide everything. I scowl a bit and begin to draw, but my heart isn't in it, as a little piece of what could have been all mine floats away in the dusty air currents of the ceiling fan that creaks overhead. And now I can think, not that I really know much more about God than I did at 4—or probably will at 40—"God, this is so unfair." For everyone else, drawing is just drawing, but for me, it's me versus him, hoping that I'll turn out a Van Gogh and he a 7-year-old, just so that I can prove that there's a difference between us.

Like opposing nations expanding across the globe, we colonized where we could and fought over the boundaries between ourselves. We marked our territories in the corners and crannies of the world we knew, in academic subjects, in hobbies, in sports. I spent the first decade of my life carving out my personality, parsing our sameness to find those things that I could call my own.

Clarity

Doppelganger: (noun), a ghostly double of a living person, especially one that haunts its fleshly counterpart.

The American Heritage Dictionary

Those years were bitter. But time, as it has a tendency to do, changed us. The stifling sameness of our younger days evaporated.

I finally found something that I was good at—I loved to write. Morgan discovered that he preferred to hold clay rather than pencils, and preferred sculpting to almost anything else.

I couldn't sculpt for my life. This was okay.

Sometimes I was less uplifted. One morning my mother called us both down to dinner. "Hey guys," she says, "I've got something to tell you. It's important. Morgan's going to Hunter next year—made the cutoff by just a point—but, hey, in is in."

She ladles soup; my heart catches.

"Jared, you missed it by the same number. I'm sorry. It's really too bad, just a point, and all."

Too bad, because in is in but out is also out. It hurts, because I've been trying to find some part of me that's just me, not lose Morgan.

More came; more was to come. I expected to feel lonelier than I did. I expected to miss the other side of my coin. What a difference the years make.

Morgan wants to go to art school. "Academics are nonsense," he says. I nod and smile and turn the page of *United States Government*.

He wants to live in England. I like it well enough here.

His clothing is mostly paint-spattered. I keep mine clean—not spotless, but clean.

To paraphrase Kurt Vonnegut, so it went. The day came when my grandfather stopped us and said, "My boys, you just don't look the same anymore." A year or two later, I believed it. I looked into an old photograph and was surprised to see just how similar we had once been. Our sun was setting, painting the sky with memories I was not sure— I'm still not sure—I wanted to lose. I lost them.

I've heard that recovering drug addicts feel extreme pain when they experience everyday problems—a stubbed toe can be agony, because they've been numb to feeling for so long. I think that this is something like what it has been for me to detach myself from Morgan. The feeling of being alone on the earth, the feeling that's said to be part of the human condition, sometimes aches. Most people have had to experience it from birth. I have not. Sometimes the newness and strangeness of it burns.

I have looked long into a mirror and seen not only a reflection of myself, but that of a person who I was once a single cell—the ethereal boundary between one embryo and the next—away from being. This the conflict, the contrast, that is at the heart of our brotherhood: that I vacillate back and forth between believing that time has driven a wedge between us, reducing our relationship to that which exists between ordinary siblings, and feeling the lingering shadows of the connection we once shared. I know that some part of me will always be part of Morgan, just as a part of him will always live in me. But, at the end of all of it, I have finally realized that I am who I am, independent of anyone else, independent even of the young man who shares my genetic code.

Everything that I know about myself I know because I have come to understand it through two lenses, my brother's and my own. I have earned my identity through the mire of a decade of blurred boundaries.

I believe that no matter what happens, the link between us will persist, over time and distance.

I will wake up one day ten years in the future, and I will suddenly know what Morgan is thinking.

I will share his heart and mind just as I once did.

We will inhabit the same square inches of earth.

We will be totally at peace to do all of it.

And in God only knows how long, we will rest easy, knowing that, forever and always, we've got each other's backs.

That's about all that I can ask for.

SELECTIONS FROM GOLD, SILVER & AMERICAN VOICES MEDALS

STUDENTS IN GRADES 7—12 SUBMIT WORK IN 11 WRITING CATEGORIES. THIS YEAR, MORE 20,000 WRITING SUBMISSIONS WERE REVIEWED BY AUTHORS, EDUCATORS, AND LITERARY PROFESSIONALS.
GOLD, SILVER, & AMERICAN VOICES MEDALS WERE AWARDED TO WORKS THAT DEMONSTRATED ORIGINALITY, TECHNICAL SKILL, AND EMERGENCE OF A PERSONAL VOICE.

INITIATION
ANNA ENZWEILER, 18

NOTRE DAME ACADEMY
PARK HILLS, KY
TEACHER: LYNN DICKMAN

What was there to herald us?
We had no oil, no stain, no knife,
nothing but the bulge and ripple of our tongues.
We sat on the floor and folded unfitting heels
beneath oddly thickened thighs,
listening for the guttural voices
in the room before us.
We spoke in impulse and blank and color,
and in the far window the skies shuttered.
Indeterminately, elbows settled to knees
and hands flew, ragged and raw,
not knowing, pale, cracking the bonds.
The first night we touched a universe was then,
although I forget the words we used.

MITBACH (KITCHEN)
YONI NACHMANY, 13

HUNTER COLLEGE HIGH SCHOOL
NEW YORK, NY
TEACHER: LORI D'AMICO

In my kitchen, there is a drawer just for spices.
When you open it, pause for a moment,
inhale. Now move, out of my kitchen
smelling faintly of cumin and cardamom,
to Jerusalem, to the Iraqi market.

Here, people sing along to Arabic music
blasting from the radio
and bulky boxes of spices flash red and sweet to hungry passersby,
while friends escape the scorching sun
at a restaurant, where the family owners cook their specialties.

Outside, pita with za'atar and hummus come very cheap,
only five Shkalim if you know the merchants,
and the smell of oil sweeps across the houses.
In the evening, mothers send their children to the Abulafia to buy
bread for the family
and bargain with the skills their parents taught them.

There will always be men shouting,
fighting for the lowest prices;
women carrying loads on their heads;
children in awe, trying to help their parents run
the family business.

ROAD TRIP
DONTE JEFFERSON, 13

LUSHER CHARTER SCHOOL
NEW ORLEANS, LA
TEACHER: ERIC FLYNT

We're going across the country again
but I'm not surprised
he got another job
something about construction.
I wonder if he could rebuild our hopes
give her another change
not blame her for something she
couldn't control
something she couldn't rid herself of,
even if he tried
we'd still be where we are
trapped
on our way to Boston.
I wonder if he even notices
the way my eyes squint when I try
not to cry
over what he's done to us
what he's done to me
sometimes I sit down and ask myself,
why couldn't it have been him?
Why couldn't she stay?
But instead I'm stuck with him
who I'm supposed to call "Dad."
But he'll never be my dad,
he'll never replace her,

no matter how much he wants
me to respect him,
to even like him
the only thing we have in common
is that we're
trapped
on our way to Boston.

CHICAGO, CITY OF WIND
ANDREW ZABELA, JR., 13

HOME SCHOOL
CHICAGO, IL
TEACHER: LUBOV ZABELA

The wind howls and whines
accompanied by the rain's chatter.
Snow the many street lines
flooded in the endless patter.

Skyscrapers rise from the ground
enveloped in the shimmering white.
With the fog are they bound
until they grow out of sight.

The wind whistles its tune
through both alley and street,
under the light of the moon
rain falls as a sheet.

Bright lights dazzle the way
that the winds will always travel,
enclosing the air in a mystical ray
that no one mind can unravel.

A lone ship made its stay
in the sprawling harbor at Michigan Lake.
Tomorrow will be the day
her return she will make.

Yet for now it shall lie
in a calm eerie peace,
broken only by the cry
of the wind that won't cease.

Morning creeps upon the city's frame.
The sun staggers above a tower
sings the wind never tame
full of unknown power.

Waves crash against the shore
roaring like a brute.
The wind will tell the lore
of how it charmed us with a flute.

As long as the song is heard
on every alley and street,
sung by the ancient bird,
a melody so sweet.

SPILT MILK
FILIPA IOANNOU, 15
HUNTER COLLEGE HIGH SCHOOL
NEW YORK, NY
TEACHER: RICHARD ROUNDY

I always mistake wizened leaves for sparrows, all lined up.
They are small and frail. Only the wind moves them.
They remind me of you.
I am stuck in place pasteurizing the spilled milk, and I
cannot stand the sight of your hiding under
the coffee mugs that line your wide windowsills lapping up
the white sunlight that I once envied.

I will continue to watch you pull yourself along by your thumbs;
they are simple, mechanical and strong in the way that your
newer, simpler life was supposed to be,
free from compulsions. You still found things to haunt you;
you were always an enigma.

You are saving me a heart under your floorboards,
ripped carefully from red paper and free from telltale gore, and
I fracture from far away thinking of the light streaming from
     windows paralyzing you,
of anxiety a grim cartographer remapping your once steady hands;
I know I cannot hear your voice.

I think back to you and imagine the lines diverging as I watch other girls,
think of how much like them you were—no, better.
The strongest, smartest 12-year-old I knew until you fell away.

I am afraid you will dissolve in the sweat that slickens what I
    thought was your cocoon.
I have come to fear that it is permanent,
under the sheets in your room, where you smell the way you always did
with the perfume oil that smelled like the way I feel about my mother,
and I wish I could lie with you forever, as the cold air descends in
    crescendos of white lights
spinning across skin.

THE MOON
BENJAMIN COPAN, 16
WELLINGTON COMMUNITY HIGH SCHOOL
WELLINGTON, FL
TEACHER: SCOTT ZUCKER

An ocean of trees,
on the side of a mountain,
                    bathes
                    in the liquid beams of moonlight
          that shower down upon the waves of leaves.

Scars and veins of rivers
     fracture into fractals
     as they meander down the mountainside,
                         slicing through
          and winding around the seas of trees
          and eventually converging
                    in silver lakes
                    that mirror the grayly splotched canvas above.

The moon's face hides in a splotch of gray paint.

Only its bald scalp protrudes from behind the cloud
                              like an old man
               peering, peeking, watching over
          the scattered remnants of civilization,
     the ursine forest inhabitants in their hibernation,
          and the bovine beings feasting on the fields
                    that they fertilized just weeks before,
               contemplating every pleasing bite as
the fruits of their labor meet their finely-tuned palates.

THIRTEEN WAYS OF LOOKING AT A VIRGO

SARA KASSEL, 18

CHAMPLAIN VALLEY UNION HIGH SCHOOL
HINESBURG, VT
TEACHER: ROBIN LAUZON

I

The only woman
The organized, worrying, meticulous
Modest temptress of perfection

II

Caught on the cusp
Of Fire and Earth leaning evenly
To both sides of a weighted scale

III

This is not my place
In the heavens
These stars that surround me, ostracize me

IV

Like a kettle of steaming water
The boiling blood wheels and dances
Steaming and crying harshly, shrilly
Silently

V
Caught forever in a spellbinding
Dance across the room
And never coupling but for
An eclipse

VI
The secret association
Mystical brotherhood of contradictions
Of complications
My modest eccentricity, and organized
Mess

VII
The dirt in my fingers is cold
And soft and hard
Rich and barren and muddy

VIII
I'm prone to drawers and boxes
To solid colors and hardwood floors
I keep time in file folders

IX
Deep in the forest I walk with my belongings
The clothes on my back
And dream of my shoe closet, long forsaken

X
Where am I going? The circles draw me in
Their even shape misleads me into tranquility
There is no blood, virgin

XI

The room full of loudness and soft smells
Overwhelming olfactory, auditory, tactile
On my toes and no one knows
The ease at which I float from
Person to person, defying all astrological
Parameters

XII

I kick off my talons at the door
We train barefooted gripping
The cold concrete for balance

XIII

The ink bleeds deep into my pores and hers
The same but feet and hands take different paths
Every day the same but within I am so
Deeply rooted in two places
The twins and the virgin lion,
Who knew?

GRINGO
AMERICA PEREZ, 14

COLORADO ACADEMY
DENVER, CO
TEACHER: BETSEY COLEMAN

Around 1994 I am born.
> *Al nacer me dan el apodo: Prieta.*
> *Todos dicen que me parezco a una mona, por ser tan peluda.*

Around 2006 my living room is filled with Christmas gifts.
> *Desde juguetes a planchas, todos quendan satisfechos.*
> My mom is told that she has tumors in her uterus.
> My brother doesn't get a birthday party.
> My family and I go see *Happy Feet.*

Around 2000 I learn English little by little.
> "Jay, jao ar yu? Mai naim is America."
> "Hi, how are you? My name is America."
> My dad breaks his ankle.
> I am the interpreter for him and the doctor.

Around 2008 my friends and I manage to make breakfast, eggs sunny-side up,
> Without hurting anyone.
> *Desafortunadamente, quemamos el pan tostado.*

Around 1999 my friends and I come home crying every day for about three months.
> We are sad because we don't understand English, the broken language.
> *Nos sentimos destrozadas.*

Around 2009 our attempt to make popcorn brings the firemen.

Around 2001 I get a pet Chihuahua;
My dad names him "Gringo."

Around 2008 I realize I'm deathly afraid of fish, clowns, and roller-coasters.
I give a speech in front of 300 people for
The Challenge Foundation.
My parents, brother, two sisters, and I play *Lo Loteria* for two hours.

Around 1998 my sister asks me for a flip-flop when we are in a pig's pen.
I give her one of my flip-flops.
I am taken to a *curandera* because I step on a nail.

Around 2006 my sisters and I obtain scholarships to private schools.
Green, gold, black, white, red, and navy blue become our school colors.

Around 2009 I will be 15 years old.
Mis amigos y familia celebrarán conmigo en mi quinceañera.
Bailaré el vals con mi papá.
Obtendre mi última muñeca.
Terminaré mi niñez. . .
Y comenzaré la plenitud de mi juventud.

TOSHIO AND THE THIMBLE
EMILY CORWIN, 18

DETROIT COUNTRY DAY SCHOOL
BEVERLY HILLS, MI
TEACHER: MATTHEW SADLER

In a Japanese movie house
she fiddles with an iron locket—
a thimble.
The porcelain lamp lights wilting
images flicker from the back room
like a lighthouse
guiding midnight waters in a four-wall room
in a geranium-pink coffee mug
the film reel chatters to life.

Once upon a time,
Toshio talked with a spaceman
who had tumbled gymnastics
in Jupiter's halo and in the fractured bones of stars,
building a new constellation—
Agoyoanye, Scorpio's daughter.

Toshio emptied the clear, citrine jar
that had once protected dragonfly nectar
and bruised, magnolia weeds
2000 yen in his lap.
He rode inside the jostling bus
like a heavily salted dinner
tossing and turning
in the seasick belly of a whale.

He sat on the Pacific's edge—
ever-changing, every hour
sands around his manufactured drawstring trousers
forming illegible Braille,
here he thought of his crippled war hero father,
his deformed body like
something sculpted from the fingerprints
of a child in ceramics class—
fresh out of the kiln.

The girl, breathless in the eighth row,
clenching onto the mahogany armrest,
suppressed the roses in her garden face.
She loved Toshio
in black
in white
in a whale's entrails
inside her thimble
in a goldfish bowl with algae vines
the astronaut, the horoscope,
the handicap, herself and Toshio,
synchronized swimming in the Japanese movie house.

CARNIVAL KALEIDOSCOPE (VILLANELLE)

NOOR BRARA, 17

AMERICAN EMBASSY SCHOOL
NEW DELHI, INDIA
TEACHER: TODD CHURCH

A popcorn pinwheel of color and music box strings
Inspire candy-floss laughter and jellybean joy
Toss up your hats, you acrobats; cartwheel into kings!

Cheer for the queer clowns as they somersault onto swings
Snooping in Technicolor tents, wistful wonder boy?
A popcorn pinwheel of color and music box strings

Fire-eaters roar dragon flames on make-believe wings
Circus girls dance their sequined smiles, cunning and coy
Toss up your hats, you acrobats; cartwheel into kings!

The ringmaster whips tigers into sizzling rings
Let fly rainbow ribbons and childish Cracker Jack toys
A popcorn pinwheel of color and music box strings

Spectacle stars twinkle music and magical things
Painted faces, glitter grins, puppet shows to enjoy
Toss up your hats, you acrobats; cartwheel into kings!

Now we jesters pack away our bags as the crowd sings
Songs of tinsel, Candyland and fairytale decoy
A popcorn pinwheel of color and music box strings
Toss up your hats, you acrobats; cartwheel into kings!

BATTLE AT WOUNDED KNEE

MELINA GOTERA, 15

CEDAR FALLS HIGH SCHOOL
CEDAR FALLS, IA
TEACHER: JUDY TIMMINS

Hundreds of us stood, frozen
as a white flag, waving naked against
the screaming yellow sky,
(swollen with rain, like a mango's threaded flesh)
bared its teeth and smiled at us,
grinning from the grip of a white-as-snow hand
hanging loose from the white-as-snow arm of
a white-as-snow man I was told not to fear.

Hundreds of us stood, frozen
as they called out to us
their loving battle cry,
"It's okay, it's okay,
you will be fine,
you will be safe,"
and ripped weapons from our hands,
bared their teeth and growled,
staring straight through my skin,
through my bones, the muscle tissue wrapped around me
(like a mango's threaded flesh).

Hundreds of us, and we were told
how this is okay, how we should not be afraid.
We were told how, you see, we had nothing to fear
but our own rotting yellow skin.

Our very skin
is wrong, you see.
Our history, written on walls,
in the thick dried mud washed away near Wounded Knee,
on the spotted palms of my mother.
It was all wrong, we were all wrong
and they were only trying to let us know.

Hundreds of us stood, frozen

as they told us again, "It's okay, it's okay,"
as they waved their white flag,
as they bared their yellow grins,
(shining dull against pale pigments)

frozen, as they smiled,
"You will be fine,"
then grabbed an old man,
ripping him apart at the seams,
much like their old white flag,
yellowing, almost brown at the tip.

Them a white flag, us the yellow sky.
I am suffocating on the sound of
guns, sparks, soaring through us,
through them.

Frozen, as our lungs filled quickly
rising and falling and back again with
sounds, deep and low,
echoing like thunder across miles of earth.
Miles of land that belong to no man, and to every man,
every woman, every child.

To the hummingbirds and the sound of the trees creaking,
belong to the yellow of the sky and the
white of the man shooting toward it.

It was all so much more than
loose cloth, stitched up white-as-snow.
And it was all so much more than
a sky tinted bright,
the yellow and red
the turquoise beneath all our skin.
It was all so much more.

Hundreds of us lay, frozen.
"You will be safe."

I WANNA HEAR A POEM
YADIRIS VALDEZ, 14

DREAMYARD
BRONX, NY
TEACHER: DANA CRUM

I wanna hear a poem
I wanna hear a sex poem
A weed poem
An "I make my wrists bleed" poem
Not no cheesy poem
But a sleazy poem
A poem that'll make your lips curl like an Elvis CD
I wanna hear a cold poem
A hard poem
A "Here, take my card" poem
A poem that'll make me go to the edge of my seat
Because it's so damn good
You don't care who or what is reciting it
I want Scooby Doo to come by and whisk me away with his
    un-understandable speak about how sad he is 'cause he ain't got
    his Scooby snacks
I wanna hear Rihanna talk about how unfaithful she is
Or Eminem's shovel digging his mother's grave
I wanna feel the hot lava of the words gushing through the margin of
the paper because the poem is too strong for it to obtain it
I wanna hear the poem of a bored watch cop
Or a mad detective
The dreams of a troubled kid
Or a lunatic mother
I wanna hear a crazy lifeguard's poem

Or a simple rock star's poem
I wanna hear a poem about a great adventure
An adventure to the outskirts of a war site
I wanna hear a soldier's poem
About his best buddy's violent death
Or that terrorist's poem whose head got cut off
I wanna hear such an extreme poem that'll make me wanna
Jump on a ski boat in six degree weather
A poem so wrong and twisted
It'll make me have nightmares
I wanna hear an unusual poem
A poem that'll make me go "hmm"
To top it all off,
I wanna hear a love poem
From a cow to a moose
A silly poem
I don't care just don't make it a déjà vu poem
Or a cliché
Show me a poem that'll make me think
Give me a poem so good, bad, disgusting
That'll make my poem seem like trash
Try, but I'll accept a friendly quit
Just give me a poem that'll take my time
Not waste it, just give me a poem
A poem, a poem, a poem I wanna hear

ROCKING
KAILANA DURNAN, 18

UNIVERSITY SCHOOL OF NASHVILLE
NASHVILLE, TN
TEACHER: FREYA SACHS

Pennsylvania mornings are thick with grackles,
so I sit on my lonely portico, in the chair Bill built.
I sit and watch them fall like night over my yard,
binoculars in my hands, steady hands in my lap.

I used to photograph them—people hate grackles—
like death! But with Bill in the Gulf, Evangeline married,
and Fritz always warbling at the end of the bar,
the blue-blacks of my landscape were my only company.

In the winter my lawn swells like a healthy moon.
I sit like a doll in Bill's chair and pine for my grackles;
in their eyes I am a million pieces.
in the snow, I am thin and endless and solitary.

Even now, I wake up to Bill feeling like a widow.
I am myself in my chair, on my bare porch. I am not alone—
grackles, too, must feel like a piece of the lonesome masses.
The grackles must wonder about the ocean, must think about death.

WAL-MART IS GHETTO
WILL DODGE, 14

CHARLESTON COUNTY SCHOOL OF THE ARTS
NORTH CHARLESTON, SC
TEACHER: MARY ANN HENRY

Halls full of seventh-graders talk and high-five
In their cashmere jackets and A&F polos
$170 jeans with the new flip-flops
Squeaks come from the new basketball sneakers
The fur cloth rubs from their North Faces
I'm different though
I wear the old, the thrift, and the unwanted
I take the $10 sneakers with thanks
And I sew the holes up on the cloth with ease,
Promising myself that one day
It would all be better.

The popular walk daintily
As I fight to keep my sneaker soles on
There is no one else like me
No one from the Ridgeville apartments
No one born on a couch
No one living in a leaking-roof condo
No one like me
Jenna What's-her-face walks by me
"Wal-Mart is sooo ghetto," she says
I want to hit her
She doesn't know
She really doesn't know.

ARIADNE'S MAZE
CLARE IRALU, 13

HOME SCHOOL
GALLUP, NM
TEACHER: TAMMY IRALU

I will write my memoir
now that we are heading to Athens
with a salty breeze in our faces
and seawater lapping
the sides of the ship.

It was mid-afternoon
and I was painting a picture of my garden
when I heard the sound
of chariot wheels on the road.
Even from a distance
I could see my father, King Minos of Crete.
There were 14 other people,
running behind the chariot.
I wondered what my father was up to.

As they drew closer,
I ducked behind the hedge.
The strangers and my father headed
for the palace's back door.
I followed silently.
Only after I went through
that large cedar door
did I realize
my father's guests
were chained together

and that we were headed
to the dungeons.

I kept hidden
while my father
locked them in.
Once he left,
I sat down
on a dirty hay-covered floor
and listened.

I gathered the prisoners
came from Athens.
They would be forced
beneath my father's palace
into a maze
to face
a beast
half-man, half-bull:
the Minotaur.
This was how
Athens and Crete
kept the peace.

As the prisoners cursed
their fate,
I heard a loud rumble below us.
Once the walls stopped shaking,
I decided the legend of the Minotaur was true.

All storytellers
in the prison cells
looked grim

except one:
Theseus,
Prince of Athens.
He claimed he had come
so that one less of his father's people would suffer.
I noticed his brave, calm, confident air.

As I hurried back to the palace,
I wondered:
could he save people
from the fate
my cruel father
had forced upon them?
I'd give him a chance.

Late that night
while the palace slept,
I crept to the dungeon
to offer him help:
a sword
to fight the Minotaur,
a ball of wool
to find his way
out of the maze.

Now I am in the garden again,
watching the rosy fingers of the dawn
creep into the sky.
I'm thinking of Theseus
and my leaving home
somewhere safe and far
from the Minotaur's lair.

WINTER
MEGAN GLASCOCK, 13

HOME SCHOOL
WHITEFISH, MT
TEACHER: JANICE LANDREAU

The earth is sleeping
white flakes fall from the sky
drifting like feathers onto the frozen ground
covering the earth in a white quilt
letting it rest protected
like dove wings wrapped across us
protected in our slumbering state.

3.0 CIRCULAR MOTION
MOLLY O'NEILL, 16
GREENWICH ACADEMY
GREENWICH, CT
TEACHER: JEFF SCHWARTZ

These days are wound too tightly, with no time
to finish things. I want it all to end
with balance and a sense of the sublime.
No more of this mad whirling that will rend
desire and keep us so dissatisfied.
The rift 'twixt what is and what ought to be
is widening. We are borne on the tide
of spinning earth and ticking clocks, and we
are trapped in such quick circles of motion
always accelerating, like ships caught
in a whirlpool on the stormy ocean.
We seek the center, for this is our lot:
buoyed by our airy aspirations,
anchored by our earthly obligations.

CREATIVE TAPESTRY
THORNTON BLEASE, 13
STANFORD UNIVERSITY EPGY ONLINE HIGH SCHOOL
STANFORD, CA
TEACHER: DENEENE BELL

"To dream the impossible dream
To fight the unbeatable foe
To bear with unbearable sorrow
To run where the brave dare not go
To right the unrightable wrong
To love pure and chaste from afar
To try when your arms are too weary
To reach the unreachable star"
—*Joe Darion*

I squint and stare through the luminous sunlight, past the golden rays of the Inca's most powerful deity, Inti, and see the ruins draped across the top and down the sides of a vast mountain area strung between two distinct Andean peaks. I inhale the meager murky atmosphere slowly through my nose and admire the craftsmanship of the fortress city. I look at the violent mountain peaks jutting up and around the sacred Inca city and everywhere I see steps, thousands of steps that appear to be impossible obstacles set before my tired and unconditioned legs. I am aware of every muscle, aware of the torture I will inflict on them as I force each leg ever so slightly off the ground to climb these formidable foes. I look at the misty clouds pulsating in a slow, rhythmically-choreographed dance around my head as I enter the gates of Machu Picchu. The swirling clouds present a mysterious façade to the ceremonial city, pulsating to the same rhythm that pounds in my head. I wonder: *Could I stay behind? Perhaps I could spend the day watching the llamas graze?*

The slight breeze tickles my forehead. I can feel the air wrapping my body in a soft, delicate jacket, yet I am unable to breathe as I should. My breathing shortens as I try to take in more oxygen. My family calls for me to keep up the pace. I try to focus on plodding ahead, but it seems that I am moving in slow motion while everything else around me moves in a rapid, staccato fashion away from me.

Gasping for breath as if a vise was methodically tightened across my chest, I attempt to climb the steps and tour the ruins. One step, two steps, three steps, four, I slowly climb. I look up and realize that these steps are a ladder to the heavens, to the unreachable stars. They extend way up into the puffy white clouds dancing for the sun god in the pure blue sky. My skin tingles; I can feel the presence of the Amerindians worshipping the brilliant solar orb and I embrace the mountain range with the same enthusiasm as I did my first class through the Stanford University Online High School.

My mind drifts. . . to a two-page book list with a syllabus and pacing guide adequate in preparation for the New York Scholastic Marathon. Mentally I type my 19-letter password to log into the virtual classroom, and my mind is engaged with hurricane force. My enthusiasm escalates as I approach my first timed and high pressure final exam. My head pounds, my heart pulsates, my windpipe becomes very sensitive. Like balloons being squeezed inside a trash compactor, my lungs tighten and my mind freezes. It is a blank slate, wiped clean, with no information available. My hard drive crashes and freezes; the computer in my mind will not reboot. I sit still, unable to move, unable to conjure information any more complex than my name. My head pounds faster and faster, my legs are numb, and my hands are shackled under the control of a malfunctioning brain.

Back on the mountain, I am frightened. I try to breathe normally, but my chest is heavy and my lungs are on strike. I am lying on a terrace, a break in the steep accordion steps. I feel the clouds kissing my face, embracing my body. I see the massive peaks rising above the earth like loaves of bread awaiting the oven. I should know that I am in Peru, yet I am in a fog. My mind isn't sure if I have altitude sickness or if I am back taking final exams. The sensations are the same, the same inability to breathe, the same pounding of my heart in my head. Gasping for breath as if I am being methodically suffocated and tortured with pins and needles around my mouth, I suspend the mission of touring the ruins for the day.

I look up and see my older brother, lithe—fit and confident— ascending the mountainside, while I struggle to free myself from my physical and mental bondage. I simultaneously see images of my class- mates easily racing to the peak of success, while I struggle to set myself free of my learning disabilities, the Central Auditory Processing Disorder that becomes obvious under pressure. My legs are heavy and weighted, my muscles cramping from movement in the low atmos- pheric pressure of the Andes Mountains, just as my brain cramps as it misfires under pressure, halting the retrieval of information bytes, reducing the speed of communication at the synaptic junctures, and keeping the information under lock and key deep within the recesses of my brain. My dream to climb to the summit of Machu Picchu seems to be an impossible dream, just as impossible as forcing the two halves of my brain to communicate with each other, and work in unison with each other rather than participate in a cerebral siege combat. I call it Helen Keller brain. My ears can hear and my eyes can see; however, my brain does both ineffectively. The path through my brain is not a yellow brick road, and neither is the ascent of Machu Picchu, a severely steep and undulating challenge that causes my body to revolt much like my brain, resulting in an inability to move spontaneously, to organ- ize my thoughts, or to process conversations.

I sit alone on the steps with only "more steps" in view for what seems to be an eternity until my dad and brother return from their ascent. Back at the hotel, I rest. The pounding in my head eases a little and I am able to enjoy the dinner and display of native dancing. I decide that I do not want my impossible dream to haunt me for the rest of my life, any more than I wish to surcease challenging mental pursuits, nor ultimately my dreams of being a writer, despite the complexities of my miswired brain. Obstacles left unchecked can prevent success. Obstacles not approached with the vigor of a quarterback can prevent the winning touchdown in the game of life. Tomorrow, I will try again.

Climbing is no easier the second day, but I finally take some serious consecutive steps; first, six or seven. And then I rest, letting a group of young adults pass me, before I wager another six or seven uneven stones jutting out like baby dragon teeth, then a third group of seven. An older woman passes by me and smiles a warm, inviting smile. An empty feeling, a sadness wallowing in the pit of my stomach wrenches my heart as I watch her long, brown hair streaked with silvery-gray swing with her steps. The aroma of White Orchid perfume dances to my nose. "Mom!" If she were here she could help me climb these angry rock monsters of Peru.

Renewed confidence rings through my body. I breathe in and out as slow and steady as the land. The jutting rocks and the pristine green terraces come into view. I imagine I am among the Amerindians of Machu Picchu running up and down these mountains, 548 years ago, building the sacred ceremonial "Lost City of the Incas" almost 10,000 feet above sea level. Although my breathing is not any easier, I persevere one step at a time.

My mind returns from its creative drift to ancient associations, back to the violent Andes Mountains, mountains thrusting out before me, thrusting toward the sky, shouting to the sun. Self-contained, with agricultural terraces built throughout, the exacting mortarless blocks were built with a precision comparable to record-setting Michael Phelps' Olympian physique. Both the Incas and Phelps accomplished the nearly impossible. Can I? Can I fight the unbeatable foe with tired and weary arms and legs? The words spoken by Phelps infiltrate my thoughts: "With creativity you can accomplish anything." I wonder: Is creativity the key to success?

My progress remains limited. Slowly—step by step—I challenge the pleated ladder of the sun. Slow and steady, I approach the unreachable star. Slow—though perhaps not always "steady"—can also describe my thought processes. Deep like the valleys cut by the mountains, my thoughts are personally and intellectually gratifying, yet fraught with difficulty when trying to share those mental experiences with others. While my father and brother, like two foot soldiers, approach closer and closer to the top, I stay behind on a terrace about a third of the way to the top. *Should I give up? If I give up climbing the mountain, will that set precedence for giving up on my dreams of becoming a writer because of my processing disabilities?* Sadly, sharing the experience of being on top of the world with my family, accomplishing the difficult feat of taming the monster mountain, is not to be.

With some more subtle creative adaptations, I am able to hike even more the third day. Crafting a story in my mind, I visualize myself alongside the character in my next novel climbing to the top with ease. Thus, by taking a different path to the solution that did not rest upon my weaknesses but my strengths, I find ways to fight back at the mountain. I take one step, then two, and a few more before stopping to rest, then my body begins to joust back. My eyes focus on the green, velvet-coated mountains. By concentrating on the beauty of the Andes, my mind free from the pumping pulsations, I relax and the main character of my new story begins encouraging me in my mind.

Soon, Adventure Jack—one of my evolving literary characters—is metaphorically by my side urging me to keep trying. Imagery brings Jack and me back to the days of the Incas. We are both worshipping the sun god. Soon the pounding in my head eases a bit, and I ccan take a few more steps into the air until I approach what could be called the Condor's Nest, the optimal view point. As I view the towers—the peaks jutting out all around me like cotton-topped armies of green marching to the sun—I am acquainted to a simple world lost in the midst of time. I see the stone waves preserved on the ground, twisting and turning, a twining tower, arching toward the sun.

Both Jack and I wonder: *Did they believe, as they constructed the stone temples, that they could reach the sun, the circular sphere in the sky that became their god?* Belief in the impossible was significant to their success and to my triumphs as well. I realized that with a creative outlook and belief in myself, I can do anything. I now can fully understand the power presented in the words spoken by Phelps: "With creativity you can accomplish anything." Slow and steady may not have won the race to the top, but I realize that I was still able to enjoy the view. The challenge necessitated that I reinvent myself, and with the assistance of my new character Jack, that is what I was able to do.

Leaning as far to the edge as I safely could brought tears of happiness to my cornflower-blue eyes. A sense of freedom trickled through me, electrifying both my mind and my body. With this feeling came a revelation wrapped around an image of Phelps reaching his hand out to the edge of the pool, overtaking his competitors by a fraction of a second. My thoughts drifted from the image of a well-disciplined athlete trained to perfection to myself: an awkward pre-teen with two lobes of my brain refusing to communicate with one another; a brain living in a hostile neurological environment, sentenced to a purgatory called Central Auditory Processing Disorder.

At that moment I realize that creativity is what has been holding me and the two halves of my brain together for years, and that creativity along with perseverance will be the key to my success in the future. Climbing the steep path—trying to succeed every day—I need to reinvent myself to adjust to my internal environment rather than attempt to fit my rather unique brain into a one-size-fits-all lifestyle, just as my body had to adjust and reinvent itself to climb Machu Picchu.

NON DIMENTICAR
ADRIAN PASKEY, 16
BOILING SPRINGS HIGH SCHOOL
BOILING SPRINGS, PA
TEACHER: W. DAVID SHIELDS

One of 52 identical siblings, she is a most familiar friend to musicians. Elementary-school students to elderly people covet Middle C, who shines her brightest through all travail. Slightly to the left of the true middle of the piano, the key reclines in bliss as a wooden prism carved like the panhandle state of Oklahoma. Unlike her demure ivory ancestors, the modern Middle C sports a fine-grained wood iced with glossy cotton-candy-cloud paint. Her intricate grain patterns are visible on the edges of the key's platform, adding mystery as she bobs up and down during concerts. In the gloriously warm sunlight, a slight yellow tinge is visible from age. Dancing to the music, the sun's rays glance at the top of her and slide airily across the pearly surface before gracefully lighting off the sharply rounded edge. The dainty sliver of sunshine darts further down to illuminate the reverberating canyon below that is filled with mallets and strings. Tickled, she giggles a mellow jingle and resumes her part in the never-ending serenade that is her legacy.

Music has been a part of my life as long as I can remember. That sounds rather cliché now that I say it, but it is one of those paradoxes that outlasts time. My grandfather was a musician, playing in the Army Cavalry band, working in a professional band, and directing several religious choirs. He encouraged my parents to find a piano instructor for me to study with when I entered the first grade. Every Sunday, I would show my grandfather what I had learned. It was an unspoken tradition that grew between us. He taught me that music is the most useful tool one can have in life, and I should never forget that it will remain deep in my heart.

"Non dimenticar." Never forget.

I thought he was just an old man who liked music, but now that music has become the most relieving, intense, and passionate entity in my existence I can see that he was right.

My grandfather encouraged me to expand upon my musical skills, and led me to voice lessons with an extremely accomplished teacher when I reached the fifth grade. I grew more and more attracted to music, and he continued to encourage me, being the only musician in my family. When I was 10, he died, but his spirit continued with me through music. The same year, I received his alto saxophone, and the music continued. I practiced before school and every day, playing the evenings away on my precious instruments. At the first opportunity, I began accompanying my school and church choirs on piano. No matter what happens, there will always be music.

Whether I am disgruntled, miserable, elated, or tired, I can turn to music. I have learned how to allow it to consume me and carry me with the waves of emotion written on the paper, in contrast to the turmoil of society. The genre I select reflects my mood and ranges amongst centuries of composers. When I sit at a piano and begin to decode the black maze that was so carefully thought out by composers through the ages, I find myself at peace.

To play alone supplies the serenity to express myself and experiment with other styles and techniques of playing. I find myself playing early in the morning, before the sunrise, or late at night after the world has gone to sleep. When I am restless at night, I don the headphones of my digital piano and play until the early morning.

I admire and respect the instruments that bring such joy to me and those who surround my life. I feel that the piano is the most beautiful and intricate instrument of all. With its combination of keys, mallets, and strings, it is fascinating. The uniqueness of the shape and grain of a piano is inspiring, as is the difference in the touch of different pianos. Familiarizing myself with the touch of a piano is similar to getting to know a person. Different ways to play each key merit different tones as well as ways to play and produce beauty. Then again, the music itself blossoms with dazzling flight.

The top of my piano glistens in the moonlight that squeaks through curtains concealing the old bay window. A stream from the moon flickers as an owl floats by, humming along with the melody that escapes from the reverberating strings within. The song grows, expanding into a convivial serenade and subsiding into a placid repetition of the bass strings that is reminiscent of waves gently rolling onto a pure white beach. I continue the familiar patterns that sparkle with clarity and fade into the comforting cloak of darkness. As the world has long since gone to sleep, only the spirit of music hears the sounds that celebrate its very existence which is entwined with my life, and subsequently everything that is dear to me. In the hush, a voice echoes somewhere deep within the caverns of my mind:

Non dimenticar. Never forget.

BROKEN GOURD
EUNJU NAMKUNG, 18
WRITOPIA LAB
NEW YORK, NY
TEACHER: REBECCA WALLACE-SEGALL

Preface:

Do you know how to start my memoir?

How about: A conversation with an old lady on bus. That's the start of my memoir.

Or: My brother throws walnuts at my head.

Now that's the first page of my life, I swear.

Or: Poverty is privilege, this is my new philosophy.

Now this is something interesting. This is my memoir.

Oh, dear God! Please let it be none of the above.

Actual Start of Memoir:

You see, my dad brings home a special branch.

Like how he brings home old cash registers that we hope to keep for a hundred years so that my grandchildren can get them appraised at the eternal *Antiques Roadshow.* I play with one for a couple of days, pretending I am a cashier to my imaginary customers. One day, however, I stop punching the buttons and opening the drawers because I realize the pennies and nickels I put into it pale in comparison to what the antique is actually worth. To think, that what I am wearing right now can be worth thousands of dollars in two, three, or maybe five hundred years. To think, everything I own will be an antique in due time. In the future I will be automatically wealthy as long as I hoard my trash, keep my possessions away from sunlight, and live a long life.

Done and done. I'll work on the latter.

Like how he brings home the memory of me, his little daughter, hoping that maybe when he comes back from work, the broken gourd standing before him would transform into his mental image. My father, not the type to tell stories, tells only one story. Just one and only story, over and over again. The story is about me, his one and only daughter, and—according to him—the term "daughter" is up for interpretation. He says I am more son than daughter, but more broken gourd than son.

The story evolves, grows tumors of extra details that were never there in years past. In fact, the story has grown so much with passing time that even my father gets increasingly more surprised by the new versions that come out of his mouth. There are hundreds of versions of it drifting in time, but no one can uncover the truth because whatever was has transformed to what is now, and whatever is now could be infinitely different then.

In the purest form, the story goes:

Eunju Namkung, age 6, punched Ian Park, age 8, in the nose. His nose bled and he cried. Eunju cried too, because she was afraid of getting in trouble.

And this is a version that has been spoken sometime between then and now:

Eunju Namkung—a mere age 6, a sweet little kindergartner—was playing with Ian Park, who was in second grade but had no friends of his own age to play with. He looked stupid with his goofy mouth and stupid big front teeth and stupid monkey ears, all curled at the edges, with the weird mole mounted on his right ear. He was making fun of her for being smaller, for being a girl. She was standing there, her cute fists balled tight, letting his voice trail off, watching him shake his head and smile a smile that asked for no forgiveness. Her braided pigtails got tighter and tighter, constricted with the power of her rage. The force spread outward and outward from the point of vindictive concentration, unraveling and thinning away, drawing away from the central fact of the stain until nothing at all was invisible. Eyes closed, without a word, she got up, came to him, gave her hand to his face—his goofy face was all lit with bonging and alarms. Her knuckles met his nose and he shrieked. As a wimp, he couldn't tolerate the pain in his nose as both of his nostrils trickled blood—a "twin nosebleed" as it is called in Korean. What made him run to his mother crying was not the pain in his nose, but the pain he felt from the metaphorical castration of his boy body.

Eunju cried too because she was afraid of getting in trouble, that clever devil.

And this is a true story that I hear as I grow up. Though the stories may have been skewed, I know it is not fiction because I can still feel the residue of the punch boiling in my hand. I know that I was, indeed, smaller and weaker, and thus nothing, and that I still am the same powerless girl of age 6. But at that moment, against Ian, I was everything. Even if it was a blind shot, Ian heard what I had to say without me saying anything. Each time my father tells me this story, it becomes more elaborate, little Eunju more brave, a little more painful. I shrink and feel his words poke me in the ribs. I am ashamed that I am not the girl of whom my dad speaks so proudly.

Like how he brings home a soccer ball whose seams have frayed. I take it in my hands and look it over, disturbed by the messy hexagons of black and white. I wonder if I should tell him what I really think. I decide not to, because I know what the soccer ball means. My father is telling me that although he isn't too happy about it, he will allow me to play soccer.

So I play soccer, but I can't even score the winning goals. I tell my parents that scoring is as hard a thing to do as defense, but they say, "It's possible." They tell me that daughters don't play soccer and sons score winning goals. I frown and moan and run onto the field thinking that the powerful red I feel surging through my body can help me in the game. I kick the ball, which, not surprisingly, goes a few feet out of bounds. Although I don't look in their direction, I can hear the intensity of my parent's necks cracking as they shake their heads, muttering, "Broken gourd. Broken gourd. Our daughter broken gourd."

I pick up on the violent competition that exists as a subset of soccer games. I learn the skill of pushing without being caught, and that is only the start. My specialty is body-checking someone with massive force but in an elegant manner that appears to be harmless and accidental. The best fouls are the ones you make but for which the other team gets penalized.

This is how it is: I throw girls onto the ground. I untuck my jersey to annoy the ref. I make sure the goalie gets hit hard even though it seems like the ball will miss the net by a mile. And sometimes I feel bad, but when I see my parents on the sidelines and remember the tattered soccer ball my dad gave me, my apologies are empty and my mind rages with a desire to get back on the field. I am, after all, a broken gourd. I stir up the dirt that makes the air hazy and hard to breathe. When the dust settles, I wonder if my dad is watching me with the eyes that he has when he tells the story of Little Eunju and the Twin Nosebleed. Usually, he doesn't answer my beckoning stares.

Like how he goes to Korea and brings home traditional tops at my brother's request and no stuffed animal, against my request. I know I am beyond the age of stuffed animals, but I want them anyway. Generally, I don't care for stuffed animals, particularly at night, when I make sure to store all of them, their beady eyes and all, in the closet, where I will not see them, and they will not stare back. I just want to see my dad walk through the doorway with large suitcases, one filled with his clothes, the other with a stuffed animal so large it would not be able to sleep in the bed with me. It is a fair and simple test that I specifically design with the hope that my father will pass. So when he doesn't bring one home for the other time that I asked him, he fails the test.

I fail just as badly.

I ask him, "Where is what I asked for?"

He says, "You never asked for it before, so I thought you wouldn't need it now."

I wonder if he will ever hear me.

At least the tops bring harmonious joy to my brother and father. They wrap the leashes around the top, tongues dangling, panting like two dogs racing for a bone. Hurling, unraveling, releasing, and launching these tops into the air. The tops scatter like dragonflies with strange hums and disturbing metallic shine. Once they land on the ground, they spin and circle each other, just as my brother and father circle around the battle of the tops. Together they are hunched, gorilla-like, literally patting the floor and punching the sky.

"Beat him!" Fist up, my brother shouts at his top.

"Spin faster!" Both fists up, my father urges his top.

I can tell who wins by his growl of victory, as the other one scurries to pick up their immobile, defeated top. Again they race to relaunch, and again they circle their tops, yelling strategies to the earless tins, and again someone growls. Then repeat, then repeat. That is, until I get hit in the head by a heavy chunk of spinning metal, which brings them harmonious joy plus uncontrollable laughter. I can feel the rage accumulating in my muscles, the cry waiting to be released from my throat, but just for my gleeful brother and father, whose ingredient to getting along are simple tops, just for this beautiful sight, I'll quietly smile. The broken gourd can risk a few more cracks.

Like how he brings home pink jackets, which he thinks I'll wear. I tell him, "No. They're only for Asian girls who wear glasses and have no lives." But of course "have no lives" doesn't translate well in Korean, literally meaning "their bodies are lifeless." So again I become the weird American child who says such terrible satanic words. But really, he's just a bit upset about my rejection of his pink jacket, which could possibly be the only time he thought to buy me clothes.

Whenever I do see pink jackets on the street—puffy with down and warm with embarrassing color—I feel a little colder and the wind strikes me across the face. Whatever I am wearing at the time—be it a brown jacket or blue windbreaker—it becomes nothing more than a veil waving gingerly in the sharp wind. My bones rattle with the biting feeling of a gust that comes not from storm, or passing wave, but from the memory of my lost chance that drifts further away with passing time. In the pink, I see the image of my father putting the jacket aside, surprising me with the lost look in his eyes.

Like how he brings home remote-control mini car racers that are supposed to be mine. They are for me, a girl. They are not for my brother, who is much older—too old to be playing with cars—but takes them anyway. I wanted to keep them—to fill the void left by the stuffed animals that were never bought; to right the wrong of the pink jackets.

I imagine my father bought the cars from a greasy Korean man wearing the black coat that every poor Korean owns and sporting tough workman gloves with red rubber palms, which—when put together, palms thrust outward—look like a baboon's ass. The man, merely a peddler, offers my father the cars and my father buys them to give to me. But is he thinking of me, or is he thinking of this other man's daughter, who for all I know could be wearing a pink jacket? We are the same daughter.

My father is giving for himself, even as he pulls out his weathered wallet with rounded corners and limp leather, even as he puts a faded green bill onto the hungry red rubber, and even as their gloves touch.

Like how he brings home black bits of rubber in his hair. He's a greasy Korean man—greasy from lying supine below cars dripping fluids, from drinking oil and antifreeze—who lies beneath a Lexus, maybe a Toyota. Brake pads, oil, engine head, pistons, cylinders, transmission, differential, tire-pressure gauge, windshield. Yes, I know such parts and can even point them out.

For a week I am his assistant. He makes me sweep, but it is not possible to fit the entire Earth's supply of dirt in a dustpan, even with multiple trips to the trash can and blisters numbing my hands. Every hour I make my rounds, picking up pounds of blackness. Black bits that eventually make their way into his hair, which has developed a nasty hybrid of black, white, and brown. Shame on him for trying to hide his wisdom hairs with commercial dyes that say, "Look, I'm aging and insecure about it." As a daughter, I sit behind him, straddling my legs onto his shoulders, searching as a monkey fingers through the fur of another to find black bugs, dinner.

One day, he brings home a cane. He goes to work in Woodside and drives back to the Bronx, bringing home a wooden stick. Maybe it was a fusion of lightning and tree that made the branch wrangled, twisted, and curved as ugly things are. But as most ugly things in nature are, it is beautiful. A shepherd could have used it, maybe the ancient civil rights activist who asked the pharaoh oh, so kindly, to let his people go. I can smell the Red Sea, feel the narrow escape. The canes's shaft has scars that tell the story of how a blessed flock was saved from beastly wolves.

The Moses stick, as it comes to be known, is sturdy and solid. It comes down on me one day, and I definitely feel the lightning and the tree. I don't feel the pain, and don't even know if there is any, because the fear within me grows like a large hole and makes everything not matter. All I did was finally talk to my dad the way I wanted to. I told him, "No, I would not like to change the channel." I said, "My friend's dad bought her Valentine's Day chocolate." I asked, "Can you put down the newspaper for a second?" I knew my words were pronounced with swiftness, a subtle chill, that I hoped would go unheard but was somehow detected by my father's soul. The one time I decide to dare and break the silence I become a silly girl fallen into an even larger well of silence, where the walls are slimy and the water dark.

The hook looms above me, drawing ellipses in the air as the other half of it colors me purple. My mother's face is in the shadows, which isn't possible in the brightly lit room. I wonder why her eyes look at me with pity when her voice echoes with anger. Dad must be in the other room listening carefully, assessing the severity of the situation. The voice, the cries, the cracking of the Moses stick, they must all satisfy him. He does not come in.

My mom's right—it's better her than him. She was right when she heard my father's growl. She was right when she dropped the dishes and left the sink water running. She was right on time when my father had thrown down his newspapers, considering for a second if a daughter could be hit. I trust that she is right as she pulls me, violently, but with a grasp of salvation somehow. She pulls me into the room, yells the words that my father would have said. I am glad it is my mother wielding the Moses stick. My father is right for staying in the other room, sitting on his couch, continuing to read his news. If he were here, I would never be able to look at him again, never be able to say I was the monkey upon his shoulders.

My father brings home discord. He sighs before he walks through the doors with a bag of newspapers, takes off his grease-bottomed shoes, and sighs again as he lies on the couch, smothering the remote, which he'll yell at me to find later. Watching the news as he reads the papers: I don't get why he tries to know the entire world when he doesn't even know his home. My day at school, the remote's proximity—he doesn't know anything.

He doesn't know my brother hit me in the back of my head so hard, so hard my face got numb. Not a sting, but a subtle numbness that washes up onto my face as seaweed does at the beach. It appears, disappears, only to reappear and remain. And thus the numbness crept. First above my upper lip, then no numbness. Then forehead, then no numbness. Then the cheeks, then nothing. Then the numbness floods in, humming a vibrato across my skin. My face felt so light it might float away, almost a pleasant feeling, if it hadn't been from my brother hitting me.

I imagine that it was a frightening strike, some sort of blitzing technique that he learned from his friend, *Monday Night Football.* Maybe it was Saturday-Afternoon, Cut-Into-Cartoons College Football: speed, pushing of door, swift strike. It's all very good except for poor little me, whose poor little head became a physics problem with his elbow or water bottle, whatever it was. He the lion, me the gazelle, our home an African dryland, seemingly peaceful but poisoned with tension. It is my life as prey.

At the sound of the collision my mother scurries in, tired. My brother's mother looks frightened to death. My mother and his mother are standing in the same spot, torn which to be first. One arm over me, the other arm holding him back, it is terrible what we are doing to her. She's dying on the inside, splitting in two, and favoring us both. My father walks in, and as instantly as his head bobs through the doorway, he bobs back out. He knows nothing and therefore can say nothing.

It's funny, because I can only think of the Moses stick. When my mom stood over me, wielding it above me as if I were the sea, I recall my brother intervening and holding my mother back. He held her back. And just like then, my father is on the couch reading the newspaper, just waiting until someone could help him find the remote. I hear the slow rustles of the black-and-white print violently sweep into the room whenever I take a breath and my crying seizes.

My father brings home newspapers. I wait in anticipation for him to ring the bell. When I hear his heavy boots climbing up the steps, I fling the door open and watch his hands, hoping they will be empty. Although he searches for my eyes to look into his own. I look at his hands. Everyday he carries plastic bags, their handles lightly wrapped around his coarse, dirtied fingers.

"Take these," he sighs. He extends his arms to me. I take them from him, and we both linger in front of the doorway for a few seconds. He expects a bow, but he should know that I stopped bowing years ago.

I consider it for a second.

I see a girl whose black hair slides off her shoulders and hangs limply from the surface of her scalp. Her bowed head looks like it is hanging from a ceiling. I decide I do not want to bow. I walk away to put his newspapers on the couch, and I can hear him closing the door, taking off his shoes, sighing.

"Broken gourd."

EXPERIENCING ADOLESCENCE AS TANTALUS

EMMA FUNK, 14

WEST VALLEY HIGH SCHOOL
FAIRBANKS, AK
TEACHER: CARRIE HEIMER

The House on Solitude

I remember moving to the house on Solitude. I carried a fishbowl between my feet on the drive. Upstairs was so big and white and open and bright. It looked like Heaven, just lightness, with one big mattress in the middle. My room was pink. It made the carpet look pink too. It was the inside of an eraser. A Necco wafer. I painted over it. Purple, like a bleached grape. Then green, like key limes and Granny Smiths. Even though it changed, it was never quite right. It was always infantile.

It has a minuscule window. I hated it. Going from the empyrean luminosity of the top floor to the Pepto-Bismol dungeon was like being condemned. Trudging down stairs covered in a carpet that does nothing to make the floor more comfortable was a jail sentence.

The yard is big, with two chicken coops and a gazebo that is covered in moss. I always wanted to live inside the gazebo, my own little house; an adult in a poofy dress, throwing tea parties. I wanted to run away from home once, so I decided to live in the chicken coop. I never did. It smells awful in there.

The best part is the raspberries. My mom looked at houses for three years. I never thought we would actually move. I stopped caring. Then we went to one. The realtor was late, so we just ate berries in the yard. I love raspberries. They are the best part. The house is a house. It has a roof. But I love the berries best. They felt like home even before we lived there.

My brother used to have a lizard. We fed it crickets. Some escaped, and now they lived under the furnace. I loved listening to them because when I did, I was in the tropics, slumbering in a hammock, surrounded by monkeys and jaguars and grand kapok trees. I always imagined that under the furnace they had a metropolis, with twinkling lights and trolleys. I miss that sound.

If You Die Before Your Dinner

Dessert before dinner. My aunt always orders key lime pie before dinner. If you die before your dinner comes, at least you'll have had dessert. I like that idea. It keeps you in the moment, optimistic. I don't understand the other things she does, though.

My aunt sniffs crayons. She has boxes and boxes: small, large, and jumbo. Thirty-two colors, 64, 128. Each one like a technicolor mountain range. They hide in their boxes, little towers, temples of friendly pigment, ready to conquer the world. But she doesn't color, she just smells them. She prattles on about them, the waxiness, and the palpable odor of color. Waxiness like candles, candy corn, the smell of dental floss without the mint flavor.

She also sniffs artificial grapes. I visited her once and she took me to a hobby store and showed me a certain aisle. It was covered in plastic grapes, a vertical vineyard. They are maroon, like albino rat eyes; black, like licorice; and green—a pale, sickly green, like snot. They are shaped like boat buoys, and overly shiny. On the two-story high wall, they are like polka dots on lush virescent fabric. They are a caricature of fruit, a travesty to the starving. They are made for kitchen tables and mantelpieces. Temptation without reward. She rubs them between her fingers, like they were long-lost jewels, found after years of searching, or bloody battles and conflicted succession. She floats her digits below her nose, like she is sniffing a fine vintage wine. She is a connoisseur of grapes and crayons. I don't know why she is so connected to her nose. Maybe smells are a constant for her, dependable. They are always the same. Maybe it's the only thing in her life that doesn't change.

My Name

I looked up my name once. It means "universal." Usual. Typical. Boring. Like paste, useful, but overly sticky and funny-smelling. Tacky—like a carnation. My name is an ugly red mug from an office Christmas party. Functional—like pea gravel. When I was little, I wanted to be named Eleanor. Like the first lady, something strong and elegant, like a tiara. Back then, I loved the color pink. Things change.

My mom told me I was going to be named Graham if I was a boy. Like the cracker. I like Graham better. She also told me she wanted me to be Grace or Iris. Yesterday I walked into a room without opening the door. Grace is not the name for me. Iris is wrong too. It is tall, slender, delicate and purple. I am a traffic cone. I am not quiet, or dainty or feminine. I do not own a dress.

My name did not set me up for success. I wasn't named after anyone. I saw in *Time* once that Emma was the most popular name in Englan. I was one of the many. Apparently Jane Austen's *Emma* was written so no one would like the protagonist. When I wasn't universally ordinary, I was unlikable. I'd never liked the name anyway.

Then I started German class. The teacher saw my name and was surprised. He said that I should have kept my name instead of choosing a German one for class. I didn't know Emma was German. I used to think of Germany: guttural language, lederhosen, and potatoes. But I love the language, and now I am special. Singular. Sensational. Now I accept my name. It is a mask of putty, hiding the color and intricacies below. Simple, but enigmatic.

Terrifying Brilliance

She is intimidating, especially to the unprepared. She talks much faster than I can take notes or even comprehend. Her mind travels from topic to topic like a pin-pong ball. She can explain anything and offer her opinion as well. She has an almost fictional strength of character. She knows who she is. She is a novel made of iron, carved with intricate designs, poetry, controversial ideas and clarity. She is a desk lamp—when asked, she swivels over to shed light on that of which I am ignorant.

She is always on time, always energized, always wearing a vest. She always writes in cursive, and she always writes with a fountain pen. She says pens are like toothbrushes: You don't use anyone else's. She always drinks Earl Grey tea, and always recycles. She is always going, gleeful, glorious, sagacious. She talks with her hands, like an interpretive dancer; literary analysis in 6/8 time.

She is Einstein, Herodotus, Ovid, and Chaucer. She would climb to the top of Mt. Everest and theorize about the ascension of a mountain being a Christ symbol. She taught me to never say "hopefully," or leap out of my seat chirping "boink!" in the middle of a novel. She introduced me to the archetype. She taught me the meaning of i.e. and e.g., and why the number 33 alludes to Jesus. She gave me Jane Austen, John Knowles, Eric Remarque, Harper Lee, S.E. Hinton, Joseph Conrad, Chinua Achebe, and—most of all—William Golding. She is the fountain of knowledge, spurting ideas and information whether it is wanted or not, like the fact that the Hanoverian royal who married into the British monarchy brought a fat mistress and a skinny mistress. She taught me that the oven is not related to the muffin.

She also introduced my class to God. She discovered we were raised as heathens. She says she grew up giving ten cents every week to save the pagans in Africa. Little did she know we were right here. She has educated us on Christian history, from the stories of David, Bathsheba, Lloyd Douglas's *The Robe;* from the Church of England and the Puritans to Martin Luther and his 95 theses. She has saved us from ignorance. She is a veritable force of nature, typhoon Susan. I want to be her.

She has taught me more than any teacher I have had. She still scares me a little, though.

Annotation

My teacher asked me where my notes were.

"On this piece of paper, right here."

"They're not in your book?"

I couldn't write in books. They were so perfect, so clean. Whiteness, punctuated by prose: so intelligent, so strong, so enviable. Who was I to mar that clear beauty? I could never match them, so wise and important as to be published. I dreamed of writing—wished and fantasized. Writers were clouds. Idyllic. Writers were statues, fixed in glory, messiahs over me, one so young and ignorant. I absorb, praying for osmosis. . . I would not dare to mutilate that poetic paragon of prose. My wobbly words were half-baked cupcakes from a box in comparison to a writer's 12-tier wedding cake replete with pearls and orchids.

How will you find a quote? How do you remember what you thought later? How will you know where to look? I could not answer. My thoughts felt stupid, childish, frivolous, undeserving of being immortalized. Minuscule. A pea next to the country of Bolivia.

But I was under orders, so I took a pen and attacked that pristine ivory. My pen was an assassin's dagger, the ink spreading like blood into the page. The page was ruined and it was conquered. Writers no longer sat on pedestals, their faces intent, philosophical and grayish. My thoughts were good enough. I had grown into someone large enough to stand next to an adult, and still keep my head above water. My word next to theirs was still a weak, pea-brained puppy next to Lassie, but it could stand on its own feet and bark loudly.

I have always wanted to find books with writing in them, to see what others thought, to marvel at their grand ideas. Perhaps someone will find, deep in a last-chance sale bin at a used bookstore, a book that I have annotated and they'll think I am clever.

Identical

"All right, Emma. Let's try 'Minuet Three' again."

I released a sigh that would have sent the Leaning Tower of Pisa tottering on its foundations.

I lift my flute up, the metal covered with sweat and saliva, like a disease. It is warm in my fingers, growing heavier with each repetition of this song. I begin to play. The notes are heresy to my ears.

"Again, again—one more time. Let's see if we can clear this part up, shall we?"

It rings in my ears, the eternal echo of my shortcomings. Her patience is both comforting and infuriating. As I continue to slide below musical perfection, I feel like I grow shorter. I am a squalling infant, incapable of what is proclaimed as simple.

And finally I reach it: tonal obedience. I have reached the standard. I sound like a recording. I have reached this perfection, but my thirst is not quenched. It is her perfection, not mine. She says in an infantilizing, falsely encouraging manner, "This is how it should sound." I must play it at the right moment. Just like everyone else. In a group, we must play at the same time. If we are perfect, it sounds like a single musician. Identical.

I stare at the flute. It mocks me from its case. It is nestled in black velvet, relaxed like an arrogant old man in swim trunks by the pool on his private island. If I raise it to my lips, I must do it correctly. It must be at the right angle. The sheet music lies there, the lines of the score as rigid as the expectations set by music teachers. The notes are flies, buzzing around my head as I try to focus.

"*Again,*" they whisper. "Do it just so."

Then I tried acting. And I was a balloon released—a butterfly liberated from captivity to stretch its sticky wings and glide into the sun. With a play, I am given a word, and—sometimes—a general direction at which to aim it. With it, I can fly. I can holler it from rooftops. I can whisper it beneath a pillow. I can mumble it in front of the class. Every time I say it, the word is different, and it is perfect for something else, just maybe not this.

A note is concrete. It is right, or it is wrong. "Here is what you say, when you say it, how long it takes you, and even how you say it." *Dulce.* Sweetly. Obediently sweet. No love. No joy. No passion. No sweetness. Only discipline, a soldier marching in time.

Then I knew—I could never work in a cubicle. I cannot do something just like everyone else. I do not want to play it over and over, only trying to achieve someone else's idea of perfection. A note is always someone else's. It never belongs to me. I can make a word my own.

Fear of Failure

"We're at places," I murmur into my headset. "Okay, Lights 103.1, go."

For me, adolescence is running the projections for the play *The Laramie Project.* My leg bounces, the only moving part of my body, anticipating that first cue. As it arrives, I twitch with anxiety, fervently praying that the screen that will appear is correct. I concentrate, for it is essential that I press it flawlessly, at the right moment. I wait in a minuscule corner, walled by hundreds of vertical ropes like vines, a pale fluorescence, twisting faces into gaunt ghosts. A hard, metal chair is curling my body into contortions. I am chained to the constant fear of having the wrong scene appear, constant dread that I can't do it right, that I will fail. That I am a failure. And then, like the inevitable sunrise, signaling another day, another show, another show to screw up, my cue comes. "Pro H, go." And I hit the button. The nine key. If it's right, I am on cloud nine. If not, there is no cloud and I fall down,

down, down. I tap it, a tap that is simple, swift, subtle. The screen advances, fading steadily and. . . it is correct. A sigh rattles my stiff body. I have another chance.

Yet when I do make a mistake—my finger too chilly to execute an action, an order too early or inaudible—Armageddon begins. An opportunity for total success and perfection is stripped away, like peeling paint being obliterated by a power washer. Before, it was fixable, it was forgiven, it wouldn't decide my future. That one misstep, that gaffe can cause the entire show to plummet. I will go home, berating my sobbing self for not reaching a goal that seems so simple, for not achieving perfection when it is dangled beneath my nose, like a melon before the face of Tantalus.

I know I can do this. I want myself to succeed. I need to succeed. I am not in over my head, though I feel suspiciously wet and light-headed. I expect perfection in timing, but I cannot achieve it. It is a glistening, golden apple. The snake says I can reach it, and I am so hungry.

In the end, the projections are simply a complement to the actors, an afterthought. But they are all I have. Progressing from screen to screen will not decide my fate, but every time my finger twitches, every moment of guilt and self-flagellation, the ashamed profanity mumbled just offstage, pulls me further from the ideal I crave.

AN IRRATIONAL BODY, A PERFECT MIND

HARI SRINIVASAN, 14

HOME SCHOOL
CUPERTINO, CA
TEACHER: ARYA BASKAR

Speech is the most commonly used form of communication in the world today. You go up to a friend and say, "Hi." Your friend responds, and you flow from one topic to another. Before your friend has stopped talking, another thought has formed in your mind and out comes your spoken output. How easy it seems.

How would you feel if someone told you that you could not utter a word all day or communicate in any form? Even if people or your best friend told or asked you something, you could not respond. If you were hungry or wanted something, you could not ask. If someone was mean to you or you didn't like the way some things were done, you couldn't talk about your frustration. That would probably be the most frustrating day in your life and you would be mighty agitated. Now, what if this story was repeated day after day, year after year?

From age 3, I've had this diagnosis of autism. And for close to eight years since, I was trapped in a silent world. I could hear and understand everything around me. I had no speech. I had a rather crazy body which I could not quite control either. I could not point to the right answers or hold a pencil for handwriting. All people saw was this kid who was in constant motion, unable to sit still, and who apparently was incapable of learning anything meaningful.

> *I Remember*
> *I remember at 1*
> *A bright baby was I, bouncy as can be*

Learning to walk and talk just as babies do
Cooing and laughing, intent upon fun
The future so bright and the grass so green

I remember at 3
The world torn asunder around me
Helplessly hearing a diagnosis that perplexed me
What is this autism they all talk about?
The future turned dull and the grass turned brown

I remember at 6
A parade of therapies surrounding me
Understanding not the person that was me
Tossed between teachers both kind and mean
The future so bleak and the sky's so gray

I remember at 9
"Why does he act so," the general cry
"This body does not reflect my mind," my silent reply
Repeating lessons that bored me to death
The future so dark and the day turned night

I remember at 12
Happiness arose as my words were typed
Potential of this bright mind now sets in
Wonder at the difference of the body and the mind
The future so bright and the sky's now blue

Quite by accident, I was introduced to typing at age 11. I always wonder why it is assumed that a person like me would have only twenty or at most 100 things to communicate. Does not a typical person say and have thousands of feelings, thoughts and wants? For me, the letters on the keyboard brought a power beyond belief—a way for me to show the world, the beautiful mind inside this dysfunctional body. It opened a whole realm of interaction, which was exciting yet overwhelming in its sheer possibility. Would I be able to pull it off, I wondered? Ever since I can remember, I have been always been observing, analyzing and contemplating. Just because I could not talk did not mean I had very little to say.

The Person Inside
Set in stone seem your opinions
Can't do this, Can't do that
What pray should I tell you?
Just reach down into this bright mind
Can't possibly communicate you say
Unless words pour from my mouth every day
What pray should I tell you?
Written words are the technology of this age.

No intelligence possible you say
Inside the body, that acts a certain way
What pray should I tell you?
Big mistake to judge a book by its cover

Help this person is your goal you say
Careers and promotions you get along the way
What pray should I tell you?
Are you helping me or you?

Human evolution is Nature's creation
Thousands of years has existed mankind
Yet, opinion is set by a few who limit
The potential of the magnificent human mind.

But do speech devices solve all communication problems for people like me? Batteries die, charges run out and devices get stuck. Some famous landmarks do not allow any electronic devices inside for security reasons. They don't work in the swimming pool or in the rain. Such devices are expensive and will break sooner or later. They are bulky to carry around. The speech on some is mechanical and devoid of emotion.

Besides, typing is slow work. Not all of us are fast 10-fingered typists—some of us type with one finger and some with two. A person can speak a lot faster than they can type. Your voice is in-built and goes with you, a device has to be carried around. You have to have access to the device, turn it on, maybe clear the screen, type, and then press its voice activation. The spelling has to be near perfect or it won't work well. Your partner has to patiently listen to your output before voicing her next thought. How stilted does this sound? And imagine a typical kid having the patience to have this really slow conversation in the middle of play. And if you add body control issues like I and many other people with disabilities have, it makes it even harder and slower.

Yes, technology has to improve but it has been a big part of the solution for me. Where would I be without it?

Autism is a spectrum disorder, which means that no two individuals have the same set of issues. It's a diagnosis based on broad observations of external behaviors while in fact there could in reality be multiple sub-sects based on underlying physiological and pathological makeup. Social interaction seems to be a broad, observable underlying similarity. Are you surprised at this, given all the emotional and physical baggage we carry?

A typical high-school friend of mine once told me that his volunteer group was initially freaked out at the thought of meeting kids like me. I understood perfectly what he meant. All of us share a nagging fear of the unknown. The main difference is our coping mechanism. When you have communication challenges, it becomes harder for people like me to ask questions and thereby get our fears and anxieties reduced. So when we are put in the new situation without having this backup mechanism, it ends up with us being in an extra-heightened state of anxiety. People with autism and other disabilities just manifest this in ways that may be considered socially inappropriate. I may start making more noises or get hyper or even get upset, even if it's an activity/person I really end up liking later on—all part of my coping mechanism and reaction to change. From our side of the fence, we do want very much want to mingle and have friends, yet behaviorally we do end up doing things that seem to give the very opposite impression. The way to lessen these irrational fears is basically lots and lots of practice on both sides of the fence.

My heightened sensations work, both for and against me. They allow me to take in and analyze details often missed by others. At the same time, they result in sensory overloads, which are difficult for my mind and body to handle and heighten my external 'autism-like' behaviors and worsen body-control and coordination.

Adolescence is quite a transition for most, as one is not an adult yet not a child either. With the changing biochemistry of our bodies comes an influx of emotions, thoughts and feelings. Over the next few years I will have to navigate this ocean of both knowns and unknowns, securities and insecurities and some strong emotions thrown into the mix. Given my existing autism-related issues, this mix is going be doubly challenging both for me and people around me.

Many times, I feel like I am not one person but two. I know I have this incredible mind. I can grasp complex concepts at speeds that are enviable. I have an innate grasp of language. Language is but a form of communication used by men—variations of communication in different parts of the world. Looked at it in this form, why should deciphering prosody of multiple languages be that difficult? My logical mind easily understands and enjoys the patterns and harmonics in math and music. Science is the pure art of discovery and is second nature to me. Nature is one of the favorite topics I like to write about. Nature is poetry and poetry is Nature. Nature is like a vast sea of intriguing delights just waiting for you to dive in, explore and experience.

On the other hand there is this body of mine. I love music, yet struggle to sing or play an instrument. My mind races along, but my fingers, controlled as they are by my body, take a long time to type a single thought. Many a time, my rational mind stands back and looks on in frank amazement at the behavior of the body—a body, which is so ridiculously illogical and irrational. Why should the mind struggle so much to control my coordination and emotions? Is my body an unresolved number like Pi, phi and the golden ratio—one that eludes a complete solution?

Me or We?

If I were a math expression I'd be
<u>*Irrational Number Body*</u>
Perfect Square Mind

A body that acts quite on its own
A mind that can only watch and mourn

Body, the numerator, mere flesh and bone
Irrational number like a math anomaly
Visible to all, pure absurdity

Mind, the denominator, profound and wise
Perfect square- like, just ecstasy
Hidden from sight, pure tragedy

Body just limited by space, movement and time
Mind without boundaries, infinite times

Two seeming identities in one unreasonable body
Perchance, I should be a 'We' and not 'Me.'

I crave the 'Me' and not the 'We'
How do I go from the 'We' to 'Me?'

Two roads diverged as in Robert Frost's poem, and I somehow found myself on "the path not taken;" the one, "less traveled by." I wonder what the other road would be like where definite maps and solutions are available for much of everyday life. My road is at times challenging and yet exhilarating, too.

I journey on my path, though I know not where it leads, even as I constantly look for solutions.

YOU COULD HEAR THE FLOWERS WEEP
AUSTYN SULLIVAN, 18

MANDEVILLE HIGH SCHOOL
MANDEVILLE, LA
TEACHER: LARA NAUGHTON

You bring birthday balloons to his grave today. You write notes and leave them on his headstone. You drop them in his flower holder. The rain tears the paper to pieces and it eventually deteriorates. Those futile words swim around in his sea of soil. The tones and syllables, idioms and phrases rest in the ground for no one to hear. You wish that he could hear them. Some days you would like to think you are the walking example of your father—the representation of what he wanted you to be. You would like to see him swim with the Koi fish in the clear, eternal sea, where the beluga whales roam, where the bright-colored fishes occupy the waters, and the swans swarm and sing.

Four years ago, you sat on the mahogany benches and watched your father lie in his coffin. His left hand rested over his right on his chest, carefully like your head did as a child. You remember lying out on the hammock between the trees, your head placed perfectly on his chest, and as the autumn scent and autumn leaves surrounded you life seemed faultless and boundless.

You approached his lifeless body. You could see the makeup coating his neck. His body was full of embalming fluid. At his collar, his skin turned blue, and you noticed the marks from the rope on his neck. When you touched his cold, heavy hands, the murky clouds crept in the sky, hovering like a sorrowful spirit, forming hands to fetch all of the voided souls soon to be forgotten.

You stood over your father impassively. You noticed the light shine down from the ceiling above him. In between his eyelids, the light caught that glare in his lifeless eyes. The flowers circled you and your father at that moment.

You could hear the flowers weep.

The priest talked, but you just stared at your hands. With your eyes, you outlined each crease, and then you got to thinking: I am my father's son. Your hands helped carry the coffin to your burial. The gust blew the bark and dead leaves through the air. You and your brothers sat in the cheap plastic seats in front of his coffin. In rows, friends and family hugged each one of you. They gave you gentle kisses, held you by the shoulders, whispered in your ear, "I love you. Never forget that." They told you, "I am sorry you have to go through this; we will always be here for you." Then you got to thinking: time goes and time goes, it is never coming back.

It started to rain, so everyone ran to their cars, and you remembered their words. You stood in the rain and stared at his coffin. You collected the flowers on top of his coffin and placed them in your coat pocket—this was the only part of him you had left. You had anticipations of making him proud—now you just have to hope he is listening.

It was in a hotel in Florida where your father had the sheets knotted around his neck—alone in misery. Could he tell the difference between the chemicals and his own feelings? To him, there was no difference between cardboard and flesh.

It was your brother's birthday. You called over and over and never got a response. The day before, your father told you and your brothers, "I am coming to see you three, soon."

He never made it.

It was in Florida, where your father lived with his new wife. It was there, after his funeral, his newest wife sold every last part of him. She flew away with all of the money. She flew away with a part of you wrapped in her ravenous palm. She had made promises for the future. You never saw her again.

You wrapped your arms around your brothers in the living room.

You told your brothers, "He is still here, he always will be." They still don't understand. Never again would death be mentioned.

After his death you dreamed, you thought, you sang dirges for his remembrance—everyone else ignored it. Sometimes you trace his face on the inside of your eyelids. It usually looks like yours. Thinking: I am my father's son.

You dreamt of his cold hands drawing his ghosts on your back. Now his ghost hovers over you everywhere you go. At night it speaks to you and tells you stories. He tells you stories about him and his father in that small town in Germany where he grew up. He talks about the dusty roads and how he used to paint on every stone he could find. He would paint on trees and all of the townspeople loved it. Besides the night stories, your father's ghosts haunts you—it hovers over you day by day. Some days you want it gone, but most days you want it there. Some days you just need to be haunted.

And the story goes like a whimper beneath your breath—never heard and never told. Your brothers think you need to stop all of those grieving thoughts. Your mother thinks you need to quit your daily dwelling. They say you need to turn to praise to save you from sorrow. They use those beliefs like bandages. The story goes on and everything is untold. This is how easily we forget. This is how quietly we mourn.

Today, with the birthday balloons in your hand, it rains down on you like the last time you saw him. Out in the grass, you see everyone's graves scattered like continents. They are all decorated with fake flowers. Your father's ghost hovers behind you, hovering over the grass. You start to decorate his headstone. You stare at your name engraved into the headstone. "The Beloved Father of. . ." The clouds creep like vultures in the fragile sky, like correlating circles.

It doesn't seem to matter that you stand in the rain. You become drenched with water, you talk to the ground. Nothing seems real; or you just choose not to believe it. You stick the grass in all of the engraved letters. You spread the dead leaves all around the stone. You place the sticks in the ground that surrounds it. You hope he notices. Today is his birthday, and you are alone to celebrate. No one remembered this vital day: a day to celebrate the selfishness of suicide. You try to never feel the hopelessness of living.

His ghost roams the graveyard. You are tired and sick from the rain beating down on you. You don't believe in much of anything today. The world stands still and you let go of the balloons. They drift through the clouds and become dots to your eyes. You no longer see those Koi fish or the beluga whales. The swans no longer sing, and the bright-colored fishes decay. The waters become black, and that sea of beauty you dreamt of becomes empty and stale. Death becomes a friend on your side. It comforts you and lets you know that it is okay to die, it'll happen some day, it happens to everyone. It whispers in your ear. Your time will come soon enough. Around each corner it skulks and watches you. One day you will hold its hand.

You can tell yourself: "When I am discomforted, I will find comfort in the sounds. When I am hopeless, I will decorate his grave. These are the things I have to do to make it right. When the clouds form a hand, ready to take me away, I'll know that I made it out all right. For now, I will sing just like a broken chord sprawling off my lips—broken melodies and broken speech. I will turn context into bullets of gratitude. Now listen to yourself: Father, there is a spot in my brain where you lie where you splice life and death together. I am tired of waiting."

Translation: I want to be in that spot in the ground next to you. This is not right.

"Just like those broken chords, nothing is ever right. We live to be longed for, so maybe the key to letting go is forgetting everything we used to know.

RASH
ALBA TOMASULA Y GARCIA, 17

JOHN ADAMS HIGH SCHOOL
SOUTH BEND, IN
TEACHER: ANN RAYMER

"Apocalypse" was the only word I could understand on the page: a reproduction of a reproduction, entirely in a dead language. Next to the text was an image of demons writhing around the ruins of hell while a radiant man broke the chains of the damned.

A happy ending for all.

I never got why humans are obsessed with such stories. If the world isn't consumed by fire, it's trampled to dust by gods. In other stories, it falls prey to giant snakes or is eaten by jaguars before a new world is born. In most, if not all, of these stories, humankind is a victim caught between its limitations and the anger of deities. The very idea that humans could destroy the world is almost taboo, even though every nation now has the power to wipe out all life. So we tell stories of death by higher forces. They clear our conciences, at least to ourselves.

At the time this story starts, I was 18. Excited yet anxious about going to college, I fretted about entering unknown territory more than a zoo-bred monkey worries when it's freed into the wild. My fellow monkeys and I felt we couldn't be bothered with anything besides getting good grades. We spent our days in study, sleep, and the occasional party. Those were strange days, all of them as similar as cans from a factory, but all permeated with anticipation at what was yet to come.

After trudging home from school one hot December day, I found my father working on business reports and occasionally glancing at the TV, which was impassively revealing the usual images of flood, fire, and war; and then the entire screen went blood red. A woman, TV reporter voice steady, told of an unknown vine that had appeared in China and snaked its way across the countryside, destroying many rice fields. The story lasted much longer than those kinds usually do.

Alerted to the story by my silence, Dad glanced up long enough to assess the world's most recent problem and snort, "You know how people are, always freaking out about everything."

He picked up the remote and switched the TV off.

He was right. Invasive species had always been everywhere, from Japan to American suburbs. As I did my homework, brown tree snakes were creeping into bedrooms in Guam, Kudzu vines were causing billions of dollars worth of damage in Southeastern America, and a thousand more little catastrophes were happening in other areas. Even I—I, in the richest country in the world—had to deal with zebra mussels blocking up our water system, an inconvenience for a few weeks. This new vine was just another pest. Who knew, maybe it would become a delicacy? My own woes, besides, left me too tired to care much about this extra irritation; there was nothing I could do about it. There had been invasive species before, and they had never stopped anyone from studying.

A week later, I heard the vine mentioned again. At school, Erin—a friend constantly mucking around with recycling bins—was solemnly describing the "Red Hydra," as the vine was now called.

"I think that it should be named after Medusa," one person said. "Medusa was the one whose heads grew back, right?"

Another interrupted "No way, that was Hydra."

Erin grew red. She always got mad when people didn't care about something she considered important.

Serious discussion on the vine continued. Erin already knew a lot. She described how the plant had engulfed both rice fields and factories in China, for the Red Hydra was extremely hard to kill. If the spiny, ropey heads were cut off, they simply grew back the next day ("That's why it's called the Red Hydra, stupid!"). It was soon discovered that unless the entire root was destroyed in one go, the vine would survive, casting out more vines to cling to the soil.

People were calling it the Apocalypse plant. Thank goodness it was only in China.

Everyone felt sorry for those who had to deal with such a pest, but—Red Hydra or no Red Hydra—there were exams to pass. I had tutoring every day in order to complete my education. Life forced me to ignore events half a world away; even so, the vine found ways into my day. Articles on the Red Hydra screamed from newspapers, theorizing that the vine was more than another invasive species that could eventually be brought under control. Everyone thought it would stay in China, but one day, or so they said, the Red Hydra started to sprout in India, no clues as to how it got there. China and India were quarantined, and news of them ceased.

Every day brought more information on the Red Hydra, whose invasion of both the world and conversation was infuriating. I stopped watching TV to shut the news out, and switched it on again only to find that the Red Hydra had spread into Australia and the U.K. Getting information on the plant soon became a daily ritual. I would come home, switch on the TV, and so discover something new about the pain the vine was causing, the crops it was destroying, the species it was driving to extinction.

Around this time, I found myself in a friend's room, hoping to take a look at the game *Devil May Cry.* As he was setting up I flipped through TV channels, searching for something amusing, but instead discovered that the Bengal Tiger was extinct, killed by the Red Hydra and the poachers who took advantage of the ones caught in its spiny embrace.

I felt worried.

"Hey, have you ever heard of *The Inferno?*"

My friend stopped setting up the Playstation and gave me a confused look.

"You know," I went on, feeling irritated, "the book that describes Hell, with demons and fire and people getting what they deserve—what Dante wrote? I was thinking that with the Red Hydra screwing everything up that. . ."

"Huh?" He held up the game box, still looking confused, "Somebody wrote a book about this?"

I realized then that—even to me—the Red Hydra existed mainly as another horror movie, for although life was now hard, spiny, and short for many people, over here it continued as scripted.

Some things, however, were different.

The Desert War continued, but now people were saying that we ought to leave and spend our energy looking for ways to eliminate the Red Hydra. I even saw a protest or two about it. Congress said that they needed to discuss the matter more. By that time, China was drowned in Red Hydra, and Australia was on its way to the same fate. Online, all many talked about was the Red Hydra. We picked up the same newspapers and read the same reports of crops and corpses getting buried under masses of the spiny red vine. The stories in the paper and videos on the Internet led to all sorts of rumors of what the Red Hydra was. Most were, truth be told, fantasies.

I cannot help, when looking back at that time, silently cursing myself and everyone else I knew—for all our talk, we stayed plugged in and did nothing.

And so, as I was plodding home from my last day of high school, I spotted a tiny patch of red among the green of the well-trimmed lawns I was used to. It was surprisingly festive, almost like a red ornament on a Christmas tree. Curious about this dash of crimson snuggled among the green blades, I walked over to inspect it. It was a vine—thick stem, spiny curled leaves, and a bulbous tip that resembled a ripe plum. Its overall appearance was almost beautiful. As I admired the plant, I realized what it was: right there, in the middle of my world, was the first head of the Red Hydra.

The rest of that day was spent in a daze. I raced home and reported what I had seen to my parents. Both started when they heard my story, and my dad phoned 911, almost dropping the phone several times in the process. The receptionist at the other side informed him that they only dealt with medical and criminal incidents and for problems with invasive species we should call a park organization. My dad did as told, and was asked if he wanted to sign up for swimming lessons. When he stated the problem, he was told to wait and put on hold.

Eventually, one of the park rangers came over to take a look at the problem. By then a crowd had gathered. The possible fates of China and India were discussed every day, but no one was sure what to do with a plant that swallowed countries whole. Rashly, the park ranger went over and grabbed the vine, only to reel back screaming and clutching a bloody hand, having forgotten that the Red Hydra was covered with microscopic needles. A gardening neighbor then tried to pull it up (wearing protective gloves, of course). The vine stretched and snapped. As a single body, my community dug into the soil, trying to eradicate every bit of that monster that we could find, only to discover the strength of the roots and the hopelessness of our task. The park ranger, hand bandaged up, called a government agent who called someone else, who managed to get the attention of a person of importance, and the whole area where that little vine was growing was soon quarantined. I have no idea what they did to the lawn; men in bio-suits covered everything from the public's eye with large sheets of white plastic, and shooed everyone away, including the family who lived in the house next to the lawn.

The sun was setting while the neighborhood was being strong-armed away. Everyone left scared and confused. My family was one of the last to leave; as my parents had been paying more attention to the news than most, the appearance of the vine in our neighborhood scared them immensely. Eventually, after an agent assured and reassured them that everything was under control—that there was no need to worry, that they would be just fine—we left. We arrived at our house while the sun was in its last death throes, only to find, among the green of our lawn, a little patch of red.

The Red Hydra, eager to conquer new territory, spread over the ground so thickly that the original land was soon dyed red. From a distance, our fields looked as if they had suddenly developed a festering rash. It even started to creep into houses, mine being no exception. Every day the entire population of the neighborhood hacked and slashed at the vine or dumped pounds of chemicals on the earth, intent on eradication. The government officials who had arrived at the start left when the Red Hydra started growing on the lawns of the White House, leaving us to struggle with the unforgiving vine. We turned to our televisions after the day's battle, hoping that someone had discovered a cure. Wars of a different kind, we found, were being fought the world over, though this time, instead of oil, human killed human over land. And then, when the Red Hydra was undeterred by even the heat of the Middle East, the troops gave up and came back, wanting to die in familiar lands. War was happening here too, war against an enemy that never slept, never talked, never thought. And so it was, until one day, in the middle of a winter that should have killed the mosquitoes, we learned that the invasion of the Red Hydra was the result of another parasite.

"It seems then," a blurry man on TV solemnly declared, "that the vine dubbed Red Hydra is an ancient species that thrived during the Triassic Period, when global temperatures were much higher than now. It went into hibernation during the Ice Age, when global temperatures dropped to the point where it could no longer function in its environment, and has remained in slumber up until now. Yes, species will respond to global temperatures in many ways, and the Red Hydra slept. Now, due to a combination of natural greenhouse gases and the carbon dioxide our machines create, the Red Hydra reawakened in temperatures warm enough for it to shake off its slumber and thrive in its former terrain. Old habitats though they may be, its former competitors are extinct, which gives Red Hydra the freedom to spread into whatever dirt it can. The temperature is again ideal for Red Hydra growth, and so it spreads at an alarming rate. According to what information we can get these days, the Red Hydra has taken up most landmasses on Earth. Species have responded to global temperatures as they always do. . ."

The screen flickered and went black.

Everyone stared at the blank screen. I was too shocked to even cry. Now, my mind is weak, my memory barely holding up, but I do remember taking my eyes from the hissing screen to the surrounding red, wondering how my species would respond.

It has been months since people gave up.

Demons and angels no longer hold meaning, for Armageddon is here and we know how it's going to end. After the TV broadcast, the humans I knew responded by going insane. The night the screen died, everyone became too scared to go outdoors because of the mobs. Looters took what they wanted and more often than not killed anyone who got in their way. I saw one gang bash a neighbor in the head, steal his wallet (though money no longer meant anything), and leave their victim's body on the ground to mingle its red with that of the vine.

When my family and I dared to go out and see how a friend of my mom's was doing, after the gangs had left, we found her on the second floor of her house, hanging by a noose from the ceiling, vines licking at her feet like tongues of flame. Yet nothing frightened me as much as the parties. Crowds would gather in the streets, everyone dressed up in their finest, and feast together, singing or talking like nothing was happening. I saw a group of such revelers put out their banquet on my street. The people there seemed wraiths more than flesh and blood, eating their feast of canned food while the Red Hydra crept closer. It was like they had completely given up on the idea of surviving, and had decided to enjoy their last days while they could.

My mom died soon after the announcement due to depression or stress or suicide, I don't remember what. My father and I laid her out in the backyard, hands over her chest like an Egyptian mummy, and soon found her covered with Red Hydra. My dad was never right after that. He started giving himself and me less food, and one day I caught him putting sleeping pills into our rations. When I refused to eat and confronted him about it, he whispered that he was trying to save us from the Red Hydra. I stayed away from him after that. A few days later, he was gone.

I live in the red-cloaked house by myself now. Humans have become as scarce as polar bears, and those that I do see run away as soon as they meet my gaze because we have become dangerous to each other. Every day is just like the last, but for one thing: every day I get weaker, and the Red Hydra gets a little closer. I am now so frail that all I can do is lie down and try to sleep or read.

Did I tell you what I'm reading right now? It is an interesting work about Martians who tried to take over Earth. They covered the world with red weeds, and almost won. . . until our diseases killed them all. They died, you see, because they weren't from Earth—they couldn't be part of our nature.

It has a happy ending.

I've read that book five times now, mainly because the only friends I have in this red world are the books in the house: this book about the aliens, Dante's *Inferno*, and a few others. Someone had written in the *Inferno* that "the weather is better in heaven, but the parties are better in hell." Looking out the window at the neighbor's house that has been completely covered, my mother's buried corpse. . . I can't help but think that such a statement is completely wrong.

The stored food is almost gone. I tried to eat the Red Hydra, scraping off the spines, which I could not see but which I knew were there, and soon found myself retching up what little food I had in my stomach and the poison in that pretty, ripe-plum head.

Hardly a day goes by when I don't think about my parents and their parents and the people before them, all working towards this end and not even aware of it. The cicadas don't even chirp anymore, though it had seemed like they were at home among the Red Hydra, finding the hated vine a comforting place. I wonder if they have buried themselves for the next several years, waiting for things to become a little more to their liking, until they can burst out and reclaim a brave new world. Maybe the very notion that they survived is just wishful thinking, and in truth they all died. I wouldn't know. These days, my brain barely works. In any case, the cicadas have disappeared. It's funny how you never miss anything until it's gone.

THE MAGNETISM GENE
KAREN NIEWOEHNER, 18

BOTTINEAU HIGH SCHOOL
BOTTINEAU, ND
TEACHER: SIENNA RUTER

Gwenyth adjusted the tubes on her scuba-diving suit.

"Are you sure you'll be all right?" asked Mr. Brown.

Gwenyth nodded, giving the response he expected of her. She knew Mr. Brown did not even slightly regard her welfare, except when it furthered his ambitions to discover the secrets of the Bermuda Triangle. On this mission, her safety was immaterial; he cared only about the Triangle's effects on her. Adjusting her helmet, she stepped over the side of the boat and let herself sink. Several colleagues watched her, whispering among themselves as she went, wondering how she could appear so calm and professional when, in all likelihood, she would never see them again. It made them nervous.

Colorful fish and plants surrounded Gwenyth, but the undersea beauty that would have caused nearly anyone to pause and gawk was utterly ignored, so accustomed was she to seeing it. Instead, her eyes focused on her gauges. She was deep enough already. It would not pay to be so far under that she could not surface quickly. Calculating the number of strokes it would take her, Gwenyth swam very slowly to the edge of the Triangle, alert for any unusual effects but experiencing none. Carefully, watchfully, she entered the Triangle. She had not a qualm about doing this, nor a thought of her past as she verged on the unknown. Long ago, when she first learned to dive, she had trained herself to focus only on the task and its technicalities while underwater. That way she would not make a mistake.

Inside the Triangle's perimeter, Gwenyth began to sink. Assuming that this effect was caused by rarefied water, she released a pair of weights. She sank lower, and wondered if she should rise or whether she ought to do some deeper observation. A quick glance at her depth gauge's acceleration was the answer. Gwenyth frantically discarded more and more weights in an attempt to get higher, yet she still sank, faster and faster. She let them all go and clawed at the water above her, trying to surface.

The edge of the Bermuda Triangle—she had to get back to it. Abandoning her attempt to surface, Gwenyth struck out toward the safe water, but it was all in vain. Mr. Brown had mentioned magnetism. Maybe some of her equipment was being attracted. She shed all nonessential metal components.

With a jolt, Gwenyth's feet hit the ocean floor. *Don't panic,* she warned herself. *Just stand still and don't panic.* There was nothing else she could do but hope something would float up and warn the others of her distress. Until then, the less oxygen she used, the better.

For several minutes she stood motionless on the ocean floor with her eyes closed to save the effort of blinking. Reading the gauges no longer mattered. The only thing Gwenyth could do was stay alive as long as possible. Around her the water silently danced and flowed, as active as any undercurrent so deep could be. A faint click sounded near Gwenyth, and she opened one eye. There was a door rising out of the ground.

I'm running out of oxygen, she thought. *I'm seeing things.*

The door swung open, inviting her in.

This is crazy.

Gwenyth sat down on the ground and closed her eyes again. She began to get dizzy and feel like she was moving. Resolutely, she huddled and tried to stop observing. Better not to observe when the things she saw didn't really exist. Nevertheless, she felt a tremendous bump and then she fell.

Gwenyth awoke to a faint light. She was in a glass box, clear glass, but so thick that she couldn't see through it. She stood up and tried to swim. She tripped. Puzzlingly, there was no water. The box was full of air. The intelligent part of her brain told her that it was all a farce, and she looked at the gauges to reassure herself of her sanity. Her oxygen tank registered empty. Animal-like, she decided to chance following her flawed impulses and drown rather than suffocate.

She tore off the tube.

Oxygen-rich air poured into Gwenyth's lungs, and she took deep, gulping breaths, swallowing all the life she could reach. Reason returned, and incredulity with it. How could it be? Why was she in a glass box, and why could she breathe? Examining it, she saw a door on the ceiling, and a drain next to it. To her left was a square of sealant on the wall that resembled weatherstripping.

"This is really weird," she said out loud, removing her scuba suit. Mr. Brown sure had some funny methods of learning. She hoped he intended to let her out soon and give her something to eat. Since Mr. Brown had never told her what he expected her to do in such a circumstance, she rebelliously ignored all scientific observation and curled up on the floor to sleep.

She awoke several hours later, refreshed. As grateful as she was to The Company for rescuing her, surely they couldn't expect her to stay here. Piling her suit into a heap, Gwenyth stood on it and opened the door. Water whooshed in—almost washing her away, filling the room up to her neck before she got the door shut again.

It didn't take a marine biologist to know that the ocean was outside that door. This was terrible. Brown had put her in danger. If he left her here. . . well, she would think about that when it happened. Gwenyth just hoped that the pile underneath her would not wash away. She was not so refreshed that she felt like treading water; In fact, she doubted that she ever would be. All Gwenyth wanted for the rest of her life was a landlocked house in a landlocked state in the middle of a big continent.

Glancing at the door, she was startled to see water flowing through the drain. Assuming that it was a leak, she stopped it with her hand, then realized that it was suction instead. An unseen force had been draining the water. Gwenyth waited until most of it was gone before she concluded her investigation of the room with the weathe stripping.

Kneeling, she detached the weatherstripping a few inches at a time, expecting a flood any second. When it was all done, not a drop more leaked inside. Gwenyth held her breath as she pushed on the glass section.

BAM!

It vanished.

She jumped back.

Convincing herself that no further consequences would follow, she crawled into the vacated space.

Several feet later, it joined a short hallway with an elevator. As she approached the latter, the doors opened and a muted mechanical voice asked, "Where to?"

"What are my choices?" Gwenyth inquired, stepping in and looking for a panel of labeled buttons.

"Scientific, Residential, or Garden," replied the elevator.

"Scientific, please," Gwenyth requested.

The elevator stopped and said, "Here you are, Tegwen."

White-coated scientists darted among long lab tables covered with bubbling chemicals. Smoke seeped out from under the closed doors with bronze nameplates that lined the perimeter. This was familiar ground. Gwenyth found a spare coat on a peg on the wall beside the elevator and wrapped it around herself. She wove between experiments, ducking at appropriate intervals as sharp objects sailed over her head and closing her eyes as solutions blew up in her face.

She found the well-stocked chemical cupboard to her left and sifted through a bunch of bottles, many of which were unrecognizable. Smiling at the broken shelf lying on the floor of a cabinet in such a prominent laboratory, Gwenyth chose a couple of solutions and a large magnet to continue a series of experiments relating to this most recent venture. She felt pretty proud of herself for accomplishing it, despite her close call. What kind of place Brown had sent her to, she did not know, but she was confident that his commendations were on the way.

"Excuse me," said the lady next to Gwenyth, just before a heavy steam rose from her beaker, making it impossible to see. "What are you doing?"

"Well," Gwenyth replied stuffily, "I've just come from diving in the Bermuda Triangle, and I'm studying magnetic effect."

The lady laughed.

"Intermolecular magnetism, you mean. Gwenyth, I'm Dylys, and you need to come with me. You won't understand, but you're in danger."

The last part was only a whisper, obscured from the rest of the world by a popping noise and another burst of steam. "Terribly sorry, guys," Dylys yelled, and—snatching Gwenyth's hand—tugged her along into the elevator. It moved without her saying a word. The door opened.

"Have a nice day, Tegwen and Dylys."

Gwenyth scowled. "Why does it keep calling—"

Dylys interrupted, "Come on, Tegwen," and dragged her out.

Gwenyth wanted to argue this odd practical joke, and began to wonder why she was following a stranger. Likely it was even a kidnapping plot. Turning, she ran back into the elevator.

"Scientific."

The lab was the same as when she'd left it. She determined to take a more practical approach this time and announce her presence to someone in authority. Mr. Brown should have warned her that she might not be among friends. It was another reminder to always take care of herself.

She knocked on the door marked "Ynyr." It was well located, and the scientists in the main room seemed to take pains not to disturb it. Mr. Ynyr must be the president of the establishment, or at the least, a very respected member.

Gwenyth knocked.

The man took his time to come to the door. When he finally made his appearance, Gwenyth was assured of her judgment. He was in his late 40s, well dressed, and his records lay neatly on tables all over the room. Gwenyth respected those who kept good records.

"Excuse me, but I'm Gwenyth Smith. I just returned from a scuba investigation of the Bermuda Triangle."

"Is that so?" inquired Ynyr, raising his eyebrows. "Won't you have a seat?"

Gwenyth smiled. This was the kind of treatment she expected. He pulled out a chair and stepped out the door.

"I must tell my colleagues that you are here. Wait one moment, please."

Twenty minutes passed.

Restlessly, Gwenyth got up and began to pace. She argued with herself over whether to peek at his records. It would be interesting material. Mr. Brown seldom sent her to common scientific conventions. Curiosity won. She read all the details of Ynyr's experiments; impressive, but a bit over her head. A few frankly puzzled her.

Ah, he was a magnetism expert. That was why she was here.

Voices from the room next door butted into her thoughts and she scowled. People would make it hard to concentrate.

Wait—they were talking about her. Gwenyth listened.

"Stop kidding me, Ynyr," a gruff voice said sarcastically. "I have work to do."

"Believe what you want. You can deal with the consequences."

"Okay, okay. But how did she get here? I mean, years ago I told Dylys to get rid of her for good, and now here she comes popping up again. Dylys wouldn't do a sloppy job like that."

"Yeah, right!" Ynyr growled. "Dylys is softhearted enough to free an elephant."

Gwenyth rushed to the door. She had to escape. The knob didn't turn. Ynyr had locked her in. Warning herself not to panic, she returned to studying the pages on the table. The trials involved molecules, genes, and magnetism all at the same time. "Intermolecular magnetism." That was what Dylys had told her. Was it conceivable that they had managed to magnetize their world and its inhabitants like an atom? Sure enough, these scientists had inserted genes that held the people of their little world to its nucleus. It was like a magnified gravity, a pulling together of things that—while not significantly affecting their weight—prevented one from floating or swimming away.

Had this been necessary as a safety measure, or was it a means of keeping its inhabitants prisoner?

Gwenyth picked up a list naming all inhabitants and their exclusive magnetic identities. "Ynyr, C5; Emyr, C8; Trahaearn, C11; Hywel, C09; Tegwen, C18; Rhiannon, N305."

Gwenyth skimmed the list. "Gwenyth, C18."

It couldn't be! She had been born here, which explained the peculiar name her birth mother had given her before abandoning her. Now, with her magnetic identity, she would be stuck here for the rest of her life.

Stuck?

Yes. Even with its faults, the world above the ocean was the only one she wanted right now.

She still could not understand the unwelcoming attitude of the scientists. Their menacing words must mean that they intended to do their utmost to dispose of her. She looked back at the list, trying to puzzle it out. Where was her name... after Tegwen...! Gwenyth sat down to steady herself. She and Tegwen had the same identity, and the scientists did not want this. Their conversation had pointed toward an attempt to destroy her in the past, foiled only by Dylys.

The door opened, and to her relief, revealed Dylys. "I'm sorry. I didn't understand."

Dylys waved her hand at Gwenyth. "It doesn't matter."

"I have to get back to Earth!"

Dylys laughed. "You're in it!" Then whispered the craziest escape plan Gwenyth had ever heard. She sized up all of Dylys's six-foot stature—from her familiar lab shoes to her wildly cropped hair—and nodded. She would have refused if Dylys's honest brown eyes hadn't begged her.

The garden turned out to be a very large and orderly place. Everywhere she looked, carrots, corn, and rice grew in perfectly straight rows with not a weed between them. The light from the dim heat lamps that covered the ceiling and reflected off foil walls and the evenly-spaced sprinklers on the ground and ceiling reminded Gwenyth of a grocery store.

A cheerful whistle made her turn toward a slight man toting a humongous basket of lettuce. He limped to the elevator and deposited the basket. "Residential," he said as if he'd done it several times each day of his life. Resuming the tune, he started back in the direction he had come from. Belatedly registering her presence, he pivoted.

"Yes?"

Gwenyth was speechless. The professional who always knew what to say to company executives could not think of a single word to explain the situation to a damp gardener with muddy shoes and overalls.

"Well?" he asked impatiently, twitching to get back to work. He could barely keep his gaze on her, preferring to consider the stage of the corn and length of the carrot-tops.

"I—," Gwenyth began. "I—." She stopped. "I know this sounds absolutely ludicrous, but I have orders to take a basket of carrots to the lab."

He raised his eyebrows and puckered them down, studying her. "I don't know what this nonsense is. . ."

"Please," whispered Gwenyth fearfully. "It's to save my life." Doubtfully, the gardener handed it to her.

The elevator slid to a stop.

Gwenyth got out, crawling behind a lab table on her hands and knees, straining her neck awkwardly to see the nameplates on the doors. She found the door marked "Ynyr" and turned the knob. It opened, thanks to the wad of paper Dylys had jammed it with. Sure enough, behind the tables with the records was a huge magnet. Gwenyth knelt beside it and began rubbing her head on it. After several seconds she felt lighter. Dylys was right. She rubbed a bit more, until she was sure that she weighed about what she had on the ship that morning. Creeping out, she crawled back to the elevator.

In her panic, Gwenyth realized that the door did not open to her with her magnetism deactivated. She frantically searched for a lever to force it open. She remembered the chemical cabinet. In an instant, the broken shelf was in her hands, wedged between the doors. She could hear running footsteps beneath her. This had to be quick. The elevator began to go down. Someone had called for it. Gwenyth gave an extra shove with all her strength and a little extra.

The door opened, and she leapt inside, yelling, "Up! UP!!"

Miraculously, the elevator rose.

With a grin, Gwenyth seized the basket brimming with carrots and spread a portion of its contents on the elevator floor. The rest she deposited along the hallway to the glass room. She entered the enclosure and put on her scuba suit, noting that Dylys had refilled it with oxygen.

The elevator door opened and Ynyr and several others ran toward her, steaming like an experiment that was going to explode at any minute. They tripped on the carrots.

Gwenyth yanked the block of glass back into place and forced herself to pay close attention to sealing the weather stripping. She heard yells as her pursuers rushed through the rolling carrots to her oasis. Then she opened the ceiling door and it all faded away. Through the clear, comfortable water she rushed, rising, reveling in the beauty of her ocean and barely remembering the need to swim quickly to the side, out of the Bermuda Triangle.

The ship was just where she had left it, and Mr. Brown was pacing on the deck. Gwenyth surfaced and yanked off her helmet, soaking her ponytail a second time.

"Man overboard!" she hollered, close though she was to the boat. "Throw me a line!"

"She's here!" Mr. Brown yelled, jumping into the air with happiness. "Guys, Gwenyth is here!"

They thundered onto the deck, cheering as loudly as they could. It echoed across the whole empty ocean. Gwenyth reached for the rope, running a finger down her face to wipe off the tear.

FLYBOY
LINDSEY MAXON, 18
LAMAR HIGH SCHOOL
ARLINGTON, TX
TEACHER: MARTHA LOU BUFKIN

The flyboy was inside the boundary between the world and the sky. To him, there was a definite line: When you are at that altitude where the land beneath you is a hazy endlessness; and the sky above you is a pure, empty, vast blue; and the horizon in all directions is made of nothing more than luminescent streaks of cloud; then you're inside the boundary. This was his favorite altitude for flying—the level where he could see as much of the world as possible without it sinking beneath a sea of condensation.

He'd decided he wanted to fly as a child, the first time he'd ever taken a trip for which a ground vehicle wouldn't be sufficient. The flight had departed late in the evening, and his eyes had been dazzled as he rose into the air and was hit with the reflections off the towers of his city. Brilliant light—orange and red and violet, sparkling off glass and metal and wires. . . He'd never seen anything so amazing before. He decided then that he wanted to fly when he grew up. And so he had.

However, he'd never expected that flying would take him to a place like this. This vast territory known as the Southwest of the United States—simply "Southwest" to the locals, he supposed—was nothing like the cities he'd flown over as a child. He wasn't quite sure where he was now, if it was New Mexico, Arizona, perhaps Texas or California, but from up here it didn't matter.

It was beautiful.

He was fascinated by the shape of the land, the rolls and the ridges that would suddenly give way to flat ground. In fact, he was so distracted by the world below him that he found it hard to concentrate on his job.

He was on a manhunt.

He wasn't quite a soldier; he wasn't exactly a police officer; he wasn't really a bounty hunter, either. Nevertheless, he had asked for an assignment—any assignment—that would take him to the Southwest. He could fly, and he could fight, so here he was. Man-hunting. Lucky that he *did* like the land so much, his superiors had laughed; most flyboys from the cities were unnerved by all that nothing. Too much rock, not enough metal. It wasn't natural, they said.

True, pure nature was unnatural; but the flyboy thought the government had overcompensated for the land's barrenness. Rising out of sand and hills, spaced at even intervals, were immense mechanical pillars, columns made of wire and circuitry. They jabbed indifferently through the clouds, ending abruptly with vast satellite dishes well above the boundary that marked the start of the sky. They were used to monitor the vast territory and track down the natives that still ran free.

Intrusive as the towers were, it was a miracle this land was being preserved at all. The territory once called Mexico was being mined for metal ores; Colorado's and Utah's mountains had been hollowed out and filled with penal institutions. Only the Southwest of the United States was protected, as a nature preserve of sorts; it was, after all, a very historic location.

There were many objections to its being a reserve—why not just put up a monument? Flatten the land, corner the natives. Trying to track them down in this vast wilderness without damaging the land was more trouble than it was worth.

True, it was trouble, but he thought preserving the land was worth it, which was why he had been willing to help with the manhunt. Plus, it gave him a chance to enjoy the landscape. So he set his jet to autopilot, and enjoyed.

Jagged ground was interspersed with land flat enough to have been steamrolled, and collapsed away into deep canyons and dry gullies that looked as if they'd been clawed out from the ground. Sitting neatly in each gully was a sinuous river of dried mud that perfectly fit the contour of the bottom of the clawed-out ground, as perfectly as if the land had come first and then someone had designed a piece of river to fit inside the already-present cracks and crevices. He could see why this land had intrigued the first explorers.

This wasn't a territory that his people had cared about until a bit over a century ago. That was when the first crew of explorers had started flying over the land and observing it, taking photos and shooting videos to send back home. Unfortunately, they were better photographers than pilots; someone had made some stupid mistake and crashed their ship, right near a native civilization. The natives had captured the explorers.

The flyboy, along with a great many other people, thought that his government had been absolutely shameful in response to the crisis. No one had even heard about the explorers until they were long dead, and by the time any useless "rescue" crews had made it to the crash site not even the natives remembered the incident. Apparently *their* government had hastily covered up the accident too. No matter— thanks to the explorers, those who came after them had discovered a beautiful land, rich with resources and ripe for taking. In tribute to the explorers, their crash site had been converted into a memorial, and their place of imprisonment was now a museum.

The flyboy himself planned on visiting both sites the first time he got a few days' vacation. First the Roswell Exploration Memorial, and then the Area 51 Museum of Terran History.

Naturally, no natives were allowed to visit either the memorial or the museum, which greatly displeased them. Actually, quite a few things displeased them: they disliked the imprisonment of their population (which he understood perfectly); they disliked their forced relocation to inland cities, away from the *nastily* humid coasts and seas (which he didn't understand); they disliked the arrest of their current world leaders and the appointment of new leaders; they disliked the destruction of their natural homes and the installation of colonies, watchtowers, factories.

The natives who gave themselves up got off easily, but those who escaped into the Southwest and tried to fight their new leaders were punished severely. Those foolish enough to try to knock the satellite towers down received extra punishment. That was why he was now on a manhunt.

Miles Arthur Adamson was the man's full name, although if the flyboy's crude knowledge of local custom were correct, he would be called "Miles" by his friends and "Mr. Adamson" by all others. (He wasn't sure what the purpose of the "Arthur" was.) He quite certainly didn't have the privilege of calling this man Miles, so he'd go with Mr. Adamson.

Below, clouds thickened from gauzy fog to solid fluff. He lamented the loss of his once-perfect altitude, then brought his jet lower. He couldn't see as far now, but he could see more details: the infrequent signs of civilization. This, he thought, was what really made the land so beautiful.

Pure nature was unnatural; alone, it wasn't anything worth spending hours gawking at. No, what truly amazed him was the odd juxtaposition of vibrant life with vacant land, of dirt and desert with city and civilization. If the rivers lying in canyons had been built perfectly to fit the curves, the few structures in the Southwest were no less perfectly placed. On the uneven sides of vast mountains, his eyes were caught by unexpectedly sparkling geometry—buildings, homes, farms. Sloped plains suddenly flattened for a cluster of low structures. Canyons had concrete roadways laid along their tortuous twists as skillfully as any river, twisting up and down along ridges and around the sides of mountains.

Native civilization both defied and deferred to the laws decreed by nature. In the Southwest, mountain bowed to man as often as man bowed to mountain, and one would not be the same without the other.

The roads balanced out the rivers, and the cities balanced out the canyons. The uneven patches of infrequent shrubbery were as often as not replaced by the geometric grids of planned vegetation, or the green irrigated disks of man-made crop circles.

He had always been told that civilization cannot flourish in complete wilderness, and nature cannot survive in the face of progress; one must succumb to the other. But here, in the Southwest of the United States, sand and steel coexisted, too thoroughly engrained in each other to be separated. Everything in the Southwest was a whole.

There—this was the place he'd been looking for. Between a range of low, jagged hills and a clawed-out canyon wide enough for a dried river and a deserted road to writhe side-by-side, was a narrow stretch of flat land. It had a smattering of empty buildings alongside a stretch of irrigated circles, growing who-knew-what alien crop. It was one of the native communities that had stood empty since the Southwest's subjugation.

He found an empty space just beyond the circles of unkempt, dying crops; swooped down; and neatly landed along the narrow rim of the canyon without disturbing any of the vegetation. He put on his helmet but didn't seal it, so he could breathe the desert air, and strapped a handgun to his belt. He had a wide variety of much stronger weapons in his jet, but he'd been advised to use minimal force. After all, as his superiors had told him before his mission, Earth creatures break easily.

The atmosphere was warm and blessedly arid, a welcome change from the area where he usually worked. His typical job was patroling the coast of California, making sure no natives had gotten boats and tried to escape into the ocean. California was just so humid—and as soon as this mission was done, he'd be returning to his coastal patrols. He took a few deep, comforting breaths of dry air as he approached the desert dwellings, with their oddly patterned walls of brick sheltering one sullen inhabitant.

He never quite knew what to expect from a native.

As he entered the town, he saw nothing but dusty streets and angry graffiti, some of which his government-issued helmet automatically translated into his own language—"Independence forever! Kill the invaders!"—and some of which his helmet left alone, saying only, "Error: Explicit Content." Stupid government censors.

The traffic lines on the road, white and yellow lines like war paint, were half-covered in unswept dust. He carefully walked on the double yellow stripes in the middle, assuming they were the guiding lines to keep travelers on the main road. This town was familiar, although he'd never visited it before. He'd studied images of the landscape, of the town, of a house, of a face; now, he'd found a house that matched the images, and inside he expected to find a matching face—Miles Arthur Adamson.

Remembering a bit of native custom, he knocked on the door rather than trying to open it on his own (doorknobs were a bit oddly shaped for him to get his hand around, anyway).

A voice shouted from within: his helmet displayed the translation like a subtitle, "Who's there?" In a moment something in the door clicked and a native appeared. It looked up, and its expression immediately soured.

"Oh. You."

Its eyebrows furrowed, only drawing more attention to the fuzzy growths over its eyes. The flyboy found himself, as always, staring at the fuzz above the native's eyes and then on top of its head. Hair always looked like an exotic hat to him.

The native crossed its arms, and took a couple of slow steps away from the flyboy. "I suppose this is about your towers?" it said.

He wished he could understand the native tongue enough to understand this one's tone, but could tell enough from its body language that it was hostile.

"Yes. Are you Miles Arthur Adamson?" he asked, and his helmet translated his words aloud into the native language.

"Unfortunately."

Well, good.

The Flyboy took a step into Mr. Adamson's dwelling and said, "I am here with orders to arrest you and relocate you to the San Francisco colony. You will be put on trial for..."

He fell silent.

"For?" Mr. Adamson prompted.

The flyboy had been completely distracted by the oddest sight he'd ever seen. Sitting beneath a glass window, in a contraption that looked similar to the bowls the natives served food in, was a cactus. A real, live cactus, in some dirt in a bowl, growing quite as well as it would out in the desert.

He stared at it in baffled amazement. He had never witnessed such a thing before, this further entanglement of civilization and wilderness. The natives had not only carved and coaxed the desert into accepting their offerings of civilization, but they had integrated pieces of that desert within their civilization.

"For what?" Mr. Anderson repeated.

He quickly turned back to Mr. Adamson, meeting those beady eyes—so strange, with their three colors; so tiny—and said, "I apologize. I was briefly distracted."

Mr. Adamson's face twisted in an unpleasant-looking way.

"Just let me guess," he said. "I'll be put on trial for trying to blow up one of your radio towers. What now? Is this the part where you haul me in?"

He suddenly spread his arms wide, startling the flyboy.

"Then do it. Go on! I held out as long as I could, I did the best I could, but I'm no moron. I know when I'm beat. I've done my job and now you've got yours, you—"

The government censor blocked out Mr. Adamson's next few words.

"Please calm down, Mr. Adamson," the flyboy said. "I wish for this interaction between us to go easily, if at all possible."

"Easily?" Mr. Adamson made a strange sound that the flyboy's helmet couldn't translate. It took him a moment to recognize it as laughter. "Nothing's going to be easy. You've destroyed my world—you realize that, don't you? You've enslaved or—I don't know—maybe killed everyone else, you sick—"

Censored.

"Why should I make this easy for you? For all I know, I'm the last human standing up to you."

"Yes. You are, in fact, the only native we are aware of still living outside our planned colonies," the flyboy said. It was noble, in a way, this native's patriotism. The flyboy had little such loyalty of his own. His government was often ridiculous; he just flew for them. "However, we would not have discovered your existence had you not attempted to destroy one of our satellite towers. There may still be many of your peers living in hiding."

"But none you know about. And if they're in hiding. . ." Mr. Adamson's shoulders made a strange jerking motion, a shrug. "So I really am the only one standing up to you, aren't I?"

"That appears to be correct."

"So all you have to do is take care of me and then you'll never have to bother with your precious historical park again."

That was something he hadn't considered—as soon as Mr. Adamson was arrested, the flyboy wouldn't have another excuse to come out here.

But he wanted an excuse; he wanted to be a flyboy so that he could explore these worlds. He wanted to see places like this, this intricate layering of opposites, this desert-within-city-within-desert. If he captured the native and took him back to California (that city-and-city-and-city-with-too-much-water-beside-it), would he ever have an excuse to come back here again?

He was not yet ready to give the desert up.

He stepped back. "Mr. Adamson, it is foolish for a wanted man to return to the last place where he was known to be living. This makes it easy for those hunting him to find him." He took another step back, exiting Mr. Adamson's home. "That is why I did not find you here. Obviously, you are clever, and are currently in hiding somewhere else. It may take me a very long time to locate you."

Mr. Adamson squinted his eyes, his fuzzy brows drawing together. "What are you trying to say? You can't be letting me go free?"

"No, I am not—I simply never saw you. I was distracted by the view."

The native shook his head slowly. "There need to be more of you monsters with that kinda attitude," he said. "Do you give me a head start or do I leave without packing?"

"I can afford you a day."

The native immediately retreated into his house, presumably to start packing.

The flyboy peered into the doorway again, at the piece of desert in a bowl. "Will you be taking your plant with you?"

"The cactus? What would I do with it?" Mr. Adamson called. "Take it if you want."

"I . . . thank you." The flyboy walked into the dwelling, to the window, and carefully picked up the plant in a pot. "Your generosity is appreciated, Mr. Adamson."

"Miles. It's Miles."

"Miles."

The native considered the flyboy his friend? Merely for letting him go free? The flyboy was not kind, just indifferent toward his superiors. Didn't the native understand that he'd soon be hunted down again?

The flyboy exited Mr. Adamson's—Miles's—home, and followed the yellow war-paint streetstripes to the edge of the abandoned town. How long could he let his target evade him? Ten, perhaps 20 days— any longer, and his superiors would assign someone else to capture Miles Arthur Adamson. Whether by the flyboy or by some other soldier-flyer-hunterto do it, eventually the last human standing would fall.

The flyboy returned to his jet, removing his helmet with one hand

and cradling his piece of desert with the other as he climbed inside. He'd report to his superiors that the native had evaded him. Miles had one day's head start.

He took off with the potted plant in his lap, carrying it in his jet up to the perfect altitude; nature-in-machine over city-in-desert, balanced in the boundary between the world and the sky.

HOOFPRINTS ON THE HEART

ABIGAIL HERTZLER, 18

LANCASTER MENNONITE HIGH SCHOOL
LANCASTER, PA
TEACHER: JANE MOYER

Scene I

*Spotlight on a **Man** on stage right. He is your "Average Joe" of an American: tall and mildly chubby, wearing faded jeans, a Dodgers T-shirt, and Sambas. He is holding a horse racing program in one hand. Behind him, in darkness, lies a single, thick white fence—the kind you find at race tracks—backed by several stair-step rows of plain steel benches.*

Man: God, I hated that horse. Every time someone came up to me and started talking racing—any part of racing, from betting to owning to just being a fan—the name Kingsom was guaranteed to come into the conversation eventually. Guaran-freakin'-teed.

He pauses, glancing down at his program for a moment, then looks up again.

Man: Okay, okay—I didn't always hate him. Fact is, I was the self-declared driver of the official Kingsom bandwagon from the time he broke his maiden. *{walks slowly to enter stage}* And by "broke," I mean shattered—that dang horse won his first race by 14¾ lengths. I still remember the stretch call. . . good old Tom Durkin nailed it.

He shuts his eyes, drops his program, and flings his arms out, reciting.

Man: "And Kingsom is starting to pull away, and pull away impressively here. . ."

Tom Durkin's Voice *picks up the stretch call and the two recite together as a chorus of pounding hooves starts to crescendo in the background.*

Man and **Tom Durkin's Voice:** ". . . He's going to win by a colossal margin—and here—is—Kingsom! Breaking his maiden by nearly 15

lengths. . . a promising start for this youngster. . . Kingsom—
remember that name."

Tom Durkin's Voice slowly fades away, as do the pounding hooves. Man slowly lowers his arms, picks up his program, and gradually works his way back to stage right.

Man: God, that horse—he was everything the sport needed, everything we the fans could have hoped for. *{shakes head}* Don't let people tell you horse racing is a happy little business rolling merrily along its way. It's not. The horses are breaking down left and right—they're bred and trained for blinding speed, without a shred of stability in the lot. Their legs snap with all the ease of a child breaking a stick in half. And it's not pretty. God, no. The breakdowns, the bad ones, they give you nightmares.

The Man shudders a little and pauses, as if in thought.

Man: *{quietly}* They haunt you, the bad ones. Enough said. But Kingsom—he had it all, man. The looks of Secretariat, the gritty determination of Seabiscuit. . . heck, he even had the rabid, fanatical followers of Smarty Jones, Afleet Alex, and Barbaro, all rolled into one.

The Man pauses again, then smacks his program on his thigh.

Man: Dang horse.

He looks away to the shadowy race scene behind him, then turns partway to the audience.

Man: He started out so good. . . the whole thoroughbred world was buzzing about him.

Scene II

The Man walks from upstage into the shadowy scene behind him, which lights up accordingly. Several spectators are seated in the benches, but they are simply background. The Man walks to centerstage and joins the small crowd at the rail: a petite, brown-haired Woman; a Father in his mid-40's and his 14-year-old Kid; and an Old Man. They are all waiting on the track rail for the horses to finish warming up and to get into the starting gate.

Man: *{to **Old Man** on his right},* You've got twenty on Kingsom, right? It'd be a crime not to.

Old Man: *{squinting at him}* 'Samatter of fact, I do, kid. But what makes you think he's worth 20 bucks? He's 30-to-one.

Man: *{grinning}* Oh, just wait. Take the money while you can, Gramps. You won't get better odds on him again, I guarantee it. You know, he fired a bullet in his last workout—58 and change.

*The 14-year-old **Kid** who has been listening in butts into the conversation.*

Kid: Wait, what? He fired a bullet? I thought you were talking about, you know, a horse.

***Man** is reluctant to leave his conversation with the **Old Man**, but responds willingly enough.*

Man: It's racing talk—means he had the fastest recorded workout for that distance of the entire day's workout—he did it incredibly fast.

Kid: *{eyes widening}* How fast?

Man: Very fast. Secretariat-like, almost. *{turns back to the **Old Man**}* His bloodlines are excellent, too. Sired by Rockport Harbor, and he's got Smart Strike on his dam's side.

Old Man: *{frowning a little}* That's an awful lot of Unbridled's Song and Mr. P. for one horse. Has he had soundness issues?

Kid: *{sticking his face between the two of them}* Soundness issues? And whaddabout those two other names, why are they bad?

Man: *{looks over the **Kid's** head toward the **Father**, raising his eyebrows as if to say "Do I have to keep doing this?" The **Father** shrugs}* "Soundness issues" means that the horse is having trouble with injuries, 'specially in his legs and feet.

Kid: 'Kay. And whaddabout the names?

Man: *{sighing slightly}* Unbridled's Song and Mr. P—uh, Mr. Prospector—are sires. Fathers of a lot of racehorses. They're pretty well known for throwing—I mean fathering—horses with soundness issues. *{turns to old man}* I know he's got history, but—

*At this point, the petite **Woman** on the **Old Man's** left speaks up.*

Woman: He's good, straight up. That's all there is to it. He's scary good. No soundness issues, no injuries, nothing. He's clean, he's dark fast, and if he doesn't win here, I guarantee he'll at least be mowing down horses at the end no matter where he finishes.

*The **Man**, the **Old Man**, and the **Kid's** heads all turn toward the **Woman**.*

Man: Well, hey. A believer. Alright. How do you—

The sound of the starting gate sings through the air—the race has begun.

Tom Durkin's Voice: Aaaaaaand. . .

*The **Man**, the petite **Woman**, and the **Old Man** speak simultaneously, their eyes fixed on the bright chestnut hide of Kingsom.*

Man: They're off!

Old Man: Theeeey're off!

Woman: They're off. . .

Kid: Um. . . ?

Father: Shut up and watch, Johnny.

Tom Durkin's Voice: They're off!

*The **Man** leans forward on the rail, pounding his fists on it.*

Man: He's not going, he's not going, why is he just sitting there? C'mon, Kingsom, catch up already!

Woman: Oooh, he does that in workouts too. Mr. Kratz was afraid of that. *{leaning forward, hands tightening on the rail}* Come on, Scruffy, get your butt moving!

Man: *{gaping}* Scruffy?

Woman: *{impatient}* It's his nickname. I'm his groom, I'm allowed to call him Scruffy. *{joins the **Man** in pounding on the rail, which is starting to quiver from the multiple fists}* Come ooon, Scruffy! Go!

Old Man: *{also starts pounding on the rail}* Well, he's going now!

Man: Come on, Kingsom!

Woman: Get going, Scruffy!

Old Man: He's pulling away! He's pulling away!

Tom Durkin's Voice: And Kingsom is starting to pull away, and pull away impressively!

Scene III

Man is back at the front gate of the stage with a single spotlight on him and a racing program still clutched in his hand.

Man: Laura—that was the name of the groom, Kingsom's groom—Laura told me later that Kingsom's trainer, Ben Kratz, had been worried about the colt's running style. Kingsom ran really slow to start off with, falling way behind all the other horses until you'd think he was completely done. Then he'd switch gears entirely and inhale his competition—which is exactly what he did that first race. And the next one. And the next. His name was everywhere, on all the top racing papers.

Several newspapers slide past on the floor, blown onstage by "the wind;" the Man stoops and picks one up, showing the headline to the audience.

Man: When he won his first seven races by similar margins—always breaking out of the starting gate slowly, taking his time, waiting until you wanted to scream at him to go, then exploding and just powering past all the other horses—he got on the cover of *Bloodhorse*, which is sort of Thoroughbred racing's version of *Sports Illustrated, Racing Style,* and the *Wall Street Journal*.

The Man picks up Bloodhorse, which shows a large picture of Kingsom with the words 'Racing's Next Great?' written beside it.

Man: And that was when things started to get nasty.

A Tall, Thin Woman in her early 20s steps out behind and to the left of the Man. Some light filters on her face, but the spotlight remains on the Man and the Tall, Thin Woman is mostly in shadow.

Tall, Thin Woman: I can't believe they're calling him "racing's next great." He's won, what, seven races so far? I'm sorry, seven races does not make you a "great." And what's all this crap about him being racing's savior? Geez, just call him "Kingsommessiah." All hail! One horse isn't gonna save the industry, and you're an idiot if you think so.

*A short, **Greasy-Haired Man** enters the stage, stepping behind and to the
right of the **Man**. He, too, receives some ligh thut is mostly in shadow.*

Greasy-Haired Man: You people are ridiculous. I'm not saying he's God
reincarnate in horse, but he's freakin' great, or at least well on his way.
Seven-for-seven—people—helloooo. "He's just good?" Please. "Just good"
horses don't win seven straight races by huge margins. I think you're
getting "just good" confused with "fantastic-amazing-phenomenal."

*The **Man**, who has been listening to both people talk, now turns back to the
audience.*

Man: And that was when I started to hate Kingsom. I know, it sounds
stupid—you're probably wondering how the heck I can hate a horse
that I liked so much at his first race. *{shakes head}* But those people
never quit. Day in, day out, all I heard were the "'Kingsommessiah'
versus 'Kingsom, the next great'" arguments. They never quit, never.
{slashes his program through the air} It was like the '08 presidential
election, you know? Maybe you supported a candidate toward the
beginning, maybe you even supported them a lot, but by the end the
bickering was so bad that you just hated the whole thing and wanted
it to be over. And that's what happened with me. Even when Kingsom
went on to win his next four races, I still heard the arguments, and I
hated him a little more, and a little more.

*The **Man** pauses, still holding his program in the air. Then he slowly
lowers it, rubbing the back of his neck with the other hand. When he speaks
again, his voice is quiet, almost deadpan.*

Man: It happened when he was going for his 16th race, and his 16th
win. He was three at this time—three years old, and he'd raced 15
times in a society where most horses get to only ten or 11 in their whole
careers. It was his second-to-last race before his preparatory race for the
Kentucky Derby. Charity, a goodwill showing—that's all it was. People
were fanatical about this horse, because he represented something that
the horse racing world had slowly been losing the concept of for
decades: a hero. A hero with owners who ran him not just for the

money, but for love of the sport. So his trainer entered him in a smaller race in Pennsylvania. Small field. An easy win, they thought.

*The **Man** stares off in the distance a bit, rolling and unrolling his program almost unconsciously.*

Man: The truth didn't come out until almost three weeks later.

Scene IV

*It is dark. Fog moseys around in long, slow bursts. Ben **Kratz**—tall, thickly-built man—is standing outside of a horse's stall in a clean, dark barn. **Jim**—a smaller, more weedy-looking man, stands beside him. Both are looking into the stall.*

Jim: Big day tomorrow, Ben.

Ben Kratz is still looking into the horse's stall, almost as if he's in a trance.

Kratz: *{speaking slowly}* 'Ya think, Jim?

Jim: Sorry. Unhelpful. Got it. *{stoops to pick up his stopwatch and a bridle}* Ben. . . he's tired, isn't he?

Kratz: Yeah, he is. *{glances up and down the barn}*

Jim: He's got to win this race tomorrow, Ben. But he was a little slow in his last race. Still won big, of course, but he was slower. And he needs to win tomorrow, and win by a lot. They're predicting that more than 80,000 people will be there tomorrow Eighty thousand. Racing hasn't seen those kinds of crowds since—

Kratz: Yeah, I know, Jim. *{glances up and down the barn again}* And that's why. . .

Jim: *{raising his eyebrows}* Why. . . ?

Kratz: . . . why he might need a little help for tomorrow.

Jim: *{looking shocked}* You're not thinking—what, you want to drug him?

Kratz: One injection to a major vein. That's all he needs to get the juices flowing.

Jim: But—

Kratz: It's not for the crowds, Jim—it's for the fans. For all those people who never saw the true beauty behind horse racing until they had their hearts stolen by this horse.

Jim: Well, we do need the crowds. Horse racing needs the crowds.

Kratz: It's for the sport. He'll be fine. *{turns to leave}* Get the vet down here in 15, all right?

Jim: Got it, boss. *{turns to leave as well, then quickly spins around}* Oh, wait! Before I forget—there's some reporters who wanted to talk with you after you were done here. Should I. . . ?

Kratz: *{starting to walk away}* You know, Jim, my boss—back when I was just an assistant trainer—used to tell me a very smart thing about talking to reporters.

Jim: And what would that be?

Kratz: It's like catching on fire and not being able to put yourself out.

Scene V

The stage is dark, except for a large picture of Kingsom—a bright-eyed chestnut colt with a large white blaze running down his face—in full running position in the background, very shadowy and dull, but visible.
Tom Durkin's Voice *voice is echoing loudly, unseen over the faint sound of thundering hooves.*

Tom Durkin's Voice: . . .and they've reached the top of the stretch—Grand Wander is fighting on the inside with Imperial matching him stride for stride on the outside Nanananabanana is making up some ground behind them. . .

The picture of Kingsom is getting brighter and brighter; the pounding hooves, in turn, are getting louder and louder.

Tom Durkin's Voice: Grand Wander still hanging in on the inside—and there goes Kingsom! The big colt was behind for most of the race, but now he's unleashing that enormous stride of his! Kingsom inhaling the field as they make their way down the stretch! Kingsom ahead by seven—by eight—by nine. . . he's putting them all away!

A sharp, loud crack—like the breaking of a dry stick. The thundering hooves abruptly halt; the lights instantly cut off. It is pitch dark for a few moments.

Tom Durkin's Voice: *{in a panic}* Oh, my—he bobbled! Kingsom is slowing down, he's weaving around, he's—

The lights start to raise.

Tom Durkin's Voice: *{quietly, in an anguished tone}* Kingsom has broken down, ladies and gentlemen. . . he's—*{he stops, then continues in a slow, horribly resigned voice}* Kingsom. . . Kingsom appears to have fractured his right foreleg. He's down. . . Kingsom has broken down.

<u>Scene VI</u>

The stage is empty again, the background of Kingsom gone. The Man is back in his original position, standing on stage right, still clutching his now dog-eared racing program, with a single spotlight highlighting his body.

Man: He fractured both sesamoids in his right leg—the same injury that Ruffian, one of the greatest racing fillies of all time, suffered. He was humanely euthanized on the track ten minutes later. *{pauses}* I was at the race when it happened, even though by then I hated the horse with a passion. I was right by the track rail by the finish line when he broke down—he literally broke his leg right in front of me. *{pauses again}* The trainer, Ben Kratz, came out with the story—told the entire world that they'd juiced racing's savior—two and a half weeks after his breakdown. He hasn't been seen since.

The Man looks down, slowly, letting his program drop to the ground.

Man: The bad ones, they haunt you. . . when a horse gives his life for the love of the game, it haunts you till the end of time.

He walks slowly offstage.

Scene VII

*Two men are seated before an old television set. One is the **Man**, the narrator—the other is a simple "**Average Joe**" American who has called the man over to watch a race on television. They are sitting on an old, beat-up couch; the **Average Joe** is intent on the television while the **Man** looks like he is simply watching out of polite duty.*

Average Joe: *{pointing}* Look, there—there! The number 5 horse, watch—
Man: *{looking off into the distance}* Hmm.
Average Joe: *{grabbing the **Man** and forcing him around}* Look, I know you're still beat up over Kingsom, but please, please watch this. Humor me, right? Humor an old friend.
Man: *{finally turning around}* Okay, fine. Fine. All right?
Average Joe: Good. *{rewinds the tape}* Now watch.

*They watch for a few minutes in silence. The **Man**, who has been slouching on the couch, slowly starts to straighten up as the horse race on the television plays on. He watches the television intently.*

Average Joe: See that? That move he makes? It's the spitting image of—
Man: *{still watching the television intently}* Who is this? What's this horse's name?
Average Joe: *{raising his eyebrows}* Don't you recognize him?
Man: Well, no.
Average Joe: It's Kingsom's half-brother.

Scene VIII

*The **Man** is back on stage right, holding a new, fresh racing program, still with a single spotlight on his face. For the first time, he is smiling a little.*

Man: Horse racing is heart, and blood, and sweat, and tears, and life. Horse racing is one of the simplest metaphors for life. . . horse racing *is* life. All of us start at the beginning, clean and shiny and new—ready to take on the world, ready to bring change. The gates open; we are unleashed. The race begins, everyone fighting for position. As the race progresses, people take different paths and use different tactics to work their way around. Some fall far, far behind; others break down and leave the race forever. The race ends at the same place it started—at the beginning, at birth. And soon the starting gates are filled again, and another race begins. It's a cycle—the cycle of horse racing, the cycle of life. *{he paces a little, gesturing}* Horse racing and life are intertwined, connected but different. Humans seek the truth of life, to unravel the great mysteries of the sun and the stars and existence itself. . . and horse racing exists only to show truth in its simplest form: that all things are created to run their race. All things begin in the starting gate; all things end at the beginning.

The **Man** *looks over to stage left, where a picture of Kingsom suddenly appears on the wall.*

Man: Horses run, they break down, they. . . die. But the races go on. New starts shine to take the place of the old ones. Someone once described Kingsom as a shooting star—"bright enough to burn your eyes but fleeting"—there one minute and the next one, gone. It's pretty true. And it's also true for a lot of horses. Ruffian. Go for Wand. Landseer. Barbaro. Eight Belles. The list goes on for miles. Shooting stars for every century. And yet life goes on, the stupid thing.

The **Man** *stands still in center stage, eyes fixed on the picture of Kingsom on the wall. Lights fade; the picture of Kingsom is the last to go.*

THE CRUDENESS OF OPERA: AN EDITORIAL
ARIA THAKER, 16

ROWLAND HALL ST. MARK'S SCHOOL
SALT LAKE CITY, UT
TEACHER: JOEL LONG

It is Friday night. I am wearing jeans, sneakers, and an obnoxiously bright green sweatshirt. I walk out of the bathroom and down the hallway of the theatre, not oblivious to the glares I receive. I am at the opera.

I love the opera, and I mean no disrespect to Puccini or Wagner or Mozart with my casual attire. I always dress casually when I attend operas, but I certainly do not wish to snub the performers. If I hope to offend anyone with my statement, it is the white-haired, passionless people who attend opera only to affirm their social status. You can see them in the expensive orchestra seats at any opera. They're the ones who fall asleep during the slower scenes, the ones who shoot me dirty looks if I whoop after a spectacular aria. It frustrates me that they consider opera to be "fancy," but they are certainly not the only ones who think so. I wish opera audiences would be as open to their passions as audiences at rock concerts. I wish they screamed, talked excitedly during intermission about the performers, and dressed as comfortably and as freely as those who attend rock concerts do. Not until we are comfortable in the presence of art can we truly appreciate it. I wish I could peel away the senseless pretentiousness and expose opera for what it is—unadulterated passion worth screaming for.

Opera plots and characters are generally ridiculous. *Pagliacci* ends in a brutal double murder at the hands of an enraged clown. But no one sees opera for the acting or the story—opera is about the music. For me, the beauty of opera lies in the way music causes me to sympathize with such comically simple characters. I experience the power of music best at the climax of an opera.

When the clown Pagliacci stabs his wife and her lover, I don't laugh at the ludicrousness of the situation. Instead, I feel a hollow ache for the murderer's pain, as the orchestra crescendos and the leading tenor's anguished voice declares *"La commedia è finita"*—"The comedy is finished." Only opera could manipulate my emotions and make me cry at such a contrived line. It is a sheer testament to the power of music that the same emotion inspired by the verbosity of a Shakespearean monologue can be elicited after a beautiful aria. Keep in mind that an aria is usually about two sentences repeated for four minutes in different musical phrases.

One cannot help but liken an operatic climax to Aristotle's idea of *catharsis.* Like Aristotle's favorite tragedies, opera transcends rationality and provides a purgation of subconscious emotion. This raw emotion, I believe, is what makes opera so beautiful. I dress casually on performance nights to underscore the fact that there is nothing refined about opera at all—anyone who attends opera should recognize that it is no less passionate or raw than a heavy metal concert. I go to the opera for the music, not as a status symbol or to prove that I am "cultured." Linnea Covington, writer for *The Brooklyn Rail,* argues that although older people still regard opera attendance as a status symbol, younger generations do not.

The opera industry can no longer rely on the patronage of class-conscious aristocrats; Covington argues that they now make their statements via "the designer apparel [they] wear or the kind of car [they] drive." It may also be argued that such speculation is irrelevant; there is a fundamental, philosophical flaw with the elitist's prudish, "fancy"-conscious approach to opera. Such attempts to put opera on a pedestal and separate it from pure human emotion result in its devaluation and loss of interest among youth. The average age of a subscriber to The Metropolitan Opera is close to 80 years old. Just looking at the sea of white heads in a theatre is enough to make me cower at the thought of my generation's lack of interest in opera.

If we want opera to survive the 21st century, the first step that must be taken is education: All opera lovers must do their best to expose children to the wonders of opera. Seemingly trivial impressions can influence a child starting from an extremely young age. The author of *Mastering Your Hidden Self*, Serge King, states that "during childhood the subconscious accepts practically everything it receives as fact and acts accordingly." Shows like *Sesame Street* often poke fun at opera, showing puppets yowling in Viking hats. Such ridicule may seem in good humor, but if one considers King's argument, it is clear that children take jokes seriously. The result? A society in which opera is ridiculed incessantly to the point where admitting a taste for it is blatantly "weird."

I do understand why opera is easy to make fun of—it can seem strange to the uninitiated. Opera singers "scream" loudly and shrilly, and it takes a bit of time to acquire a taste for the unnatural yet beautiful sound of a silver-voiced soprano. However, the strangeness factor should not deter educators from teaching children about opera. In fact, opera's sheer unusualness should be considered a positive attribute for educational purposes. Carol Bengle Gilbert of Associated Content recounts her experience of taking her 8-year-old daughter to the opera, stating that the very fact that the opera was not explicitly targeted to children "opened the door to discussion of important life lessons" and the unfamiliar language "contributed intrigue" to her daughter's experience. Parents concerned about the suitableness of opera for children should be reassured that opera can be very age-appropriate for young children—there are plenty of charming, comedic operas such as the *Magic Flute* by Mozart. Though it has become fashionable for parents to play Mozart to their babies to "make them smarter," this induction into the world of classical music ends abruptly and inexplicably after children cut their first teeth. Well into adolescence, children should be taught that opera is not weird but wonderful.

The second step that must be taken to save opera is adaptation: the opera industry must adapt to the changing culture of entertainment so that young people will stay engaged in and excited about the opera. Producers must not give in to the comfort of doing things as they have always been done. Obviously, the current packaging of opera is not working to attract the youth, and given that the average age of a Metropolitan Opera subscriber is around 80, the art form will suffer immensely if a clear attempt is not made soon to attract young people to the theater. Production budgets will deflate, fewer operas will be presented, and the art form will stop growing.

A common complaint about opera is that it "drags." Movies have adapted to our impatience by making most scenes last about 45 seconds, as opposed to the five-minute scenes of the old times. Opera directors could stage productions in a more visually exciting, fast-paced way. To make operas more relatable, directors might take creative license and shift the setting of *Le Nozze De Figaro* from an 18th-century mansion to a 21st-century hotel, complete with an elevator and a pool room.

Perhaps the most important adaptation the opera industry must make is to become more aggressive in its advertising. Currently, advertising for opera is spare and overly subtle, especially in the United States. This is because operas rely on the old, faithful clientele who do not need ads to lure them in. If producers wish to attract the young and uninitiated, however, they need to invest in effective ad campaigns to inform and excite the public.

Julie Bosman of *The New York Times* ridicules the Metropolitan Opera's disdain for advertising, describing how for 30 years, The Metropolitan Opera has "wrinkled its elegant nose at advertising campaigns, preferring discreet sales tactics like direct mail." In reform, the opera industry must recognize that it has every as much right to advertise for its opera production as a band does for its rock concert. Throwing pretension to the wind is a necessary step the opera companies must take before meeting success.

It is not enough for the opera industry to change, though. Like any industry, opera is consumer-dependent, and if the current audience responds negatively to attempted modernization, all change will be quelled and reversed. This is why the third necessary step is acceptance: self-named "purists" must accept that change is a prerequisite to the popularization and success of opera. Often when a director chooses to translate an opera into the region's dominant language, purists claim it is blasphemy. If such harmless attempts to make opera accessible are condemned, no producer will ever take bigger risks that might actually cause the youth to take notice.

In 2007, Russian soprano Anna Netrebko came out with a simple music video for Dvorzak's *Song to the Moon.* John Steane, classical music critic for *Gramophone Magazine,* was extremely complimentary to Netrebko's singing, but his response to the video itself was surpisingly harsh, with Steane derisively drawing the comparison between Netrebko and an "MTV star" who performs "terrible lip-synching."

This is a common pattern with classical music elites—they take issue (either consciously or subconsciously) when their music threatens to become "impure" with success and popularity. These "purists" need to stop clinging to elitism, because the only road to wide popular appeal is an open an unpretentious one. The more successful an opera star is, the more the purists will try to discredit her. Anna Netrebko, Renee Fleming, and Natalie Dessay—all modern opera stars who have attempted to popularize opera—have been bashed harshly in both the professional critic and the blog worlds. This jealous reaction might be human nature, but it should be consciously rejected. Purists need to stop their crusade against popular influence, because if they do not, the art form that they love so much will slowly fade into nonexistence.

I am not naïve enough to think that everyone would (or should) like opera. However, I do wish that there were more opportunities for people to learn about it and then determine whether or not they like it. Sometimes I wonder what it would be like to be able to flip to a cable channel called OTV—Opera Television, or what it would be like if opera stars become popular enough for pop artists to collaborate with them. Too often, I think, we ridicule opera, imitate the "shrieks" of its singers and laugh at its classical 19th-century melodrama. Too seldom, I think, do we educate our children about opera and honestly grant it some respect as a complex yet raw art form. We ought to appreciate the powerful pathos and the heartbreaking climaxes that form the real heart of opera. We ought to recognize that this stupendous genre has survived more than 300 years, and it would be a shame to hear its echoes fade.

Covington, Linnea. "Until the Fat Lady Sings: Can Opera Survive the Twenty-First Century?" The Brooklyn Rail. June 2006.
King, Serge. Mastering Your Hidden Self: Guide to the Huna Way.: Quest Books, 1985.
Gilbert, Carol Bengle. "Teaching a Child to Enjoy the Opera." Associated Content. Dec. 17, 2007
Bosman, Julie. "The Metropolitan Opera's New Stage." The New York Times. Aug. 29, 2006.

HOT MINT TEA IN JULY
MARISSA DEARING, 16
MARET SCHOOL
WASHINGTON, D.C.
TEACHER: CLAIRE PETTENGILL

"Feen?" Sara asks.

"Qareeb min al-burtuqal."

Near the orange, I tell her, because I can't remember the plural for "orange." We are meeting our friends, and the fruit stands are the designated meeting spot. Sara nods and smiles instead of correcting me and leads me by the hand through a sea of brilliantly-colored kaftans: oranges, pinks, teals, and reds. Clutching my purse and her hand, I stammer *"smehli"* and *"semhili"* (the masculine and feminine forms of "excuse me") in every direction as we squeeze through the tangle of clothing, children, motorcycles, and taxis. We stop in front of a row of ten cobalt-blue carts piled high with oranges, identical except for the man standing behind each. My sunglasses slide slowly down my nose as we wait for our friends to arrive, and I can feel the back of my neck starting to burn. The chanting beat of a song blares from a nearby stereo, mingling with the calls of dinner specials, jewelry prices, *"Allah akbar,"* and *"Hello, American princess."*

I let my hair down, having forgotten my sunblock.

This past summer I went to Morocco to study Arabic and explore Moroccan culture as one of a group of 20 American students. The immersion program, hosted by Legacy International and funded in part by the U.S. State Department, involved intensive Arabic instruction and home stays with Moroccan families in Marrakesh and Rabat. There were side trips to Zagora, the Sahara Desert, Essaouira, Fez, and Casablanca, as well as guest speakers, intercultural dialogues with Moroccan students, and community service opportunities. When I heard about the program, I was entranced by the idea of spending the summer in an exotic location, immersed in a language I had come to love. I knew I had to apply.

My excitement was mixed with concern that my language skills would be tested far more than they had been in my twice-weekly Arabic lessons. For two years, I had studied homemade flash cards, pored over Modern Standard Arabic grammar, and listened to Arabic dialogues on my computer. I had come a long way since my initial fascination with Arabic culture. Still, would I really be able to communicate with my host family? I redoubled my efforts to absorb as much as possible before the trip. As I packed and exchanged emails with other student participants, I couldn't help thinking: Will I like my host family? Will they like me? Will we connect?

But from the start, I knew that six weeks would not be nearly enough. In Marrakesh, my host family embraced me with open arms and stuffed me with food. Their home was small, but beautifully exotic. I loved the room where we shared our meals, a room bordered by couches covered in rich fabrics. We watched movies together, sometimes in French and sometimes in Arabic. I looked on as my host mother wrapped her scarf over her hair, color-coordinating her scarf-pin and heels.

In addition to my host sister Sara, I met brothers, uncles, aunts, grandparents, and cousins on weekend visits to nearby towns and cities. Over the abundant feasts these visits invariably entailed, I spoke in my still-shaky Moroccan dialect, and marveled when the relatives seemed to understand me.

At first, my host mother drove me to school, afraid that I would be "stolen" if I rode alone in a taxi. (She reminded me of my mother at home.) Later, I would navigate taxis with ease. We attended school every day except Sunday. There, we studied not only Modern Standard Arabic, but also the less formal Moroccan spoken dialect, called *darija*—a mix of French, formal Arabic, and modifications (usually contractions) of formal Arabic. Our teacher was very animated; he moved around the classroom, gesturing and calling on us, encouraging us to speak. Although the pace was much quicker than it had been at home, the atmosphere was relaxed and the students eager.

When I had studied Spanish, I was hesitant to speak until I was sure I could do it very well. But having class every day and being able to practice my Arabic with people around me made a tremendous difference. I strained to hear and understand all the conversations around me, and tried out the language every opportunity I got. It was nerve-wracking, exhausting, and exhilarating.

I spent endless hours at the *Djemaa el Fna,* the famous open-air market in Marrakesh, where bargaining is an art form. In many ways, it was my language laboratory. Initially, Sara did all the negotiating, but soon after my arrival, I dove in. Some of my most meaningful conversations were with merchants and shopkeepers, debating politics and global health. I remember one shopkeeper telling me that language makes a world culture, and that America is a place where every culture can flourish.

One thing we could always talk about was food. I think I daily ate my bodyweight in Moroccan bread, which is dense, delicious, and plentiful. Breakfast went on forever; dinner sometimes began at midnight. The tagines—beef, chicken, lamb, all slow-cooked—were ubiquitous. In Rabat, we ate without utensils, sopping up the rich sauces with bread.

On Fridays—holy days for Muslims—we had couscous with nuts, chickpeas, and sweet onions. Occasionally, there were sizzling chunks of chicken or beef mixed in. Feeling adventurous, I ate snails for the first time. They were a cumin-and-saffron paradise. I discovered dates, *harira*—a traditional Moroccan soup—and *bastilla,* made with squab and a great deal of brown sugar. I devoured almond-filled pastries and caramel flans and fell in love with mint tea, the national beverage. I loved feeling the steam of the still-boiling tea on my face as I inhaled the mint. I bought a set of tea glasses for home.

I immersed myself in the rhythm of daily life in Morocco. Time is not as fixed there as it is at home, and I savored the slower pace. I discovered haunting *Gnawan* music (a mix of Arabic, Berber, and African influences) and danced onstage at a concert alongside musicians wearing hats with tassels that whirled in circles. I was enthralled by the music of Umm Kulthum, an Egyptian singer famous throughout the Arab world.

At school, we listened to a talk given by an *imam* (the religious, social, and political leader of a community) and learned about the Muslim faith. I bought a Koran. I watched street vendors spiral dirty hands with intricate calligraphy, and took a calligraphy lesson (far more difficult than it looks). Everywhere, I waded through traffic, having learned to make eye contact with the drivers, to wave and smile.

I dressed more conservatively than at home, although there was a great deal of variety in dress in the larger cities. We saw *burkas* and skin-tight jeans walking side by side. I bought one of the lovely embroidered blouses I had seen the girls in Marrakesh wearing. On a trip to the Sahara Desert, I donned a *jellaba,* a long flowing shirt that stretched down to my ankles. Sitting on a camel for the two-hour ride to the dunes, I enjoyed the added protection of a turban.

Led by our Moroccan teachers and guides, we explored the diverse Moroccan landscape, crossing the Atlas Mountains and visiting beautiful cities and villages: the colorful, palm tree-dotted city of Marrakesh, the humid city of Rabat, the blue-and-white fishing village of Essaouira, the cultural and spiritual jewel that is Fez, and the soft, reddish dunes of the Sahara, which burned during the day and felt like cool iron filings at night. We slept on those dunes, blanketed only by the still-warm desert air. I watched the sun rise from behind an enormous dune and admired colors my camera could never, ever capture. I took hundreds of photos every day and still felt like I missed a million opportunities.

We tutored Moroccan students who were eager to learn English, painted blackboards at a school in Essaouira, and visited children in an orphanage in Marrakesh. I had brought pencils, stickers, and little toy cars from the States, and gave them to the children. They clamored for the goodies. I noticed a little boy smiling shyly at me, and I drew a smiley face on his hand and gave him my pen. Afterward, he was beaming. I spoke to the kids with the darija that I knew, but mostly we communicated with hand gestures and smiles. We talked at length with Moroccan high-school students, exchanging Facebook and e-mail information. We made friends.

My experiences in Morocco will stay with me for a lifetime. I miss hearing that my eyes are beautiful while wearing reflective sunglasses, and having my conversations leavened with "thanks be to God" and "to your health." Answering blind panhandlers with "May God make it easy for you." Forgetting the English words for things. Waking up covered in sweat and not looking frantically for a fan. Feeling overwhelmed and excited and ashamed and grateful all at once by the constant and excessive hospitality. Saying "Thank you" more often than blinking, and meaning it.

THE DAY LISLE GOT MARRIED

XUEYOU WANG, 17

HILLCREST HIGH SCHOOL
MIDVALE, UT
TEACHER: MICHELLE SHIMMIN

Anja checks the mail one Saturday morning with her threadbare bathrobe tucked around her. The sky outside is a pearly pink taking on hues of golden orange, and she has a letter from her sister.

Anja is surprised. She sweeps her hand through the mailbox and gathers all the papery envelopes into the crook of her arm, as if she were holding a baby. She shuffles inside, carefully carrying the bulky stack to its designated resting place on the counter. She pours herself some cereal and turns on the television, because her thoughts are too loud and the house is too quiet. She takes a moment to appreciate the pleasant crackling sound of milk washing around with the brittle cereal flakes. She tries, and fails, to remember the last time she has been in contact with her sister. She chews her cereal with loud, crunchy gusto and wonders how long she can restrain herself from looking at the stack of envelopes, so tidy and persuasive, which has taken on more appeal than ever before.

Anja reaches out and takes her sister's letter. She runs her index finger curiously around the weathered corners of the envelope. She allows her eyes to take in the black pen inked into the fine paper.

You have traveled all the way from Berlin, Anja thinks, patting down the envelope. *Just to see me.*

She thinks about the last time she saw her sister. June 15th, four years ago; a perfect, summery, cloudless blue day, intoxicatingly fresh and baby-faced. A day of chilled ice cream cones, sun-soaked sidewalks, and sounds and smells that jumped and meshed together. Back when her sister still spoke to her; before they became estranged.

Estranged.

The word itself looks like strangled, like choking, tangled muscles and collapsing throats. Anja finds that she can speak about it detachedly, without a stirring of emotion; and that when she does so, it makes an impressive impact. *My sister and her daughter are estranged from me. In fact, they find me repulsive. A round of apologies, and expressions of sympathy.* When the phrase sinks into her brain at night, it is almost sad. It is almost realistic.

Anja thinks about her one and only niece. Lisle. Pretty, vivacious, doe-eyed. Seven years younger than Anja, and seven years dumber. She wonders if Lisle ever got married. Lisle would make a precious bride, with a name so antique and distinctly German. Her name, to Anja, is the image of a girl in a pinafore, munching on bratwurst and sewing a handkerchief. She hooks her thumbnail under the envelope flap and prepares to open it.

*   *   *

Anja was only seven when her sister, Margot, gave birth for the first time. At first, Anja didn't understand why Margie began living in a special house.

"Margie isn't sick, is she?"

"She's having a *baby,*" the nearest adult would chide in hushed tones, looking knowingly around. "She has a baby *inside* her."

And so Anja spent countless hours in her sister's little white square of a room, in her new home. She took to reading aloud to Margie from colorful storybooks, bringing Margie movies to put in the hospital television, cooking her food from home, in case the hospital food was disgusting. When she got new plastic black shoes, she brought them to show to Margie, who would appraise them as enthusiastically as was possible.

"Why do you have to lie in bed so much, Marge?"

"Because I don't feel so good."

"Are you sick?"

"No."

"That's what everyone else is telling me. But I'm not sure I believe it. How do you know they're not lying to you too?" Margot looked away, and didn't say anything for the rest of the visit. That night, Anja, who secretly didn't believe in God, crouched down beside her bed and prayed. *Dear God, please make Margie not sick. Make her be better and not so fat and then she can come home again and we can play dolls.*

One day when Anja went, he was there. He—the one who met Margot at the door with flowers; the one who drove his shiny little car into their driveway and took her away. The boy who Anja's parents spent much time muttering seriously about over the dinner table long after dinner was over. The one who made Margie so sick. *Schwanger,* they called it. Pregnant.

Anja never saw him again.

Anja was there the day that Margie started screaming, and little red rivulets ran down the insides of her calves like liquid snakes. And after the doctors ushered little Anja outside, she wondered if her sister was really going to die.

*   *   *

Anja is exceedingly careful with the envelope; she thinks of this surprise letter as a limited-edition item, possibly the last of its kind. It should have been marked Handle With Care. She realizes her fingers are sweating and wants to scream. Then she wants to laugh, because what kind of grown woman treats a letter as if it was a chocolate bar containing the Golden Ticket? She tries to breathe normally, knowing her cereal is getting soggy. She wants to see what her sister has sent her after four years of estrangement. She does, and she does not.

*   *   *

When Anja was away at college in America, her sister sent her lots of letters.

Dearest Anja, I miss you and hope you are doing well in New York. Lisle just turned 9 today, it was so fun.

Anja would read them and write back as dutifully as possible, although that usually meant a short scribble on a notepad-size sheet of paper for every dozen three-page letter Margot wrote her.

She never fully read every letter; she only glanced and digested snippets.

The doctors have told me I'm going to have to undergo surgery and I'm not even 40 and I can no longer have children and please come visit me during Christmas if you are not too busy.

Anja had small fragments of Margot's life in those envelopes; they weren't enough to piece together a small window into her life. Anja marveled at how Margot could so deeply love Lisle, rather than resent her. Lisle, the burden left by the man who couldn't stay, and who in turn left the burden in Margot that almost killed her.

*   *   *

Anja is shaken.

She puts the envelope down again and roams aimlessly around the house. Anja's fingers are trembling of their own volition. She scrambles to find a cigarette, but remembers she hasn't smoked for three years. She rips the envelope open and decides not to look at the paper. She will not look at it.

*   *   *

June 15th, four years ago, Anja flew to Berlin to see Lisle, freshly turned 21. She also met Lisle's fiancé.

He is jovially cute, and Anja is sparkling—pretty in her floppy white hat and square black sunglasses that rest just-right on her cheekbones.

"Can I have a smoke?"

She likes that he asks in his broken English, bulldozed with a heavy German accent, so she hands him a smooth cigarette and sticks one between her own lips. He lights her cigarette, like a real gentleman—like in the movies with Audrey Hepburn. They smoke in companionable silence.

"How long have you been with Lisle?" she asks interestedly, mentally complimenting her niece on her impeccable taste in men. He is tall, somewhat on the stringy side, but irresistibly adorable. Like a French bulldog, she cannot help but want to keep him as a little pet.

"A year," he says uncomfortably, sucking on his cigarette.

"And you love her?" Anja smiles. "Lisle is my favorite niece."

"She is your only niece."

He looks questioningly at Anja. He seems so young. His cheeks have a hint of baby fat. This suddenly seems like a bad idea to Anja. She wants to yank the cigarette from his fingers.

"She is *sehr schönlich*. Very pretty."

"Yes."

"Do you love her?"

"Why do you ask?"

"Does she love you?"

"Yes," he says instantly, looking embarrassed.

"Every happiness to you both, then."

"*Danke.*"

"You don't seem happy."

After a long pause, he finally says, "I am."

"What's your favorite color?"

"What?" He looks confused. He drops his cigarette and grinds it into the pavement.

"*Lieblingsfarbe.* Your favorite color?"

"Blue."

"Moody," Anja says instantly. "You are compassionate, and feel very strongly about certain things. You also have severe mood swings. You are quick to anger, jealousy, and frustration. You are low on patience and like to be admired."

"What are you," He gives her another quizzical look. "A fortune teller?"

"A woman of much wisdom," Anja jokes.

"Can you predict what I will do next?" He asks suddenly.

"Sure," Anja says. "You will get up from that garden chair, walk inside the house, and kiss Lisle. You will tell her you love her. You'll give up smoking."

He stands up and leans over Anja.

"I am very attracted to you," he says.

His breath smells like peanut butter, which Anja associates with a small child. He leans closer and suddenly all she can sense is

peanut butter cigarette smoke air

rough skin on her cheeks

eyelashes brown dark

pink upper lip like a bow

small black dots stubble

soft fingers coming closer closer closer closer to her face

hot sticky encroaching

puffy pink chapped lip

white square teeth

and then she pushes him to the ground and stands up to leave, because she feels disgusting and dirty, and her face feels like there is a cloud of smog blanketing it, and her nostrils are filled with the smell of peanut butter mixed with cigarettes.

But she can't leave, because in the window of her sister's house, a thin, freckly face is pressed against the window, looking scared and innocent, and her eyes are wide and very, very brown, like her mother's. And then it is gone again, and Anja cannot hear anything because time feels twisted and warped. She does not know what to do, until her sister stalks onto the lawn and her face is twisted and grotesque. Her face is shades of every purple and red, and she is wielding a spatula with a piece of *spaetzle* still hanging on the end. He is like a stupid little rat, curled in the light of the 1 train on its way downtown, but Anja realizes that he is still not as stupid as she is.

She throws down her cigarette next to him, where it smokes and dies. There are red lipstick prints around the end where she put her lips around it.

*   *   *

A wave of remorse washes over Anja as she finds a single, weathered cigarette in the pocket of a jacket she hasn't worn in four years. Like a token of time. In a moment of immense regret, Anja decides to write Lisle a letter of her own, to apologize. For whatever happened four years ago. She is still not sure. She does not know what happened, really. But she is so desperately sorry it pulls painfully at her heartstrings. She imagines her body as a violin, the strings strung taut from her neck to her knees. It is as if someone is trying to rip them out of her. She also feels that if she apologizes maybe everything will be better again. Anja decides that she cannot read the letter. She does not deserve to.

And so she lights her first cigarette in three years and burns the letter, envelope and all, until it is nothing but a pile of ash.

*   *   *

Lisle wonders why her *Tante Anja* did not come to her wedding. She decides the invitation was lost in the mail and moves on, as people do.

THE SAME DAY FOREVER
ANNA WONG, 13

GEORGE H. MOODY MIDDLE SCHOOL
RICHMOND, VA
TEACHER: PATRICIA WALKER

Sixteen, 18, 20. . . I'm counting my Great-Aunt Edna's moles. There are so many I have to count by twos. Little brown dots are scattered all over her pale flabby neck, which jiggles like a piece of bologna every time she talks.

"Target owes me 20 dollars, you know," she says for the hundredth time. "The man told me on the phone, but I never got a dime. People these days," she mutters in a peevish, wheezy voice. I sigh heavily, restraining the urge to roll my eyes and scream. This is torture.

I have been sitting with Aunt Edna in front of the television for over an hour, a valiant feat in my opinion, as she is 90 years old and severely senile. My mom and my little brother Johnny and I are spending spring break with her. Mom needs to settle some bill discrepancies, while Johnny and I just have to maintain our sanity as best we can. Perhaps I would be more tolerant if she was somewhat pleasant, but she is one bitter grape that never ripened. I can barely stand to look at her.

Her shriveled lips are pursed, and I can make out the sour expression etched in her face of wrinkles. An outdated pair of glasses with inch-thick lenses is perched on the bridge of her enormous nose, and her watery eyes are wide as a bat's. Her artificially curled hair is limp and so thin that she might as well be bald. Of course, I'm not allowed to say that to her, even though the idea seems incredibly appealing to me at this point.

With a heavy sigh, I heave myself up from the sofa. I stretch out my arms and shake out my legs; it's as if all of my joints have gone numb. Johnny, who is sprawled on the rug in front of the TV, looks up from his video game.

"Hey, Mary, did you want to go out for a swim now?"

He has asked me this question repeatedly throughout the morning, but he just doesn't seem to comprehend that I don't particularly feel like swimming.

"No. I'm too tired," I tell him irritably. "I'm going to get my book."

"Oh, come on. It's really nice out today," he says. "It's the only worthwhile thing in this old-people neighborhood," he grumbles under his breath. Aunt Edna is oblivious as she glares moodily at the television screen.

"I said no," I snap. I don't know why I am being so mean to my brother. Maybe it's because my patience is already being worn down by Aunt Edna's endless complaints. Because the scorching humidity of Florida is melting my brain. Or because all of my friends are back at home, lounging at our neighborhood pool, having a fun spring break without me. I know it's not very divine of me to sulk, but my less-noble side prevails. I have good reason to be grumpy.

I stomp noisily over to get my bag, which is sitting in one of the two bedrooms of Aunt Edna's petite residence. She lives in a condo complex with a bunch of other old people neighbors. Everything here is so ancient and dusty—the walls are totally obscured by cabinets full of old porcelain dolls, and I swear their beady eyes follow me wherever I go. Antique paintings of naked children hang lopsidedly on any uncovered wall too, which is just creepy. No matter where I turn, I can smell my aunt's musty old lady scent. When I get to the guest bedroom, I just flop down on the bed and close my eyes.

I decide I am too fed up and tired to read right now. Drowsiness crawls into my head and stays there for a while, and I'm faintly aware of Aunt Edna whining to Johnny about her Target suspicions again.

"Hey, honey." I hear my mom's wary voice and open my eyes. She puts her hand on my back, rubbing it gently. "Time to get up."

"Umph," I grunt.

"Mary, we're having lunch with Aunt E's friend, Miss Clara," she says.

"I don't want to go," I groan.

"Get up, Mary," she says firmly. "She's in the kitchen, and she wants to meet you. And you'd better fix that attitude, you understand?"

With that, she leaves the bedroom.

"Fine," I scowl.

Reluctantly, I get up from the bed and follow her.

Miss Clara is sitting at the kitchen table next to Aunt Edna. Though she is no doubt past her golden years of youth, her face is round and wrinkled in a less crazed, demented way than my aunt's. Her snow-white hair is a fluffy halo on her head, and she is wearing bright red lipstick.

"Well, hello there sweetie. You must be Mary," she greets me with a toothy grin. She has a gruff but sweet voice.

"Yeah. Hi," I say with a shy smile.

"I just met your brother, Johnny, over here," she nods behind me. Johnny appears at my side, smiling at Clara. "I want to tell you that it is so nice of you to come visit your aunt. She loves you all very much."

"Yes, yes, I've told them," Aunt Edna says hoarsely. I nod, but I bite my lip. It was hard to remember how much she loved us when she could be so annoying.

"Well, lunch is served," my mom says as she carries over a plate of sandwiches. Johnny and I sit as far away from Aunt Edna possible, scooting our chairs closer to the more amiable Miss Clara. Mom pulls up a chair next to Aunt Edna to close the gap, but she shoots us a look. Lunch is actually okay. Clara is really nice, a much friendlier old lady than Aunt Edna. She speaks kindly to Aunt Edna, and just says patiently, "Yes Edna, you've told us that already," with each of her redundant comments.

When we've finished our sandwiches, my mom says to Aunt Edna, "Why don't you go get your wedding album? You can show the kids the pictures of you and Tony."

"But everything was borrowed. I couldn't even afford my own dress," Aunt Edna muses wistfully.

"Oh please, you were beautiful. Go get them," my mother insists. "Alright, they're in my bureau."

She hobbles out of the room.

"Kids, why don't you go to the den and wait for her? Miss Clara and I will clean up here," Mom says. Johnny hops up, eager to resume his video game. I know that Mom is trying to get rid of us, though. "Go on, Mary," my mom says, a dismissive tone leaking into her composed voice.

"Okay." I leave my seat at the table, but I linger in the hallway outside the kitchen to eavesdrop.

"So how have things been, Clara?" my mom asks.

"Oh, poor thing. She's becoming so forgetful. Not bathing, not eating either. . . As far as I can tell, all she's been eating is that coffee cake before you came," Clara answers.

"Edna is a mess. You actually don't have to tell me that, I figured it out as soon as we arrived Thursday," my mom sighs in exasperation. "This whole week, I've been trying to clear up her paperwork. . ."

"Is it that bad?"

"She hasn't been paying her bills!" I hear my mom lower her voice, whispering like a person shouts. "If I hadn't gotten here, her electricity would have gotten cut off. And so many scams are preying off of her. . . she's so vulnerable."

"I want to help, but she's so defensive these days. I don't want to push her, though, because then she'll shut me out. She'll have no one," Clara says quietly. A surge of affection runs through me for Clara. What a selfless woman.

"Oh, dear." Silence fills the kitchen. I press my back against the wall, waiting for the conversation to resume. I feel a pang of guilt as I realize how much my mom is helping Aunt Edna. This spring break is even more excruciating for her, and yet she's still kept a sweet face for Johnny and me.

"You know, as far as the bills go, I could check on her every once in a while. She's in charge of her mailbox key, but I can help her sort it," Clara offers.

"That would be wonderful," my mom exclaims. "If only she lived closer, I'd look after her, but we live up in Virginia. . ."

"It would be no problem."

"Clara, thank you so much. But who will take care of you? All you do is worry about Edna, you need to worry about yourself, too."

"Hon, I'm in great shape."

"Mmm-hmm," my mom trails off, uncertain.

"We should check on Edna," Clara says. "I wonder where she is."

Both of their chairs squeak against the linoleum floor, and I dash down the hallway to the den to join Johnny. I slide onto the sofa, grabbing the remote and flipping on the TV.

"Edna?" my mom calls as she and Clara walk toward her room. "You okay in there?"

"Yes, I'm fine," Aunt Edna replies, emerging from the doorway.

"Did you find your picture book?" asks Clara.

Aunt Edna blinks confusedly.

"Find what?"

"Never mind," Clara tells her. "I'm just leaving, actually."

She starts to walk over to Johnny and me, and we scramble to our feet.

"Bye, Miss Clara," we say.

"Good-bye to you both, it was so nice to meet you," she says. Her rosy, crinkled face draws nearer to ours, and she reaches her hand to pinch each of our cheeks. "You both have the prettiest smiles."

"Thanks," we mumble, embarrassed.

After Miss Clara leaves, my mother beckons Aunt Edna to sit down in the love seat across the room from me.

"Aunt Edna? I need to talk to you," she says. They take their seats, and my mom shuffles a pile of papers in her lap.

"We need to discuss the matter of you paying your bills. You haven't been doing it, have you?"

"Yes, I did, I paid them last Sunday."

"No, you haven't, actually. I have put most of them on automatic pay now, but you need to go through your mail every time you receive any."

"I do."

"No, you don't. And Miss Clara has offered to help you. So, every month, she will sit down with you and review what needs to be paid, all right?"

"I don't want her to do that, I don't trust her." Aunt Edna shakes her head, her face falling into a pout.

For a moment, my mom is speechless. "And why is that?"

"She's too nosy, and I don't like it."

"Edna, I cannot believe you said that. Clara is trying to help you."

"I don't trust her. You know people these days, they'll take advantage of you just like that."

"Clara is one of the people who is protecting you," my mom says sternly. "She is trying to help you, as am I."

"I understand. But people these days. . ."

"Neither of us can help you unless you let us." Mom folds her arms across her chest and looks grimly at Aunt Edna, who is ogling into space with a vacant expression.

Aunt Edna breaks the silence. "You know Target owes me 20 dollars? The man told me on the phone, but I never got a dime. People these days, you can't trust them."

"Edna, we have settled this already. That debt expired because you did not go to the store to retrieve the money."

Mom's voice quivers.

"Is that so?"

"Yes," my mother says tightly. "But we are not discussing that now. We are discussing the problem of you not paying your bills, because you cannot remember."

"I can't help my memory. It's so hard these days."

"That is why we are getting Clara to help you."

"No. I don't trust her. She's too nosy, and I don't like it."

"She is trying to help you!" My mother raises her voice, and it shoots up a couple octaves. Johnny and I catch each other's eyes—we hear this tone whenever Mom's temper is running thin. My elbows dig into the scratchy sofa, because I am equally upset.

Aunt Edna is being absurd. She's being an insensitive, flabby-necked nutcase. How could she not trust sweet, loving Clara? Not trusting Clara would be like not trusting my mother, who has spent this whole "vacation" laboring over stupid Aunt Edna's stupid paperwork.

I hate Aunt Edna. My furious hatred boils under my skin.

"She's too nosy, and I don't like her. You just can't trust people like her. She's jealous of me, I can tell," says my psychopath aunt.

"Shut up! You don't know what you're talking about!" I explode, leaping from the couch.

Shock freezes my mom and Edna's faces. Aunt Edna's watery eyes, magnified through her glasses, are pathetically outraged. She gasps, and puts a hand to her chest. What is really sick is that she seems surprised at my anger.

"Clara is the nicest lady ever, and she just wants to help!" I shout. "My mom is doing everything she can to help you and all you do is complain and nobody would ever be jealous of you because you're—"

"Enough, Mary. Go to the bedroom, now," my mother says before I can finish, and I notice that there are tears streaming down my face. I stalk out of the living room, and it takes all the willpower in the world not to turn around and wrestle my Aunt Edna into a headlock and rip off her mole-infested face.

Once I shut myself in the bedroom, I grab a pillow and scream into it. When I'm done using it as a sound buffer, I squish it into a lumpy form and lob it at the wall. To my satisfaction, it hits one of her creepy naked child portraits. I feel better, but not much.

"Mary? I need to talk to you," my mom says tiredly at the doorway.

"Fine."

She pushes open the door and comes to sit by me on the bed. "What you did is something I've been wanting to do."

"You're welcome," I grumble.

My mom laughs.

"I'm not saying it was right. But I understand."

"I hate her. She's so stupid—how can she be so. . . ugh!"

"Honey, I know. Your Aunt Edna is old, and she's losing it."

"You can say that again," I say under my breath. "Evil hag."

"Mary. It's unfair that you criticize her like that."

I'm about to protest, but my mom lifts a hand for me to listen.

"When Aunt Edna grew up, she was a lovely southern belle. Then Uncle Tony came home from war to find himself a beautiful wife, so he whisked her away to a fairytale life.

"She was spoiled. She thinks that Clara's jealous, because truthfully, other women envied her at one time. When Uncle Tony died, she didn't understand what it was like not to have everything she wanted. Now she's 90, and she's stuck in that state. Me, Clara, and her few other relatives need to take care of her, because she can't take care of herself."

"Well, she can learn," I interrupt.

"No, she can't. Her memory is terrible, and she's physically impaired. Even if she learned to one day, she would forget the next. Honestly, I don't understand how she can live alone."

"How is that living at all, then? If she can't remember anything, isn't that like living in the same day forever?" I interject.

"Exactly. That's why it's useless for me to yell at her. It's like yelling at a 2-year-old, you know? Besides, she wouldn't remember."

I look at my mom, regretting the petulant attitude I'd had throughout the week. I'd had no reason to be grumpy at all, I realize.

"I know it's hard, Mary. But she's still a person, and no person deserves to die alone and suffer just because they're old."

"Okay," I mumble. She pats me on the leg and leaves the room.

My Aunt Edna had waited too long to mature, and now she never would. At this point in my life, I always take tomorrow for granted, hoping that it will be better than today. Change is so easy to procrastinate.

Now I understand. I don't want to be an old lady like Aunt Edna, in a nursing home with no family who is willing to care for me. Tomorrows could run out at any moment, and my todays are already numbered. I need to become the person I want to be now—that way, if I ever get stuck in the same day forever, at least it will be a pleasant one.

After reflecting another moment, I walk over to my suitcase, digging around until I feel the right slippery fabric in my hands. Swimsuit in hand, I walk out of the bedroom and start down the hallway to the living room. On my way, I bump into Aunt Edna.

I take in her sorry appearance and feel a wave of remorse. "Sorry about that," I say.

"About what?" she croaks.

I sigh in relief, though there is still a part of me that is disappointed she does not remember my frank disciplining. But I remind myself that she has taught me a valuable lesson this spring break.

"You know what Aunt E? Thanks." I say this with a smile before walking past her, leaving her clueless.

Johnny is still lounging on the floor of the living room with his video game when I get there.

"Hey, Johnny."

He looks up at me warily, cautious after my explosion.

"Did you want to go swimming?" I ask.

"I thought you didn't want to," he says in surprise.

"Yeah, but I think we should," I tell him. "While it's still sunny."

THREAD
AYESHA SENGUPTA, 17

INTERNATIONAL SCHOOL OF DUSSELDORF
DUSSELDORF, GERMANY
TEACHER: SUSAN BEVINGTON

Something about the way she cries into the phone reminds me of the time I tried to merge our skins together by pressing my hands into the soft of her cheeks. She had opened her eyes then, swept my baby fingers away like dust from freshly-washed dishes. I forgave her, thought maybe it was an accidental reflex, uncontrollable. I pushed closer to her again—my eye to her nose—her ear to my mouth, but then she stood up. Sighing, she pulled on a sweater. She had just needed a few minutes to escape reality, to slip into peace and dreams, but it didn't seem like I could let her have even that much. I was her anchor, she told me from the way she picked me up. An anchor that held her down as she sank.

"How can you forget all those years. . ." she tells me now, her voice higher than usual, painful and fragile to perceive like cracked porcelain. I clutch the receiver. Finally, a thread that cuts deeply enough to hold us together. My hand shakes. I catch a tear on the tip of my tongue and wonder if hers is as salty as mine. Is it hereditary, the taste of sorrow?

We are silent for some time, and I hear her sobs recede. I recall a day on the beach when I ran after the ebbing tide, too slow to keep up with it, until it disappeared into the next wave. I had let it escape, lost it, powerless.

"Are you still there?" I whisper.

The flood is over, and now she won't talk anymore. I am not sure who cut the thread this time.

In the empty echoes of a wordless phone conversation, I want to, need to, hang up before she does. Yet in her reticence, I find a motivation that keeps me waiting, hoping, for just one more word.

Isolation, perhaps, so that I know we are together in being alone. So that I can be sure that sometimes, in the darkness that settles before sleep, she hears the voices of all those other children who used to surround me while I watched her retreating back, wondering when I would be old enough to go with her. The years ripened, the children grew up. Yet I still fell short, still stood rooted as she walked away, still lacked whatever it was that would allow me to leave with her.

Maybe *betrayal,* so that she could tell me she feels the way I did when she forgot about me on the curb for five hours. Sitting on the sidewalk, I told myself she had asked the drizzle to watch over me, to act as a shield, as a guardian, should anything bad happen to cross my way. Eventually, the sun emerged from behind the clouds, and I wondered if the rain had to babysit someone else.

Or just *sorry,* because she might be too proud to say it, but I will come running back to her if she tells me she wants me. If she whispers how she misses me, I will tell her I miss her too. If she asks me if I am happy by cutting her out of my life, I will say "no." I know, though, that should I say it all first, she will tell me she needs to hang up now, she needs to go, because something else is waiting to be done. And I will be left with the tone, the monotone, of being alone again.

So instead I say nothing and wait. I wonder if, like I am doing, she is sitting with the receiver pressed to her ear, scouting for the slightest noise—a shaky exhalation, the brush of hair against the mouthpiece, fingertips touching the phone and almost my face. I wonder if she has left the phone on the table to take a pot off the stove before the food burns, to take the washing out of the dryer before the wrinkles dry, or to close the windows before the moths creep in as the sun sets.

I wonder if she thinks I will still be there when she comes back. I press the red button, my lower lip quivering, and tear the thread to shreds. I might be younger than she is. I might be more unwanted than she is. I might be weaker, frailer, and more desperate than she is. But I am

learning to let go. I am learning to turn away and leave, and I know—
I think—I hope—I am doing it the right way.

I stand up and set the receiver back in its base. It glistens in the light, wet. I slide my wrist across my cheeks and glance at the clock. This conversation was several seconds shorter than the last. I slam the door shut on my way to the bathroom, so that if the phone rings while I am in the shower, I won't hear it.

Because I learned from the best.

THE BURNING
KAITLIN JENNRICH, 13

NEW GLARUS MIDDLE-HIGH SCHOOL
NEW GLARUS, WI
TEACHER: RACHEL RYAN

I'm sitting in Algebra when the fire alarm goes off.

One kid grumbles, "Are you serious?"

Another says, "It's 20 freaking degrees out there."

But the teacher isn't sighing impatiently or glancing at the clock, thinking *Is it really that time?* No, she's got a worried look on her face and I watch her dither for a moment. My school has too many pranksters to take fire alarms seriously, and about halfway through the school year, teachers stop paying attention to the drills.

But now we're smelling smoke, and unless the Chemistry lab blew up again, there's a fire.

"Alright, class!" the teacher announces, taking control. "Let's go now. Just like we've practiced."

A couple of people snort and I see lots of eye-rolling. We're 14 now, too old for baby games like fire drills. Groaning, we abandon our books and begin to sluggishly file out the door. I hear one girl mutter to her friends, "My textbook *better* be incinerated when I get back." They snicker just like they're supposed to and she grins triumphantly, but I bite my lip and shoot a glance at the boy next to me, Matt, who waggles his eyebrows in reassurance. He's a jock and popular and funny and a flirt and everything I'm not, and here he is, fluttering his eyes at me. It doesn't help.

I'm afraid.

"So?" he says, conversationally. "D'ya know why there's a fire?"

"Chemistry lab blew up?" I guess and he shrugs.

"Maybe. Or the furnace exploded!"

I'm laughing now, and as I reach to turn off the lights in the room I continue the guessing game.

"Suicidal teacher had enough?"

"Lunch ladies forgot to turn off the oven?"

"Art students forgot to unplug a glue gun?"

"It's not really a fire! It's just a smoke bomb!"

"Shut up!" someone snaps, and I turn to see Lily Hales frowning at me with a fierce expression on her face.

"What?" Matt says innocently and I snicker. Lily glares and says, "Didn't you hear?"

"Hmm?" I ask.

"Do you know Evan Kennedy?" she inquires softly, her voice lowering to a dramatic whisper. I smile wryly as I imagine her as a gossiping old woman, sharing the misdemeanors of the townsfolk with anyone who cares to listen.

"Evan Kennedy?" I repeat, trying to match a face to the name. Matt furrows his brow and says, "Hey, I have Spanish with him. He's a little off, but he's pretty good with *Español*."

"Well," Lily says darkly, "He's more than just a *little off*—I heard from this guy I know that he ran out of English, threatening everyone."

"Threatening?" I inquire, smirking. "What, 'You're going to regret ever making me do this essay!' Did he give them the finger?"

"No!" Lily says, giving me a dirty look. "He said something like, 'You just wait! I'll blow you all up!' They've been looking all over for him."

"Yeah, I'm sure," Matt says. "So why haven't they issued a lockdown?"

"Because one girl said she saw him run out of the building," Lily explains. "And they trust her, which is dumb since I know who she is and she lies all the time but anyway, they thought he ran into the city but he's *probably* just been hiding in school."

"Yeah?" I grin at Matt, relishing my closeness with this strange confident boy who seems to think I have something worth saying. "So, what? He's been crouching in the janitors' closet with a bomb?"

"I think he's going to set the school on fire," Lily whispers, and I see that behind her self-assured mask, she's afraid too.

"Oh, please!" Matt snorts and I'm relieved, because I don't need a scary story when I'm scared enough already.

"What a loser, this Evan kid. They should get him some help and get him away from here!"

"Matt!" I laugh. "Don't be mean!"

We're almost to the doors now and I can see outside, snow piled a foot high on the ground and icicles pointing menacingly from the school roof.

"Ugh," I moan. "It's so *cold.*"

"I smell smoke," Lily whispers, but I don't pay her any attention because Matt is busy figuring out how to sneak back into school so we don't freeze our butts off, and he has such gorgeous green eyes.

Suddenly, Lily screams and I whirl around.

"What?!" I snap, and she's pointing down the hallway with a terrified expression pasted on her face. I barely have time to blink when there's a mountain, a cloud, a wall of billowing fire rushing toward us.

There's no time to run outside, because in a millisecond the flames will be here and I've never wanted to be burned to a crisp, so I dive into an adjacent hallway, pulling Matt and Lily with me. The fire roars past us and tries to fly outside but the freezing weather and icy snow halt it right in its path. So it turns and finds three pairs of legs sprinting down a long empty hallway. The fire is starving, so with a big gasping breath it follows the prey down the hallway, roaring hunger and fury.

I hear voices screaming, though whether they're coming from outside or just in my head I can't tell. *This isn't happening.*

"My-father-in-heaven-hallowed-be-thy-name," Lily recites frantically, and I realize she's praying. That seems like a good idea to me but I can't think of anything to say.

"God, please get us out of this alive," I entreat. "I'll be good, I promise, just please get us all out alive. Amen."

It's a pitiful attempt at prayer but at least it's something.

Matt's faster than Lily and me, which comes from being star striker on the soccer team, and he's sprinting ahead of us. The fire's almost licking at my heels and for a moment I have to roll my eyes at the incredulity of the situation.

Who would think I'd be chased by fire? Just a few minutes ago, I wanted an excuse to get out of math class. Well, I guess I got one.

"Come on, Lily!" I shout because she's lagging behind, way too far behind and there's fire licking at her heels. Why is it burning so fast? Shouldn't fire be slow and steady? *This can't be happening.*

Lily speeds up, but just a little bit, and I don't know if she's going fast enough. I know she's fast but she's scared and that's turning her legs to blocks of ice, pillars of salt. My only fear involves me falling, because I'm moving so quickly that I can hardly stay vertical.

The fire's screaming in my ears but I see another door that leads outside up ahead and if I can just go a little faster, then it'll be okay.

At least, that's the mantra in my head. *I'll be okay, I'll be okay, I'll be okay.*

"Come on!" Matt shouts, and I lower my head and grit my teeth and try to channel all that pent-up energy teenagers are supposed to have. Adrenaline is not my friend, as my legs begin to slowly turn to jelly. *I'll wake up and this'll be all a dream.*

The door is maybe ten feet away, and I'm getting ready to veer right and jump into the snow and be safe and Matt's nearly there and getting ready to open it when I hear the most awful screaming noise.

No.

"Lily!" Matt yells and there's real terror in his voice, something I'm not used to in this cool-headed boy.

I whip around, still backpedaling because that fire's awfully close and awfully hot, and I see Lily. She's finally fallen, fear getting the best of her, and the fire's gobbling away at her legs like it's famished.

I swear—which is not poetic or romantic or heroic of me—and then I start screaming. Heat comes at my face in waves, and I'm afraid that the fire's going to eat me alive too, but it's gotten its prize and seems content to burn quietly.

"Lily!" I shriek and reach for her.

She grabs my hand, another cry of pain escaping her lips, and I try to get her upright. But, oh God, her legs aren't even functional. Matt leaves the door and freedom to come grab her other arm. Even though the fire's quieting down, it's been creeping closer and closer and suddenly it snaps, reaching for me. There's the most curious tingling sensation and suddenly my arm is on fire.

I swear again and practically hurl Lily and Matt toward the door, so determined to reach that cold, cold snow. Lily starts screaming again and Matt flings open the door and I see faces—hundreds of shiny faces with open mouths staring at us—and I see several teachers reaching for us but then I don't see any of that as I fall into the snow and everything turns blissfully, quietly black.

*   *   *

I'm sitting in Algebra when the principal's voice booms through the loudspeakers.

"Could Matt Joseph, Lily Hales, and Jessica Evans please report to the office?"

Several people glance at me, then look away. Someone coughs; another shuffles their feet. The teacher bobs her head, refusing to even meet my eyes.

"Go on, then," she says and begins scribbling more equations on the board.

$4x + 12 = 42.$

I leave my books on my desk and Matt takes control of Lily's wheelchair. It's a bulky thing, full of levers and buttons that do who-knows-what and only Lily is allowed to joke about it. Normally, I would fight to take possession of the wheelchair, eager to push it down the hallway and maybe see how fast it can go, but my arm is currently resting in a sling with second-degree burns. I keep insisting that I'm fine, but the doctors and my parents say that I can't put any pressure on my arm, even though we've already established that I can move all my fingers. Two more weeks with my arm encased in scratchy fabric and I'll be wishing the fire had just killed me, because if I have to live a month with this I could possibly spiral into the depression the guidance counselor keeps talking about.

It's a quiet walk down the hallway, interrupted only by the quiet clitter-clatter of the wheelchair on the tiled halls. Matt holds his nose and I half-smile. Most of the school had been singed, but the fire hadn't left much of a mark except for a horrid smell and burns on the wall. They were predicting that construction would be done in a month or so, and a lot of our classes had been moved to different areas of the building. My Algebra class, for example, was being held in the Chemistry lab.

What great irony: I suppose the Chemistry lab didn't blow up after all.

We don't have much to say to each other; we've spent a week talking in therapy and another week just talking to each other in the hospital, when we went and visited Lily when she was getting grafts. Matt claims the best thing he got out of the fire is a chance to quit the basketball team, because they always lose, but I know he's lying. The basketball team needs him, but Lily and I need him more.

"So what's this about?" Matt finally says and I shrug.

"Maybe we're in trouble," I say and we smile grimly at each other. As far as the school was concerned, if we acted out it was a sign that we were being normal. The guidance counselor, Ms. Marsh, had let us all know that they'd understand any behavioral issues but we should come to her immediately if we were feeling suicidal or depressed.

Matt said that he was feeling depressed just thinking about having to spend Tuesdays and Thursdays, for the next three months, in her office.

We weren't even the unlucky ones.

Two kids had died: the star quarterback, who'd gone to the bathroom and decided to skip the fire drill, and a junior who had fallen asleep in the library. Their friends were also in counseling, and we saw them coming in and out of Ms. Marsh's office during lunch period.

Matt, Lily, and I were the special ones, though, and we got counseling after school in case our sessions took more than an hour, which they rarely did. None of us had much to say.

And it turned out that Lily was right and Evan Kennedy had snapped. He stole gallons of gasoline from the gas station and poured them all over the hallways, then lit a match. You'd think I would've smelled the gasoline and thought, "What's that smell?" before the flames had come, so I'd have some warning about what was about to happen.

I guess life really isn't like the movies.

We arrive at the principal's office, already wary. Matt thinks we've developed an unhealthy fear of authority figures. Maybe it's all that time in counseling.

"Matt!" the principal says warmly, beckoning us in. "Lily! Jessie! How are you?"

"Fine, thank you," Lily says politely as Matt wheels her in. "What's all this about?"

Matt and I grin. Lily always cuts straight to the point.

"Why don't you have a seat?" the principal says instead of answering, gesturing at a few chairs in his office. Lily's placed in between us and I squeeze her arm with my good hand. Ms. Marsh is in here too, and that never bodes well for us. There's a third person—a boy with dark greasy hair and beautiful blue eyes who's crouched in his seat and staring guiltily at Lily's ruined legs. Matt's sitting eerily still, knuckles turning white as he clenches the sides of the chair and eyes turning hard as they bore into the boy's head.

That's when I notice the police officer.

"You jerk!" Matt suddenly shouts, launching himself out of his seat and flying at the boy. He lands one good punch before the principal and the police officer restrain him and force him back to his seat.

"Oh," I say. "You're Evan Kennedy."

He nods and focuses on his scuffed-up shoes. Evan's wearing jeans and a ratty T-shirt, which surprises me because I thought all criminals wear orange.

"Evan wanted to say something to you," Ms. Marsh says softly.

I'm waiting for her to place a calming hand on his shoulder, something she always does to me, but I guess Evan doesn't need her help.

Evan mutters something in the general direction of his sneakers and Matt says sarcastically, "What's that, Kennedy? Gotta speak up. Don't think the ladies can hear you."

This is a new side of Matt, nasty and cruel, and I think he slips into it far too easily. I shoot a warning glare in Matt's direction and he sullenly retreats.

"I'm sorry," Evan blurts, and Lily gives him an impassive stare.

I wait for more—an explanation, a reason behind the madness—but he resumes scrutiny of his shoes, seemingly satisfied with his apology.

"Evan was being bullied at school," Ms. Marsh explains for him.

I look fiercely in Matt's direction and he pretends to be engrossed with his hands.

"He was feeling pressure in his classes and at home and he felt like there was no one to help him. He felt like he needed to defend himself."

"So he blew the entire school up?" Matt says. "Great plan. Bet you're sorry you only killed two people, huh?"

Evan looks ready to cry and I reach over and slap Matt on the back of the head.

"Shut up," I say darkly, and to my great surprise, Matt actually quiets down.

The police officer says, "Our time's almost up. We have to get him back."

Ms. Marsh turns to us. "Is there anything else you want to say to

Evan?"

I know Matt has plenty to say but he holds his tongue.

I look at Lily's legs, swathed in milky white bandages, and at my arm, folded up awkwardly against my chest. Matt's begun playing with the stapler on the principal's desk, unhinging it and shooting staples into thin air. He turns and shoots one at me with a small grin, and I have to smile as it falls gracefully into my lap.

Lily breaks the silence. "I forgive you, Evan," she says, always the merciful one.

"Me too," Matt mutters.

"Me too," I parrot.

Evan looks relieved and even when the police officer handcuffs him and leads him away, he looks like he's been granted a reprieve, that from just a few simple words we gave him freedom.

But I lied. I hadn't forgiven him.

We're walking back to class when Matt says, "I'm glad that's over."

"Oh yeah," Lily agrees and pats her legs. "I'd be gladder if I could walk."

We chuckle mirthlessly, because that's one thing the doctors were very clear on. Lily will never walk again, and it was a miracle that they didn't have to amputate.

But that's another lie; I know as well as Matt and Lily do that this is far from over. Just like the fires that still linger in my dreams and the terrified look that Lily sometimes has when you catch her by surprise, maybe we'll never be cured.

The burning was a blessing as much as a curse.

I'm probably scarred for life and may soon contemplate suicide. Then again, I'm probably stronger.

And, as I am returning to Algebra class, I have a startling epiphany: $x = 7.5$

LINDISFARNE
LANE BAKER, 14

COVENANT DAY SCHOOL
MATTHEWS, NC
TEACHER: ROBI REGO

June 8, 793 A.D.

Dawn.

It was a time of stillness and tranquility, when the sole sounds to be heard were the distant calls of seabirds and the gentle flowing of the tides. It was a time of prayer and silence, when black-robed monks shuffled noiselessly into the halls of common prayer, when the first rays of sunlight struck the bell tower of Lindisfarne castle.

But to James, it was a time of escape. While the brothers of the monastery knelt to pray, the young teenage boy made his way through the empty courtyards, keeping an eye out for others. It did not suit him to be meandering about when it was time for prayer, but James had endured far too much of the Holy Island's practices to be concerned. As he turned the corner, his destination was reached.

The monastery gates were open, as usual, for any pilgrim in need of refuge at any time. James crossed over from within the high-walled monastery onto the sloping hill that led to the sea. Grass swayed in the wind, carrying with it a curious scent that sent shudders down James' spine. He waved it off and continued to the pebbly shore, letting out a sigh.

As James savored the peace and solitude, his desire for travel was reawakened. The sight of the mainland not far off in the distance sated James' appetite for discovery, and he considered the lands beyond the staggering monastery walls and the shores of the Holy Island. How cruel of God, he thought, to drive him here from England to this prison of an island. Under his breath, he cursed the Bernician raiders who had pillaged his home and forced his family to the one place where refuge could always be found, the monasteries. James watched as a sudden surge of water splashed up over the causeway that connected the island to the mainland, momentarily blocking the path.

In less than an hour, the Holy Island would once again become an island, as it did twice a day.

As James watched the sun emerge from behind the sea, a dark obstruction on the horizon caught his attention. Although nothing more than a small splotch against the radiant morning light, it piqued his interest. As he looked on, the shape began to take form, and James' suspicions were confirmed—a ship was coming! A thrill of excitement raced through him as he considered whom the ship might hold. He scurried back up to the gates, dashing along the pathways toward the central chapel.

The Morning Prayer had relented, and monks had begun to disperse from the sanctuary. James caught sight of his father, Godwin, emerging from the oak doors with an aggravated expression upon his face.

Nevertheless, James approached Godwin, letting his excitement about the ship overshadow his apprehension. Shuffling to his father, he was met by an angry glare.

"Father, a ship is sailing in from the north!" he exclaimed, earning him an inquisitive glance from his father. The sternness that had gripped Godwin seemed somewhat lifted by the news.

"I cannot excuse your disobedience and neglect of morning's prayer," scolded Godwin, "but I suppose that can wait. This is most excellent news. The north? Strange, I would not expect pilgrims from those parts. Still... I will alert Brother Robert immediately." His father turned and, with James at his side, proceeded to reenter the chapel.

Brother Robert stood by the altar, his form contrasted against the luminescence of the stained-glass window behind him. As Godwin relayed the news to Robert, the monk smiled.

"Wonderful! Let us go down then to greet these visitors and see what has brought them here," he said, beaming. Calling out requests to several lingering monks, Robert strode down the aisle to the great oak doors.

In little time, the trio and several inquisitive monks had passed through the gates and out onto the open land to the beach below. James struggled against the light to make out the vessel and what appeared to be more behind it. What he saw shocked him.

It was unlike any ship James had ever seen—long, thin, and flat, with bright shields adorning its sides, a sickening serpentine figurehead tipping its prow, and long oars swinging at its sides. Its crimson sail flapped vigorously in the wind, mingling with the frenzied shouts of the men aboard, a sound that instilled fear and dread in James' heart. Weapons were waved in the air above the men's heads and war drums were beat. James knew these were no pilgrims.

These were marauders.

"Back to the monastery, all of you," ordered Robert, his voice laden with trepidation. The monk sprinted back to the gates as quickly as he could, James and the others following after him. The first ship was nearly to the shore.

No sooner was James halfway back to the gates did a great clamor and thundering of feet announce the arrival of the invaders. He quickened his pace as the shouts of the raiders resonated across the hill. Gasping for breath, he tumbled into the monastery just as an axe whistled past his head and embedded itself in the ground several yards ahead.

James scrambled to his feet as Robert shouted frantically to shut the gates. Steadying himself, James caught a brief glimpse of the leading attacker: a gigantic, armed figure draped in animal skins. The man locked his fiery eyes with James' for a moment before the massive wooden doors were slammed shut and bolted securely. All around him, the terrified monks began to move about in search of anything that could hold the gates. As James leaned back against the stone wall behind him, Godwin suddenly grasped his shoulder and drew him into eye contact.

"Who are they?" whispered James immediately. "What do they want?"

"I don't know," sighed Godwin. "But they bring violence and fear with them. James, I want you to find your mother and Katherine and lead them to safety. Take them across the causeway to the mainland. There you'll be able to escape into the countryside."

"But what about you?" whispered James with shock. "Do you expect me to flee while you stand and fight alone? Let me stay and help you!"

Godwin sighed and bored his eyes into James'. "These men will kill without hesitation, so it seems. It's not safe for you here," he said. As if in response to his claims, the gates shuddered violently and the sounds of metal striking wood filled the air.

"I fear my time may be brief," continued Godwin gravely. "Please, listen to me and flee. I love my family. It's what's best for you all."

James noticed a tear forming in his father's eye. Reluctantly, he nodded.

The gates shuddered again, straining the wood further. The shouts of the men had grown in intensity, filling the air with a stream of barbaric-sounding words. James turned to Godwin one last time as his father drew a long knife from within his robes, poised to defend. James finally tore himself away and fled to the cells. As he ran, thoughts of his father wracked his mind, and doubts about his mother and sister swarmed about in his thoughts.

As James turned around the next corner, a reverberating crash of wood shook the ground and the first screams of the attack echoed through the monastery, heralding the beginning of the end.

How could this be happening?

"*Mother!*" shouted James as he burst into his family's cell. His mother and sister lay huddled in the corner of the room. Tears streamed down his mother's face as she rocked Katherine, attempting to soothe the infant.

"We've got to get out!" shouted James. "We're under attack. Marauders have broken through!"

"The omens were true," whispered his mother hoarsely as she cradled the young child. "We should have heeded them. Now it has come to this. . . "

"Mother, come now!" James exclaimed desperately. "We have to get to the gates and off the island! It's what Father wanted." His words seemed to motivate her, for his mother quickly rose and made her way toward him.

"Lead the way, my son," she breathed. "You're our only hope now."

Creeping out from the entrance and into the courtyards, a horrific sight met James' eyes. Monks ran in all directions, searching fruitlessly for any safety or defense. The barbarians followed on their heels, swinging swords and axes with devastation. His stomach churned as he saw bodies on the ground—nothing more than crumpled, lifeless forms in the dirt.

"Father told us to escape by the causeway," he breathed, his heart threatening to burst from his chest. "If we can make it to the main gate, we can run south and flee to the mainland."

His mother only nodded.

As the marauders disappeared behind the next corner, James indicated it was time to move. He led his mother and sister across the courtyards and into the cloisters, carefully avoiding the mutilated corpses that lay strewn across the grass. Cringing at the sight, he turned away and began to run in the direction of the gates.

As James and his family rounded the next corner, the true peril of their goal became clear. All around him swarmed a mass of helpless monks, ducking for cover as the barbarians sacked the monastery. The attackers had torn torches from the walls and were now seting ablaze anything in their path. James watched, transfixed with horror; only when the bread house next to him went up in flames did he return to action. Ducking for cover, he fumbled for the only weapon he had, a small food knife in his tunic. He glanced at his mother, who clutched Katherine tighter than ever.

"The only thing to do is to try and break through them," shouted James. "If we can weave our way through, we can get to the gate. It's the only way."

"We'll surely die," wailed his mother helplessly. "But if we must. . . I will follow you."

James nodded. Then, bracing for the worst, he charged into the masses, ducking under the stampeding marauders and slashing furiously with the knife. He looked back once to see if his mother was still there.

She ran in James' footsteps, Katherine nestled in her arms.

Just as he glanced back, he struck something hard and thick. Stumbling to the ground, he caught a glimpse of a large hulking figure just before it hurled him against a wall. Pain shot through his head and he crumpled onto the ground.

As James' senses returned, he whirled his head around, searching desperately for his mother and sister. Nothing but fleeing monks and hulking marauders met his gaze. Tears welled up in his eyes as he scanned the masses.

No. . . he thought to himself. His stomach clenched, his heart pounded with a force he had never known. They couldn't be gone. As the marauders slowly moved off to other areas, they left behind piles of dirtied corpses strewn across the ground.

Did he have the courage to look for them?

James' heart sank as thousands of brightly colored glass fragments suddenly rained down around him, littering the ground with reflective points of light. Rising from his position, he gazed into the chapel through a massive gaping hole, where the brilliant stained-glass window had once been.

Inside, an awful scene had unfolded—pews lay overturned and sacred writings scattered across the floor; treasures of the monastery were thrown into sacks like firewood and carried away greedily. Stepping over bodies, the barbarians made their way to the altar, from which a cluster of men fought valiantly against them.

James' father was among them.

"Father!" cried out James as Godwin furiously beat aside an attacker. His father's head turned instinctively, and his eyes grew large as he caught sight of his son. For an instant, James could see a wave of sadness emanate from his father's face at the sight of only James.

"James, go!" bellowed his father in fear.

He whirled back immediately as more marauders thrust themselves upon him. Robert stood with his back to Godwin, warding off attackers with a shield and small axe as the savage men continued to drive forward with their weapons. From across the chapel, the barbarians' leader had appeared in the door frame, eyes set on the altar. A tremor of fear shot through James as he recalled the fiery blaze that had consumed the man's eyes in their earlier encounter.

"James! Go and I will follow!" howled Godwin over the clamor. James felt himself cry out to his father, but his screams were lost in the chaos. As the berserker charged, Godwin turned to his son a final time, urging him on in desperation. Necessity radiated from his every feature, and—as James looked upon him—the son made his choice.

Nodding, he fled from the building.

Through the frenzied marauders and monks, James stumbled toward the splintered gates. As he dashed out from the monastery onto the open land, he caught sight of small rowboats by the shore several hundred feet away, packed with frightened monks and refugees. James broke out into a furious sprint as he saw his salvation.

The causeway had been flooded over, leaving nothing but stirring waters between the island and the mainland. Those assembled by the shore were desperately setting off from the beach in the tiny boats, grabbing oars and rowing with an almost maniacal frenzy. James skidded to a stop at the beach, immediately turning back in the direction of the smoking monastery.

His father wasn't coming.

Fear gnawed at James' heart as he waited. Each second seemed an eternity as he remained on the shore, ignoring the escapees around him and the shouts from behind the monastery walls.

"Come with me," a monk behind him urged breathlessly.

James did not respond. Images of his father surrounded by barbarians on the bloodstained altar stabbed at his mind, and anxiety threatened to consume him—he had to be coming soon.

Just then, screams erupted on the beach and the monk behind James pulled his arm. A hulking figure was thundering down the hillside to the ocean, sword raised high. James stumbled and struck the beach as the rowboat left shore, slipping from the man's grasp. The monk groaned with horror as he drifted away from him.

James' nerves seemed to slow as the powerful warrior rose above him, face contorted in a snarl, sword raised high. James did not scream as the sword fell—he could not even force a whimper as his end drew near. But as the wild man brought his blade down, his body suddenly lurched and he crumpled into the surf.

There behind him stood Godwin, haggard and pale, but victorious.

"What happened to Robert?" asked James as he recovered from the shock. His father only shook his head gravely. Godwin grabbed James off the ground and tossed him into the nearest rowboat, stopping only for a moment as he looked back toward the monastery. Then he sighed and leapt into the boat, pushing it free from Lindisfarne Island.

As James steadied himself and looked to Godwin, he recoiled at the sight of the bitter sorrow in his father's eyes. He had the appearance of a man whose heart had been crushed, a frail, hopeless shell. Finally, after several interminable moments of silence, Godwin hoarsely asked, "What became of them?"

James' stomach clenched as he recalled his mother and sister. He sank low in the boat as his lips moved to form the words.

"Th-They were lost in the attack. Swallowed by the confusion," whispered James, holding back tears. "I'm so sorry. I failed you." He anticipated a response, but met only silence. For several seconds, only the lap of the waves and the fading din of the attack could be heard. Slowly, he raised his head to his father.

The man James had witnessed not but a second ago was gone—the deprived, gaunt face had been replaced with wide eyes and a disbelieving smile; the color on his father's face was returning. Godwin gazed beyond James to a cluster of other boats ahead of them. James turned hastily to them as well, unsure of what to expect. What he saw stifled his breath in an instant.

Amongst the black robes of the monks, it was the tan tunic of his mother's that caught his eye immediately. Although dirtied and pale, her face shone with joy as she smiled at James and his father. Katherine lay in her arms, fast asleep. The sheer impossibility of the sight rocked James and, a confused but joyful grin broke out on his face. How is it possible?

In that moment, all life was restored to James. He looked to his father, beaming in elation.

"I never did actually see them die," he bubbled with excitement.

"God has spared our family," spoke Godwin solemnly into the midday air. "A great grievance has been done today; an attack on England's holiest island is a sin near unthinkable, yet we have survived it."

"We were blessed, I'm sure," breathed James. "So much has happened. . . I can hardly believe this day is true. I suppose my wish was granted, but not in the way I would have chosen. It's all. . . confusing."

Godwin smiled. "Who are we to try and comprehend the ways of the Lord? I have learned many things on our stay at the island, among them that God is good. He will always provide for us as he has today."

James took up his oar. As he silently thanked God, he began to row fiercely and with newfound confidence. For with each stroke, he grew closer to the bright horizon and reunion with his family.

And with them he knew he would find hope, peace, and a future worth living for.

ALL THE MEMORIES
ALICE MARKHAM-CANTOR, 13

WRITOPIA LAB
NEW YORK, NY
TEACHER: RACHAEL EPHRAIM

I woke up that morning trying to figure out what day it was and what I was supposed to do today. To ground myself before I began, I thought of three simple things:

1. Grass is green.
2. Sky is blue.
3. Today is. . . ? That was too confusing, so I changed my topic of thought to food—my favorite subject other than sleep. It's easy to talk about—no one quizzes me on what I had for lunch eight years ago. But I couldn't remember what there was in the refrigerator, so I hoisted myself up out of bed. As I was about to open the door, I caught sight of myself in the mirror. Who was that old woman staring back at me, with the wrinkled cheeks, the laugh lines, and the sad eyes? Could it be me? I shrugged. Must be a dysfunctional mirror.

I shuffled out to the kitchen. I live with my daughter and her husband and their three kids, and I have a room on the first floor—I can't go up and down stairs. I'm 94 years old. . . wait a minute, no, I'm not 94, I'm. . . how old am I anyway? Oh, never mind. I hobbled to the fridge, opened it, and looked around for something to eat. I found a bowl of cold chicken soup, took a spoon from the drawer, and went back to sit on my bed. I turned the TV on and picked up a book; reading, eating, and listening all at the same time. I'm still a good multitasker.

I was finishing up my soup when I heard the commercial, and I looked up quickly at the screen, cricking my neck in the process. I gazed intently at the television, thinking that this could be the answer to all my problems.

"Attention senior citizens!" came the annoyingly cultured voice of the announcer. "Do you often forget things? Do you feel no one takes you seriously because of it? We have the answer to your problems in our new program—One Step to Remembering! Every day, focus on clearly remembering one complete memory, and write it down. If you have any questions, just call 1-800-REMEMBER. One Step to Remembering! Risk of damaging your memory if you're not 70 or older."

A process to help me remember! If it worked, that would be wonderful. Everyone always treats me like I'm senile—well, I guess I do seem senile on the outside, but it's just because I can't remember anything. On the inside, my mind is sometimes clear, I just can't get the words out, I can't find what I want to say even if my thought is not shattered into fragments. But once I've dredged up the word, I've forgotten what I was going to say. It's as if I'm lost in a huge swamp of memories. I'm so small in this vast, unconquered life that's supposedly mine. Nobody ever takes me seriously anymore. It's hard to believe that I used to have a job, that people once looked up to me and admired me.

I decided to try this new process. Starting now. A car whizzing by almost shook me out of my concentration, but then I sank back into my mind, deeper and deeper.

"Where are the car keys?" Jenny says frantically. I don't know what she said.

"Keys? What keys? Did you say keys?" I ask. I can't be sure, because my hearing isn't the best these days.

"Yes, Mother, I said keys," Jenny says exasperated, searching for them.

"Bees? Where? I'm allergic to bees!" I begin to panic.

Now, how did that memory help me? Let's see, it told me that I'm a partly deaf, senile old woman. Wonderful. I already knew that.

I wrote down my memory in my notebook, sure that this was the answer to my prayers. Then my middle grandchild burst in.

"Granny Milla, it's my birthday tomorrow!" Ashley cried. "I'll be eight years old!"

It was? Oh, right. "I know, sweetie." I hugged her.

"What are you going to give me, Granny Milla? You always give me the best presents."

I made a mental note to get Ashley the book she wanted, that her parents wouldn't get her yet because it was still in hardback.

"Remember last year, when you took me to see *The Lion King* on Broadway?" Ashley was practically bouncing up and down then.

"I do."

With one last ear-to-ear grin, Ashley skipped out of my room. I smiled after her. I would get the book tomorrow, and to ensure that I wouldn't forget, I wrote Get Ashley's Book in big letters across my notebook.

At dinner that night, I told my family what I was doing.

"I think it'll work," Ashley said firmly.

"I don't know," Annie, my oldest grandchild, said skeptically. My son-in-law, Sam, grunted. "It won't work," he said bluntly.

I tried to insist, to tell them that it would work, but when I opened my mouth Sam interrupted me.

"It won't work."

Well, I would prove him wrong!

The next morning, I set out to remember more. I searched through my mind, trying to find a memory among the faces and fragments. There—was that my memory? It didn't seem like it. No, that had to be from a television show, what was it called? *I Love Lucy.* What about that memory? No, that had to be from a movie or a book—or had I really been in love? I couldn't remember. I peered in all the dark corners of my mind to find a memory of mine, but to no avail. Oh! There it was! But I couldn't get to it, it was too high. Then a light breeze seemed to flutter through my mind and my room, lifting me up into the memory.

I ran along the sand, once again a girl of 9, the salty air whipping my hair. The sea crashed down, splattering me with spray in all its splendor and glory. The waves rose high, then thundered down, missing me by inches as I raced for the sheer joy of it, feet splashing through the freezing, shallow water.

I came out of my memory as if from a trance, or a deep dreamless sleep. I liked that memory.

It was Ashley's birthday and if I wanted to get her that new book she wanted, I had to go now. I took the car keys off their hook by the front door and left a note saying where I'd gone. I heaved myself into the driver's seat and started the engine. I pressed down the gas pedal and off I went. I smiled as I drove, thoroughly pleased that I'd taken matters into my own hands But as I turned a corner, I pressed the brakes. I had completely forgotten what I was doing, where I was going. Why was I out here in a car?

Oh, well, it was quite a nice day. I had probably just decided to go for a ride.

I drove around for a while, enjoying the sunshine and the people out walking on the busy sidewalks. Then I started home, confused, but not unhappy. I pulled into the driveway, parked the car, and stopped short. Ashley was sitting at the table with her sister and younger brother, and her parents were bringing in a cake.

I groaned.

Ashley's birthday present! I went and sat with her, then excused myself before they opened presents. I wanted to remember another memory to get my mind off of it. I looked for a happy one, but nothing came to mind. But then, I was sucked in—to a memory just as discouraging as real life.

"You blew it, Milla. How could you have done that?" My husband shakes his head.

I feel tears begin to gather. "I just want my daughter to be happy."

"Sam does make her happy. And you just yelled at him. Loudly. And in front of her!"

He walks out sadly. What have I done?

I looked at all the memories I'd written down, and was confused. Was this my notebook? This didn't seem like my life. Well, it did, but only small reminders of them remained in me, small, brightly colored birds that flitted in and out of my baffled mind. Was this really me? If not, who was I?

I went back out and sat by my granddaughter as she opened her presents. After she was done and the others were preoccupied with clearing the table, I apologized to Ashley about not having a birthday present. She said that it was fine, but I still sat down, sad. Sad that all my hoping and waiting had been in vain, sad that I couldn't remember anything, sad that I had forgotten Ashley's present, but sad most of all that life would go on as usual, with me in my role as old, crazy granny, and no one would take me seriously.

Ashley saw the tears gathering in the corners of my eyes and was taken aback. "Really, I don't care about the present!" she said quickly, alarmed.

"It's not really the present—it's more that if I keep on not being able to remember anything, no one is ever going to take me seriously again."

"I take you seriously, Granny," Ashley said softly.

"You do?" I asked.

She smiled at me. "Yes. Even when I was really, really little."

I was reminded of the memory I had written down last night.

The dust settled slowly on the cracked, smooth paint of the windowsill, then rose as my small granddaughter blew it once again. She took a deep breath in, her small face puckered with concentration, then blew it out with a big whoosh, and the dust went flying. Her short, reddish-brown hair bouncing, she turned to me with a huge smile on her dirty face.

"Look, Granny Milla," she said happily. "I can make the dust dance!"

I smile back at her. "Of course you can, Ashley." I took her hand and together we left the house to go get ice cream.

"Will you always take me seriously?" I asked.

"I will," she vowed.

I took my granddaughter's hand, and we left the house together.

"You still like chocolate ice cream, right Granny?"

THE SONG OF AN UNOPENED BLOOM
AUBREY ISAACSON, 18

CHARLESTON COUNTY SCHOOL OF THE ARTS
NORTH CHARLESTON, SC
TEACHER: RENE BUFO MILES

Rodney was known for playing his banjo. He'd sit on the front steps and pick nonstop, and you'd see he was just like the instrument: one peg shorter than the rest and couldn't keep his strings tuned. You could watch him all evening and forget he was even playing—fingers wild and eyes steady. Daddy was born and raised on bluegrass, and even he was proud of Rodney. He'd say to the neighbors, "The boy ain't good at much, but he can play the banjo, that's for sure."

No one liked to think Rodney was a problem kid or anything, he was just always alone. I never spent time with him, seeing how I was four years older and always had a boyfriend around, but I could still see what was going on. You couldn't ignore someone with eyes like his, wide and open but not really looking. He didn't have friends, didn't have grades. Some days he came home with his shirt ripped or a black eye. The bigger guys at school would tease him for sitting alone on the bus, or never going to football games. I never took to him well, mostly because I hated that he never did anything with himself. He wanted to disappear as much as he could with each day he wasted. The only time Daddy would ever talk about it was when he looked out the kitchen window at Rodney sitting in a rocker while he picked on the banjo.

"If he don't do anything else in his life, at least he played music."

*   *   *

No one in Waynesville had a whole lot then, just acres for farming. Seasons changed with the harvest. Wintertime was brought in by Christmas trees, spring had strawberries (they were always my favorite). Tomatoes gave us summer, and fall, pumpkins. Years were marked by how good the crop was—Uncle Dean got married the year the Tentons sold the most Fraser firs, my best friend Kate moved to Boone when Dad wouldn't let us carve jack-o-lanterns 'cause he had only enough to sell.

Pastor Dave was one of the three pastors in town. He built his own church that sat a mile or so behind 70 acres of Christmas trees. Farmers showed up to church if they could afford to, both time and land being sacrificed. On Sundays, when the plate came 'round for offering, some people would throw in a few dollars, maybe a check—never much. But at the end of each season, if a farmer had had a good crop, you'd see him scribbling on the back of an envelope, "3 acres, 1036 Cherryhope Road, Wes Burgess." They'd only offer their land if they had just finished a selling harvest. They wouldn't even think of giving the pastor dead soil. You'd see that on the General Store's sale bulletin board the next day for a large sum of money. I asked Daddy one time why he never gave Pastor any land. He said, "We ain't had a season worth giving to the Lord yet."

*   *   *

There was a competition in the town to find the first pumpkin of the fall season. It wasn't official or anything, just a game that started at the Farmer's Market one September. Our dads would bet—put money, land, even hunting dogs on it. It was our job as sons and daughters to actually find the pumpkin. You'd drive by farms and see small heads weaving in and out of vines, looking for the tiny thing. When we were younger, me and Rodney always thought it'd be full-size the first day we found it, like we'd wake up and see it round and orange when we looked down the hill. The first and only time I found the pumpkin, it was dark green and no bigger than both of my fists put together. Daddy would never bet any money. He just patted me on the head and mentioned it in passing to Mister Anderson at the deli, who had lost five German Shorthair puppies the year before.

He loved it when we searched for them, seeing his kids and income

come together, everything he lived for growing before his eyes. He told us to count all the pumpkin flowers we could find, saying a good farmer always knew how many blooms there were; it was most important to him. Of course it wasn't—how something begins to bloom can never tell how it will finish growing. But we believed him just the same and would count yellow petals on our fingers, tallying every ten in the dirt.

This was before anyone noticed something wasn't normal about Rodney. It was the fall we counted more than 200 blooms, line after line drawn on the ground beneath our feet. Rodney was 6, and I was 10. The sun had almost set behind our house on top of the hill, the eyelid that slowly closed over daylight earlier every day. Momma had called twice for us to come in, but I was still crouched in the vines counting flowers.

Rodney had gone and sat on the porch steps. He just sat there staring at his leg in front of him. It was mid-October, the time when ticks leave their homes in the woods and skin to hide in dirt 'til spring. When I came to Rodney, he was watching one burrow into his calf muscle, growing bigger from his blood. I moved to get matches from Daddy's tool box to burn it out, yelling that Momma would whip him for sure if she knew he hadn't picked it off the minute he saw it. I started to light a match when Rodney told me to stop, saying it needed to eat, it had a long winter ahead of it.

"It ain't a grizzly bear," I told him, pushing his arms away to get to the vermin. He yelled at me to stop, and sat as calm as could be, watching it wiggle its body into him. I told him I wouldn't be sorry when he got a wooden leg after his real one got cut off, then I went inside. I didn't tell anyone.

He told Daddy the chain link had cut him when a scar started to shine where the tick had been. Daddy searched the front fence looking for a wire end to fix. I didn't have the heart to tell him he wouldn't find anything. I don't think he could have stood the idea of anything hurting his son that he couldn't see, even more that Rodney could have stopped it. Something so easy to pluck away, but he let it eat at him, slowly making him disappear.

Daddy had always been a farmer. It's all he grew up knowing, so it's all he grew up to be. It wasn't a bad thing, but it's hard to base life off of something you don't know how to predict. He believed the usual farmer's myths: a bad season of strawberries means a good one for pumpkins, rain the day before you sow means thicker Fraser trunks, and other sayings that had no real reason attached to them. But I think they were more like prayers, a way to convince yourself that everything will turn out better than you think. Farmer gossip was the most heartbreaking thing sometimes. They were always so hopeful. They'd grab at any kind of straw when their income came from the sun and rain. My friend Mac Thomas's daddy would water his strawberries with moonshine on Easter Sunday. He said it added to the color and flavor. I think he was just a drunk.

But every time I overheard a story about a new way to grow pumpkins or trees, I thought of Rodney, and how we always wanted to believe that he would be okay. But no farmer's false hope at the beginning of a season could match what we had for Rodney.

The hardest thing was seeing Daddy's face that October. He held up a long vine with holes big enough in the leaves to see his disappointed face on the other side. "Some kinda bug," was all he said, kicking off his boots at the back door. He didn't eat dinner that night, so me and Rodney ate in silence with Momma, except for the occasional question about school she had for him. Momma was never a talker. A lot of me thought she didn't really want to be living with us.

I had a story set up in my mind that I expected to happen: We'd wake up to a note on the kitchen table where she always sat for meals, written the morning after Rodney graduated from high school, and that would be all we had left of her. I knew why she was still there, though. Rodney was holding her back. I could tell she favored him over me, for sure. She just wanted to see a diploma and know he would get on okay without her. Rodney had just started high school, and I was working at the General Store selling makeup. I wanted to tell her about the lipstick sales that day, the new shade of powder we had gotten in last week, anything that would relate us in the world of womanhood, but she continued with questions for Rodney. It was useless, really, with answers all generally the same. "I don't pay attention to girls, much, Ma," "I don't listen too much in class, either." She'd look down at her sweet potato with the same disappointment Daddy had in the pumpkin leaves, with even less to hide behind. Momma had plans for Rodney the way I did for her, 'cept hers had an ending with a good future and pretty wife for Rodney. At least my prediction was somewhat realistic.

Eventually Momma got up to fix Daddy a plate, humming an old bluegrass tune. She had a way of doing that—putting herself in the background like a low-volume radio that became unnoticed static. Rodney got up to play his banjo outside, and soon enough, the song that Momma had been humming floated through the screened door, mirrored perfectly and crying.

The next day, he woke up early, just like he did every day. There wasn't ever a real reason for him to wake up before the cock crowed, but he did just the same. He had a purpose that morning, though. He was out in the fields, even before Daddy. He was crouched over, hands disappearing into vines and leaves every few steps. He finally came in for water, and Daddy asked him what in God's name he thought he was doing. I knew he had started looking for the first pumpkin, something I thought we'd outgrown after elementary school. In high school, boys placed bets the way their dad's did, growing up before their bodies had time to catch up. Rodney must have put money on it; he was always one to stash allowance. He went back outside without a word, Daddy not far behind him with the tractor keys. He had planned to till everything up and start a late crop in place of the failing one. "They'll be ready to pick just before Thanksgiving," he said. "The other ones just bloomed too soon. The soil wasn't expecting 'em yet." Daddy said he'd wait 'til tomorrow to finish with the tractor, just to make Rodney happy.

That night, I heard footsteps come across my room. They were slow and heavy, waking me as soon as they were beside my bed. He smelled like fermenting fruit. "I found it," Rodney said, leaning down by my pillow. I told him to go to bed, that it was just a damn pumpkin. "I got it, though. I found it." He kept saying that, and wouldn't leave 'til I got up and led him out of the room. "Just wait 'til I go to school tomorrow," he said before I closed the door.

*   *   *

The next day, Rodney came home while I was getting ready for a date. A guy that worked in the hardware department at the General Store was taking me out, and he was gonna be there any second. Rodney walked into the kitchen. I hadn't even heard the screened door when he came in. His clothes had orange clumps sticking to them and tiny pieces of white. He smelled twice as bad as he had the night before. He got closer to me, and as he turned to go upstairs I realized it was the inside of a pumpkin. I almost started giggling. I had no idea how he could have gotten the guts of a pumpkin all over himself. I opened my mouth to say something rude most likely, but instead told him that I was leaving as I heard a horn outside. I remembered later why he had come into my room last night. My date asked me what was wrong, said my face turned blank when I realized that the first pumpkin in Waynesville had been covering my brother.

*   *   *

The next day at the makeup counter, a few high school girls with too much eyeliner and blush leaned against the glass cases. I overheard their conversation.

"Could you believe it? The retard at school found the pumpkin, and he actually thought they'd give him the money!"

"Yeah, Tanner and Miller said they smashed it and really let him have it. They said it was rotten. Must have come from a dump of a farm."

"I heard he bet his life that he'd find it."

They thought that was funny.

Momma found Rodney in the tool shed. "Only one bullet went through him," the police said, "nothing else to call that but suicide."

Daddy threw the handgun Rodney'd used into our lake out back, metal sinking into mud. Me and Momma cried, but for different reasons—there's different tears for a son and for a brother. She left two weeks later, and I could almost feel my heart sinking the way the gun did through pond scum—slow without knowing any other fate. I couldn't tell you if Daddy took her leaving well—the only feeling he ever wore on his sleeve was pride. Everything else was buried below the dirt he lived off of, the same way as his son.

"Only 15 years old?" the sheriff asked as he got into his car. He really said it to me like he couldn't believe it. "Didn't even get through the first year of high school."

I told Daddy about the boys at school, the story I had heard at work that day. I almost saw him flinch at the thought. I tried to picture what was going through his head—two things that seemed to be growing fine on the outside but were dying on the inside; the two things he wanted to love, his harvest and his son. In the end, they came together, head on, and revealed what had been rotting inside of the other. At dinner I'd mention something about him, say I missed the banjo music from the front porch. Daddy'd grunt in a way that meant "I know," and that he was thinking of his childhood, "the real bluegrass days" he called it—the time that he looked back on and the time Rodney blew away. He kept farming and didn't bother to clean the blood off of his wrenches and screwdrivers.

I went out later one evening to wash them, finding the silver beneath his blood. I cursed his ghost in that tool shed, saying, "I hope you're happy with this bet you lost to yourself."

*   *   *

At the end of December, I found myself looking over Daddy's shoulder at church one day as he scrawled his offering of all but one acre we owned on the back of a grocery receipt. He had told me the night before that he used to have dreams at night about farming. He had seen himself riding a tractor, hearing it pop from just being oiled, the green tips of leaves poking through the soil, the big orange harvest we sold on the roadside, and his two tow-headed children parting vines to find tiny yellow flowers for him. He said that none of those pictures came to him anymore. He said, "The day it don't come to me in my sleep is the day it ain't a part of me."

But I knew what I was watching as he placed the crumpled paper in the plate that was being passed from pew to pew. Daddy was letting go of all he had wanted since he bought our farm 20 years ago: a wife who kept her vows, a son who would take up the farm after him, fields of pumpkins that would only spread with time. Nothing came at night anymore. There wasn't Momma to slide under their sheets after dinner, wasn't Rodney to come in my room with good news like the night he'd found the pumpkin. He was leaving his ex-wife, dead son, and ruined soil at the Lord's house—a place he wouldn't return to for the rest of his life. I never asked him if our land was good enough to give to God, because I knew it was. His son was good enough, and the land where he lay was too.

RESURRECTION
YVONNE YU, 18

HONG KONG INTERNATIONAL SCHOOL
HONG KONG, CHINA
TEACHER: JASON HINOJOSA

When Thomas left I began to forget him, so I started to make a game of it. I competed with myself: every day, just one more memory. Something new. One more little quirk of his personality. Even now I still keep a list of the way I remember him, and the way I hope he remains. In my head, he still has extremely precise diction and carries a pair of reading glasses—more out of paranoia than out of any real need. His words are few, but carefully chosen. He laughs without inhibitions. He underlines his favorite passages in books with a slim line and returns to reread them later. He dislikes fish and loves the sun. He isn't superstitious. He loves buildings with tall ceilings and books with proper bindings, and stained glass and old tools and lavender. He doesn't own a single pair of sandals. And in his hand he holds his Bible. I try not to remember this part—but he always had his Bible.

The Thomas I try to remember is my brother—my brother with a smile that opens a sliver wider on the left than the right and shines crookedly in his angled face. But it's been so long that sometimes I only remember his face in movement—when he lays his head in the hinge of his elbow to read the paper, when his mouth spills open at the sides and he jerks his chin upward in laughter.

You start to lose your colors first.

I can't remember him in red anymore, only in blues and greens (the colors of his favorite shirts), a muted turquoise blur through a plate-glass screen. I don't remember if the Thomas in my head is the same one that used to tap battle hymns out on my door, or if he is just a composite of what I want now and what I knew then—it's amazing how fast you can forget someone who once meant the world to you. Now all I have are small details and minute gestures, studies in motion and shadowed glances.

This Thomas in my head is a mish-mash of trivia and random facts that settles down in the margins of my mind and smiles contently. Real Thomas is probably trying to find work at a soup kitchen and crushing receipts into his pocket some 50,000 miles from here. Maybe I've lost him forever, I don't know. The idiot has gone to find himself, when I am the one who needs to find him the most.

Before Thomas left, he wrote something on my forehead while I was sleeping, in a metallic eyeliner I'd left on the bathroom counter. It was almost ridiculous. When I came up from brushing my teeth in the morning, it was there in the mirror, all silvered and beaming. The words went the wrong way round, printed in his neat block script, but I could still make them out. Hebrews 13:5. I had to pull out my old St. James from beneath the sofa cushions and flip through the cracked pages, from Eden to Solomon and past and back again until I found it. *I will never fail or forsake you.*

I threw the Bible against the wall. I guess it was his idea of a joke.

If he left a note or a sign (other than that last mockery of a stamp on my head), I never saw it. All I knew was the cold rush as I washed the letters from my forehead and the cold silence as I ate breakfast alone, before my parents returned home. My brother had left me for God, and I was eating dry cornflakes and reading cartoons in the paper. Even without a note, I knew why he was gone. There was never any doubt.

Thomas was never really one for games. I was the boy of the family from the very start, little 6-year-old Celia hollering and running through the backyard in pursuit of a football while her teenage brother sat on the patio and watched. He wasn't a complete shut-in—he had a runner's physique to match his swimmer's appetite—but the sports he preferred were individual, almost contemplative, and quiet. Fifty lengths of the pool, five rounds of the neighborhood, the only sounds the beats of his heart and the steady rhythm of his legs. It all worked out well for my parents in the end; two healthy children, a boy to play soccer in me and a budding cleric in Thomas.

I don't remember just when or how Thomas fell in love with the Bible. I say "fell in love" because when they were together he seemed older than his few years, reunited with the second half of a separated whole. I can think of no better way to describe what I have never truly understood. Our parents took us to church, but they were by no means radically religious. There is really no logical reason why a young boy would develop such a strong attraction to the word of God, and I've never believed in miracles.

Thomas would memorize his favorite Bible verses as soon as he found them. He was a quick study from birth, a real smart kid, but he didn't like to show it. He always had a phrase or two on hand to cover every situation, every image. He could throw them out without seeming condescending or presumptuous, because they just flowed out of his mouth in natural arcs. My mother's church group loved him. They called him "the little reverend" and asked him to recite Bible passages each week, which he was happy enough to do.

The words were just so close to him that it was easier to reach for them than for any sayings of his own; to Thomas, the Lord's words encompassed so much more than his own humble tongue ever could. I remember one summer we spent in Canada—we were lying on the grass, with the waving stalks and the humid wind in our faces, and he threw a handful of dew at me. I squealed, soaking out my own fistfuls and throwing them back at him. "He who refreshes others will be refreshed!" he crowed, and the look on his face was bright and open.

When I came to him once with tears and bitterness, he told me "With God, all things are possible." I didn't think this could be a direct quote—something this simple—but it was. Matthew 19:62. Jesus' disciples asked him who was to be saved, and he replied. Thomas didn't know that I looked up the passage afterward, that I read Matthew 19:27 and onward, where Peter says, *"I have given up everything to follow you, Jesus, what shall I have?"*

Peter got his place in the kingdom of heaven. But I didn't want a place in God's vineyard, I wanted to turn the page and see Thomas' name splayed across the verses. I wanted the words he quoted so freely to be part of his own gospel, and not someone else's. What kind of teenager loves the Bible this much? What a freak.

Looking back, I've made it seem like Thomas was a walking Bible machine, practically a living Disciple, spewing out quotes every second of the day. To be fair, it wasn't nearly that bad. In most areas, he was a perfectly average older brother—teasing, dominating, and annoying. But it is so much easier to remember the extremes of the missing. For Thomas, it was his overwhelming capacity for good—his patience, his perseverance—and it was also his pastor's tongue, spread in the praise, the glory, the clotted cream adoration. This "God thing" was only a phase to me. But to Thomas it was his world, and I hated that.

I told him that once. We'd fought over something or other, and I couldn't stand the look on his face when it eventually softened and opened up to reach for me. "You're the reason I hate Jesus!" I yelled, slitting my eyes and choking back the dark parts of my throat. "You're the reason God hates me!" and I slammed my door in his perfect pious face. He called my name, but I let his calls melt into the oaken outside and swiped the furious tears of my eyes.

That night, a little part of me wondered if I would meet Christ, but he didn't come. Instead, I held my breath until I moved very slightly and quietly in my dreams.

The next morning, Thomas slipped an envelope under the door. In it was a piece of paper. He'd written: *1 Corinthians 15:51: Behold, I tell you a mystery, We Shall not Sleep, but we shall all be changed.* Underneath it he wrote, very small, *This is all I know how to say. I'm sorry, really. Please believe me, God has you in his heart, and nothing you or I do will ever change that.*

I resealed the envelope carefully. Jesus, it's not fair how much love you can have for someone, even when you hate them more than they'll ever know.

A couple of months after he left, I met an old friend out in the city. He'd graduated the previous year and gone off to some high-powered university. He was a few years older than me, and we'd only been casual acquaintances, but we were both so eager for a trace of our old world that we instantly set a dinner date for the next night at seven. His name was Richard, and he'd played guitar in a band his senior year.

I don't think he remembered that I was Thomas' sister, but something in my words or my face must have reminded him. "I heard that Thomas kid ran away," he said to me. "You know, the really Christian one. Went off to be a missionary or something. Can you believe that? He used to be in my class. We took calculus together." He shook his head. "Can't say I'm surprised, but I hope he's doing alright. Wonder how his parents feel."

I wonder how his sister feels. I didn't say anything, just smiled and went on eating my rigatoni carbonara in small bites. It surprised me how easily I could take it.

Nowadays, it gets dark earlier and earlier. The nights are colder, and I sleep in thick cardigans and long socks. In the morning I put on a kettle of tea or heat up some milk and then think of one more Thomas fact for my list. I can usually do it by the time I'm done with the tea, though sometimes it takes two cups.

A "HOW-TO" GUIDE FOR TODAY'S TEENAGE GIRL

LAURA WEISS, 18

REDWOOD HIGH SCHOOL
LARKSPUR, CA
TEACHER: TOM SIVERTSEN

THIS IS A WORK OF SATIRE AND SHOULD BE READ AS SUCH

Introduction:

The following is an excerpt from *The "How-to" Guide for Today's Teenage Girl*. The premise of the book is to synthesize all of the information teenage girls receive into a well-researched, credible guide. If all of the guidelines in this book are followed, girls achieve womanly nirvana, or peace within themselves because they are the "perfect" woman. These five sections are abridged, so not all guidelines are covered. If you would like to purchase the complete version of the *"How-To" Guide* (Impossible Press, New York, 2007, 937 pages), contact us at our toll-free number.

The Perfect Appearance

As exhibited in multiple Pantene commercials, hair must be long, silken, and flowing. You must also devote a certain number of hours a day frolicking in parks with other silken-haired maidens, to the tune of Natasha Bedingfield's "Unwritten."

(An aside: According to Elizabeth Cady Stanton, all men and women are created equal, so men should also possess equal hair opportunities. Bearing this in mind, Pantene has developed a hair-care line specifically for boys, which includes a camouflage-patterned hairdryer, masculine hairspray, and a muscled, sinewy brush. Girls, now you know what to get your boyfriend for Christmas! For instructions on how to perfectly wrap a gift, a skill all budding beauties should know, see this month's issue of *Allure*, on stands now.)

In terms of clothing, you have many options, depending on the brand of male you would like to attract. If your male counterpart plays football and guffaws constantly, you must wear an Abercrombie miniskirt, tank top, and Juicy Couture sweater. If your male counterpart listens to independent rock and wears skinny jeans, you must also wear skinny jeans, along with flat shoes that offer little to no support for the feet, along with multiple layered tops. Some styles have fewer requirements, but outfits must not be wrinkled or color-coordinate, and these should not include anything from your grandmother's closet. Please note an important caveat to these guidelines: Do not, ever, *ever, ever,* wear the same outfit two days in a row. This will result in social ostracism and other unspeakable horrors.

When possible, you should do everything in your power to most closely resemble the Victoria's Secret model of your choice, the perfect ideal of beauty. To you, Victoria's Secret is not only an undergarment haven where all your supportive underclothes must be purchased to achieve womanly nirvana, but a requirement to your female education. You may want to take notes during your pilgrimages to the store.

If you do not follow these suggestions, you may become like one out-of-vogue 56-year-old mother who says that there needs to be much less emphasis on appearance. However, this archaic viewpoint should not be heeded, because if every woman followed the rules in this book, they would be perfect, and thus, better than men.

Though this plethora of information may seem daunting, you are actually more knowledgeable about the topic than you think. Dressing up and brushing dolls' hair as a child have prepared you for the task of being beautiful.

The Perfect Health

Staying thin is important. Since 1992, the number of weight-loss advertisements in magazines such as *Cosmopolitan* and *Redbook* have doubled (according to the Federal Trade Commission), and as our society progresses, we must take this statistic as a sign that, as more women become conscious of their weight, the world will become a better place, where all women will have the chance to cavort with wonder through grassy meadows to the tune of "Unwritten."

Famous supermodel Adriana Lima is five foot ten and wears a size 4, with an ideal waist-to-hip ratio of 0.7. You, too, should strive for such a formula to achieve previously discussed female nirvana.

In terms of food options, Barbara Dafoe Whitehead, a feminist expert, says that the "best" girls refuse to eat anything but "pesticide-free, fat-free organic food." According to *Good Housekeeping*, a healthy diet includes delicacies such as spinach salad, low-fat yogurt, four-ounce portions of seafood, asparagus, "veggie-dogs," plain sliced turkey, and Healthy Choice low-fat soup. Next time you see a man or homely woman gorging on a hamburger, avert your eyes to avoid catching their disease. The grease on their fingers symbolizes their inferiority to you in all respects.

Whitehead also points out that "Good girls work out." As you listen to Fergie while pumping iron, take advantage of the subliminal messages provided to you by the media and let the manta run through your mind: ".0 7 waist-to-hip ratio, 0.7 waist-to-hip ratio. . ."

Be forewarned, however, that the perfect health goal takes more effort and commitment than the beauty goal. Your required reading includes *Cosmopolitan*, which you must highlight and annotate, and *Healthy Living*. The bikini-clad actress, grinning with ecstasy after achieving womanly nirvana, should motivate you on your treadmill expeditions. All this information may outweigh your mental capacity, so don't beat yourself up if you make a mistake. In fact, reward the extra calories you ate from that piece of white bread (a questionable offense; for a full list of offensive foods, see the index on page 737) by running on the treadmill for another half an hour, an exhilarating routine.

The Perfect Relationship

A good man is hard to find. The following is a sampling of the list of masculine requirements. If you are ever confused, consult your army of other accomplished beautiful women, as seen on *Sex and the City*. Your perfect man must be unique to your own tastes, but have:

- Commanding eyes, preferably blue, but other colors are also passable.
- A height that is three to eight inches taller than you, allowing for heel-wearing, but not so tall as to jeopardize kissing opportunities.
- A stylish wardrobe. Men are automatically disqualified if they own Member's Only jackets, wear tightie-whities, shirts of any derivative of neon, or wear socks with sandals.
- A high-paying job that will support your consuming needs.

If you have any questions about this very complex section, consult Chapter 15, titled "A Good Man Is Hard to Find!" All man-scouting must be complete before the age of 30, and all child-birthing must be accomplished before the age of 35. When your child reaches adolescence, you must also be 35.

However, as a teen, these rules are more lenient. Another set of rules applies to you. Your first step is nabbing that dreamy-eyed boy. According to howtogetaboyfriend.com, there are proven methods to achieve this goal, but such methods require a $50 fee. Here's an insider's scoop on how to do it for free:

- Every great high-school relationship begins with *flirting*. What is flirting, you may ask? In the words of Barbara Dafoe Whitehead, modesty is no longer a necessary ideal. In the blissful days of gender equality, girls are now allowed to be as profane and sexually frank as men (so long as your appearance commandments are followed). The discussion of "sex," in all its variations, is considered "flirting."

• Your ancestors may have explained to you an ancient phrase called "dating," which involved meals, eaten in awkward silence, where the man and woman sat approximately one foot apart. You don't have to add that silly phrase to your notes. "Dating" has long since been replaced with "hooking up." Hooking up is a practice that commonly occurs at parties, in houses, or in automobiles. The term is ambiguous, and thus, in today's modern age, you have the power to define it. According to Tom Wolfe, hooking up can constitute anything from deep kissing to "going all the way." Names are not necessary for this practice. Finally, girls won't have to deal with nosy men who ask ridiculous personal questions over painfully awkward meals.

• The next step is up to you. Your relations with that steamy dude may end after the practice explained above. However, sometimes hookups can result in something called a *relationship*. A relationship is a cooperative contract involving conversations, agreements, and romantic involvement. For more information, turn to Chapter 16.

As a young girl preparing for womanhood, your new cooperative might run into a few snags. When you inevitably cheat on your boyfriend with his dark, sexy best friend, you must apologize profusely but continue your appearance regimen. It is also important to take supposed insults that less-qualified minions may throw at you with a grain of salt (but not too much salt, because salt is not healthy and may contribute to skin problems). One example is the word "slut." Searching through ancient texts, etymologists recently discovered that "slut" is actually an acronym: S is for sexy, L is for lovable, U is for uber-amazing, and T is for tan. Naysayers are merely jealous of your sun-kissed complexion.

Achieving the perfect relationship is a constantly changing process. This will prove to be one of the most difficult tasks in life, but a commonly utilized math procedure can be applied: guess and check.

The Perfect Education

As exhibited by several femme-muses such as Marissa Cooper and Summer Roberts of *The O.C.*, you must never attend classes, but instead engage in intense emotional moments in hallways during unexplainably lengthy passing periods. Following in Summer's footsteps, you must also get into Brown University.

According to Christina Hoff Sommers, girls currently have a better chance at succeeding in school today than in years past. According to the U.S. Department of Education, today's girls outshine boys in terms of grades, educational aspirations, and rigor of academic programs. This is because early on, girls are trained in the art and method of applying makeup, logically planning and composing outfits, and exactly what kind of brush best suits the textural composition of their follicles. These mentally straining challenges have prepared girls for succeeding in school.

It was predicted in 1996 that by 2007, 9.2 million women would be enrolled in college, compared with 6.9 million men. This trend was illustrated on *The O.C.* as well, when Summer's boyfriend Seth didn't get into Brown, though it had been his life's dream. Poor Seth could have benefited from Pantene's male line.

The Perfect Career

After graduating from college, if you live in New York City, you should marry a rich lawyer and move to the Upper East Side and breed upper-society children while volunteering at the National Charity League. If you live in Los Angeles, you should become a fashion designer and—later—a mother. If you're really ambitious, you could even be a magazine editor or a painter. If you live anywhere else, a teaching career shines in your future. You will teach young children for a few years then go on maternity leave and never return.

Some incredibly ingenious women are able to juggle their appearance regimen and a career as a doctor. Like Meredith Grey on *Grey's Anatomy*, your scrubs will fit tightly and you will have multiple affairs with hot doctors. According to one teenage girl, you will use your "womanly wiles" to get what you want. All while your hair shines in the fluorescent operating-room lights.

For more information on careers, go to Chapter 8, a comprehensive list of job options for perfectly coiffed females.

After your career has lasted ten years, tops, you will retire to the home. Check out Chapter 10, "The Housewife," for more support in this endeavor. You may also do additional research by watching an episode of *Desperate Housewives* to see these desperately joyful women dance along suburban streets to "Unwritten."

*   *   *

The information listed above, though valuable, is a highly shortened version of necessary guidelines to achieve womanly nirvana. To buy the full version of *The "How-to" Guide for Today's Teenage Girl,* call our toll-free number. Price upon request. But be careful dialing. Chipping your nails may prove fatal to your new lifestyle.

COLLEGE BOARD RELEASES NEW SAT

WILL MANTELL, 16

HORACE GREELEY HIGH SCHOOL
CHAPPAQUA, NY
TEACHER: ANDREW CORSILIA

THIS IS A WORK OF SATIRE AND SHOULD BE READ AS SUCH

The president of The College Board, Gaston Caperton, announced yesterday that the organization had released a "new and improved" version of its Standard Aptitude Test, to be used beginning in January 2009. Among the changes will be:

The addition of 17 new sections and the replacement of 5-minute "snack breaks" by 30-minute lunch and dinner breaks during the test: Said Caperton, "A four-hour-plus test was just not long enough. Studies have shown that being able to take a 22-section, 17-hour test based on general knowledge and aptitude proves useful for students in a college environment." Other provisions of this new SAT "rule" include the allowance of a number of previously forbidden items inside the test room. These include a pillow, a microwave oven, a flashlight, and a small tent, for comfort during breaks and for when students, as Caperton himself said, "just want to hit the sack." In accordance with these changes, the College Board has changed the SAT's official slogan from "The Longest Test Ever" to "No, Really. . . The Longest Test Ever."

The allowed use of a Number 3 pencil:
Caperton is freely willing to admit that this was the only easy decision The College Board had in revising the SAT. "For too long," said Caperton, "Number 2, Medium Soft, has had a monopoly on the testing game and over all other pencils. It's time for a change. Some people just prefer the way Number 3, Hard, contours to their hand,

the way it fills those beautiful dark circles on the 68-page Scantron."
And with the SAT's new focus on comfort, this decision really does
seem like a no-brainer.

*Perhaps the most controversial change will be the initiation of a program
that guarantees that each ethnic group living in the United States will
have at least one reading passage that specifically caters to them and their
values:*
Caperton didn't wish to elaborate on this change, only offering that,
"Even with all our changes in past years, this test is still way culturally
biased. Those of the Baha'i faith have just not been performing on par
with members of other ethnic communities." Caperton then mumbled
something about legal action and asked to move on to the next question.

*The addition of a one-hour section on the history, language, and obscure
lexicon of the Central Asian republic of Turkmenistan:*
Said Caperton, "It's an obvious choice. Our exclusive studies show that
for college administrators, a student's knowledge of Turkmenistan reads
like a road map of likely college success." When asked what the hell he
was talking about, Caperton, the former Democratic governor of West
Virginia, digressed into a long-winded explanation, eventually admitting that the new section was just The Board "having a little harmless
fun."

The appointment of a Republican "co-president" to serve with Caperton:
Caperton noted, "We may be the largest monopoly in America, but to
be accused of cultural bias would just be devastating beyond belief."
(Note: In the above remark, Caperton's tone was A) composed yet
unassuming, not C) pedantic and iniquitous.)

And finally, the fee for the test will be doubled from $45 to $90:
Asked how The College Board came to this decision, which has the
likely result of making the test beyond the means of some low-income
students, Caperton shrugged and responded nonchalantly, "Who's

gonna stop us?" When this reporter made the mistake of suggesting it might be cultural bias, Caperton abruptly left the room, tears streaming down his face.

Meanwhile, a day after one of the most important presidential elections in history, few students in Westchester County have any idea who won. They're more concerned about the new SAT. Said one highly motivated junior at Horace Greeley High School, "I used to have 12 tutors; now I'm going to have 13."

THE RITE OF SPRING
ALEXANDRA FRANKLIN, 17

JACKSON PREPARATORY SCHOOL
JACKSON, MS
TEACHER: PAUL SMITH

I have seen her spray perfume into the hollow of her white throat. It is impossibly lovely and thrilling as a secret to know that she holds the sandalwood and rose, there, in the kissable niche between the prows of each collarbone. Her heart lives there too, quickening and beating. I have never seen anyone else drink tea the way she does—eagerly, desperately, as if she has fallen in love with the eggshell bottom of the teacup and misses its stained face. She has a habit of watching the pot while she waits for her water to boil. She's encouraging it, letting it warm up for its audience of one.

You're not supposed to watch it, I say. *It'll never boil, and then I'll have to stay here all afternoon. All night. I love you*, I say. *I wish you loved me.*

I don't say that. I wonder what would happen if I did. I count down from five and back up again, each time expecting to hear my voice saying *I love you*. I expect to hear it drowning out the symphony pouring from the radio on the table. The radio is old, made out of scratched mahogany and looks like a little church. Its thin screens like cathedral windows are seething Stravinsky.

"*The Rite of Spring*," she says suddenly, and the radio announcer echoes her. "It's a ballet."

"Did you. . ."

"No," she says absently, rolling her ankles back against the kitchen cabinet. She rises on her toes a few times and pulls her cinnamon hair away from her neck in a damp mass. "I've never danced it. It's not a real ballet. It's pretty radical. Pretty. . . you know. It's weird."

"It sounds beautiful."

"No," she says strangely, giving me a sideways glance. "It doesn't. Not at all. Didn't you hear the dissonance in the beginning?"

I wasn't listening, I was memorizing the freckles on your shoulder and the pale scar on your right hand, and I was wondering why I never asked you how you got that scar. I was thinking that maybe that was the key the whole time, that scar, and knowing, and if I had only asked...

"You have to have dissonance to have harmony," I say, and immediately my ears turn red. I sound like some sort of greeting card, but not really, because Hallmark has not wised up to the divorce market yet.

She laughs appreciatively. "I guess, sometimes. Did you bring the papers? Do you want some tea?"

I am momentarily stunned by her abrupt shift in direction. I accept the cup of Earl Grey and take out the smooth sheath of documents that spent most of the preceding month in the glove compartment of my car.

She stands behind me to read over my shoulder. "You haven't signed yet?"

I am defensive. "Why rush things? We rushed into a lot of things. Why rush into this?"

Her bow-shaped lips part slightly, revealing a pale line of her straight teeth (she still had braces in our wedding pictures, and even now, I think, she has only been without them for a month or two). There is a tiny beautiful chip on one of her front teeth. I know she is going to say something and I am going to break and sign my name on the line next to hers, but she does not say what I expect. Instead she asks, "Have you been dating?"

"Yes," I tell her. "Remember your roommate during our sophomore year?"

She looks surprised, but she laughs again. Her lightness vexes me in ways I cannot explain or justify. "She is not your type."

I know that. I really do, and I am not prepared to deny it. But I deny it anyway. "I don't know. She's nice. We got along well."

What I mean, of course, is that she kept drinking wine as long as I kept ordering it, so she was happy, and she was a quiet drunk, so I was happy. By the end of the evening, I only had to call a cab for her before walking to my short-term apartment 16 blocks away. All things considered, I sustained fairly little damage from the outing, except for the cost of multiple bottles of Chardonnay.

"Okay," she says, skeptical but smiling. "So sign. Just get it over with."

I see nothing to gain from stalling, so I sign the paper, and she waves it triumphantly overhead. "See? Was that so hard? You're still alive, aren't you?"

Am I? Is this living?

"How is Kate?" I ask cordially. Kate is the year-old collie we bought on a whim while on our honeymoon.

"Bad," she says. "Good, I mean, but she is bad. She's still chewing on everything." Her long body falls into a tense triangle with the wall; her slender-fingered hands clasp loosely around the teacup. I had forgotten how much tea she drinks. "She's with my mother right now. You're not upset that I have full custody, are you?"

"I hate that dog," I say tenderly. I choke on the last few sips of my tea. "I should go."

"You probably should," she agrees. Her eyes soften and her lips part again, hesitating, and one hand rises to the translucent pink shell of her ear. We pause for a moment. "Okay." She smiles affirmatively.

I love you.

"Thanks for coming by."

Okay. I love you.

On my way downstairs to the lobby, I bruise my hand between the rungs of the banister. It's an accident. It's all a happy accident. The doorman looks at me sympathetically, and for some reason I'm having trouble flagging down a cab today.

INSOMNIA
KATHY ZHOU, 15
PLAINVIEW HIGH SCHOOL
ARDMORE, OK
TEACHER: RHUI ZHOU

Of the two of them, she has the worse insomnia. It's not really caused by anything; she's just unable to close her eyes at night. On nights like these, it's like her thoughts are on fast forward or rewind; the colors spin by like billions of pixels of refracted crystal devouring her mind and her dreams. On nights like these, she drifts around the apartment like a ghost, like a—

"—vampire. You're a damn vampire. Get some sleep, will you? You're driving me nuts."

It's him. Mickey. Mickey the amnesiac, the anemic, the narcoleptic. Mickey who forgets who he is in the mornings; takes hour-long showers; and believes in living in the moment, Shakespeare in the basement, and coffee creamer. Despite his lapsing narcolepsy, he's awake every night until she falls asleep. He claims he can't sleep with her wandering around, but on nights like these, he makes his coffee black and hot while she generously tips sugar and creamer in hers (tonight *dulce de leche*, tomorrow hazelnut biscotti).

"Why are you still awake?" he asks, voice slightly groggy, eyes slightly puffy. He gulps absentmindedly from his slightly chipped Mickey Mouse mug, not even seeming to notice the scalding liquid he is pouring down his throat.

She shrugs and wets her lips from her own Superman mug. Even though his complaints are frequent and loud, his company is appreciated. There is something about his presence, the way he pulls a blank sheet of lined paper from an errant folder with fumbling fingers and looks at her expectantly from the piano.

She sits down next to him and plays a few notes, then a trill. He answers with a chord. Chord, note, harmonization, point, counterpoint. It goes on like this until they stumble on a melody—this time a jazzy tune that trips and stumbles over the keys of the piano. As his long-fingered hands drift over the keys lethargically, she hums along, something intimate and raspy. Her own hands dance sporadically over black and white on the upbeat.

Usually, it's quiet except for the piano and the soft snores of their dog, but tonight, it's raining. The liquid sound of the rain is like a soft blanket blurring the night and setting a cool breeze whistling through the humid summer heat. Rain drips from the eaves and spatters on the balcony, intrusive and yet belonging—creating an erratic rhythm that slips easily in and out of the wave of the music.

Mickey stops playing and glances at her watch and then her. "It's three in the morning. Can you sleep now?"

She bites her lower lip and shakes her head silently. He sighs and steps outside. She doesn't stop him. Instead, she lightly fingers a lone daisy in a vase that forms a singular arch above the piano.

"You're supposed to be quitting," she says when she finally joins him out on the balcony. A solitary thread of smoke drifts past the falling raindrops. "Your voice."

He smiles sadly at her before snuffing the stub out on the wet balcony railing.

"And you're supposed to be sleeping."

She looks at the shine of his eyes, the skin stretched so taut and thin over the space between his collarbones. She wonders if it will rupture if he breathes too hard—if she memorizes the translucent color and thinks too often of the life pumping beneath it.

Standing on the balcony in her bare feet, she feels he's just a little more real than the rest of them; he cares a little bit more; he loves just a little bit more recklessly. The rainwater splashes on her toes and trickles between them to tickle at the bottoms of her feet while he inhales what is left of the musty smoke mixed with the tangy rain-saturated air.

She likes to wear t-shirts out in the snow to make him mad and he likes to drink enough coffee to send him through the roof. He falls asleep in the shower so that she has to go in before he drowns or uses all the hot water. He filches her pants to wear and looks so good in them she's obliged to give them to him. He sings in his sleep. And when it comes to it, he steals her kisses at four in the morning.

She knows when they go back inside, he'll set his lips on her gently and he'll taste like stolen drags from a Marlboro and black coffee. They'll fall asleep tangled together on the piano bench and she'll whisper in his ear as the rain makes their world just a little lonelier: *Someday, I'll do something silly. Someday, I'll tell you that I love you.*

HOPE
NICOLE THOMASON, 14
DOERRE INTERMEDIATE SCHOOL
KLEIN, TX
TEACHER: KATHY SHIPPER

Slowly, almost cautiously, I open my eyes. The many machines in the room hum softly, singing an odd, mechanical song. I exhale slowly, waiting.

But nothing comes.

No pain. No hurt.

Which is a nice change; I figure that I probably haven't woken up completely yet, and so I can't feel the tingling, scratching, near numbness in my leg.

All I can feel is a deep, gaping hole in the back of my head. Or maybe it's my heart. As of now, I can't tell which.

    *   *   *

A scream caught itself in my throat. So much smoke. . . I coughed, my lungs feeling as if they were about to explode.

Asphyxiations, I thought grimly. How ironic that as I'm trapped in a burning room, all I can think about is my vocabulary word from last week.

I dove to the floor, a soft whimper escaping my lips, as one of the strong, wooden beams that lined my ceiling fell to the floor with a crash. Flames engulfed the wood, and I backed up, sending anxious glances to the door.

My mind screamed at me, *Blocked. It's blocked. . .*

    *   *   *

They don't know I'm awake, I can tell. They never talk about me when I'm awake.

I can hear them whispering. They say that my chances are slim and that I'm probably going to die. Not that I hadn't already figured that out on my own. I don't even know why I'm even fighting anymore; I should just let it go, let myself slip away.

But I can't. Part of me still wants to live. I want to feel the warm sun, have the grass tickle the bottom of my feet, and smell dinner cooking on the stove.

It's strange how when the end seems near, it's the simple things in life that matter the most.

*   *   *

I ran in the direction of the window.

It's my last hope, my last hope. . . I thought. The door was blocked by a pile of fallen wood, and although I'd never know for sure, I'd guessed that even larger flames were behind it. Right now, they were probably licking the dry wood, waiting until the right moment to break through.

My vision obscured by the thick smoke, I reached my hand out warily, hoping and wishing that my fingers would touch the thick glass window and not a burning splinter of wood. What seemed like an eternity passed as I walked blindly through my room, each second seemed to weigh me down and kill my chances of finding the window.

Soon, I felt my fingers brush a wall. Relief seeped through me as I quickly pulled myself closer to it, inching my way across the wall, trying to stay as low as possible.

Hesitantly, I reached my hand out sideways. . . and touched glass.

*   *   *

"How is she?" a quiet voice asks. The response is mumbled, and I can't make out the words.

I open my eyes, curious as to who is talking, and then shut them again quickly, not wanting anyone to know I was awake. But they notice. They don't come over to me, just hesitate, and I listen closely as heavy footsteps head toward the door. Grudgingly, I give in and open my eyes.

The doctor is gone, and I can see his shadow through the glass door. The nurse is still here though, flipping through a folder filled with papers. She's trying to smile, but it looks forced. Just like it always does. Whenever I see her she has this big, fake-looking smile plastered on her face. I think she uses it only around me. It's probably some psychology junk. Maybe, if people are smiling, it's supposed to make you feel better.

Yeah, right.

I hate it. I hate it when she smiles.

Actually, I'm more jealous of the fact that she's lucky enough to have a reason to smile.

She's not the one lying in a hospital bed.

*   *   *

I nearly died of relief as I fumbled around for the latch. There was a chance. If I could just get the window open. . .

The fire crept ever closer, each second my lungs gasped for air, each breath made them hurt even more as they filled with thick smoke.

Just don't look back, I told myself, don't look back.

But the heat on my back just kept getting stronger, and I could see flames out of the corner of my eye. Large, menacing flames, waiting for the right moment to pounce and devour me like a wild animal.

Something wrapped around my leg, but I barely felt anything. The only emotion I even came close to feeling was panic.

My fingers grasped the latch tightly, and I pushed it open. By now, the flames were right on my back, only a thin sliver of space separating them from me. But I could see the sky. In that one, quick second, I'd seen the sky. I couldn't help but grin.

Then there was a loud crack, a thump as I felt something hit me, and then nothing. Simply nothing.

All around me, there was just blackness that stretched on for forever. I felt blind, blind and deaf, but at the same time strangely calm.

*   *   *

As I lie in the hospital bed, I start to regret things. Like how I'd always complained. The rules were too strict, I couldn't do anything. . . ff it wasn't one thing it was another. I don't regret feeling the way I did. Nothing could have changed the way I felt, but I regret all the complaining. In an odd way, the complaining just seemed to make me feel even worse.

And I'd shoved my problems ont others. They'd all had their own problems, and I'd intruded on their privacy, bothering them with my trivial, petty problems.

How I'd wanted to escape. It would have been nice to get away, to have a place where I could just be me. I'd always felt. . . trapped. A prisoner to my own mind.

Sure, I'd wanted to escape from all those feelings, escape from the pressure.

I felt none of that now.

But I'd take all of those emotions plus some back just to stand on my two feet and get out of this hospital.

*　　　　　*　　　　　*

Instantly, I was shoved back to consciousness, thrust from the black abyss into a world filled with color and noise.

It was all a blur from then on. I felt myself being strapped to some sort of moving stretcher and thrust into an ambulance. My mind kept drifting, and I wasn't really sure if I was conscious, or if this was all some sort of twisted nightmare.

There was a rush of sirens, which seemed dull compared to the thoughts that rattled around in my brain. People surrounded me, each face blurring into another, my eyes crossing from what was probably exhaustion.

And then a calm voice broke through the noise. "Rest. You will be all right."

*　　　　　*　　　　　*

I feel relieved as the nurse tells me that my family is going to be alright.

I don't ask because I know that she doesn't know. But the question bothers me. . . *Will I be all right?*

And then I know the answer.

It's my choice. I can fight, I can keep holding on, or I can give up and let myself go.

But I want to live.

For I still have hope. Somewhere deep inside of me, there's hope.

They can take everything from me, tell me all the numbers that show how low my chances are, but I'll always have hope.

Hope's all that's gotten me this far, because without hope I'd be dead right now.

Only now do I realize that hope is more than just a word.

TATTOO
LORETTA LOPEZ, 17

AMERICAN SCHOOL FOUNDATION OF GUADALAJARA
GUADALAJARA, MEXICO
TEACHER: CRISTINA FAULKNER

The cursive writing on his back tells a story of a late night full of loneliness and boredom. I ask if he regrets it.

He sighs and wraps a towel around his wet body.

"A little." His typical candor is absent. I feel I have known him for a long time after a few hours but realize that this conversation will be bounded by this afternoon. His scarcity makes the words that drift along the pool special. He probably will not let me know him for long so I ask questions eagerly in hope of remembering him vividly.

"Why did you get it done?"

" I was just curious I guess." His smile tells me otherwise. It meant something at some time: *Rocío García Sanchez*.

"Who is she?"

"An old friend. We don't talk anymore." His fingers play with each other, signaling that I should talk of something that does not make him dive into a distant and regretted past.

"Good thing it's on my back, that way I don't have to stare at it all the time." He grins showing white teeth.

I have heard that name before, maybe whispered in hallways of our school, and maybe shouted through the streets in search of a girl who deserved to be engraved in swirls on rich brown skin.

His eyes grow sad for a few seconds, drifting toward the cool drops sweating down his beer bottle. The sun makes his skin beautiful while only making mine burn into a shade of uncomfortable red.

He takes a sip, distancing himself from the awkwardness I have created, and I suddenly feel ashamed for trying to squeeze out the secrets.

The pool shimmers, and I sink my feet into the tempting water, allowing him to remember the name in silence.

Rocío García Sanchez lives on his back; she is a heavy pair of wings that do not inspire flight. She keeps him on pavement, making his every step linger, eliminating the leaps from his agile body.

Sometimes he can feel the cursive handwriting on his back, sore like the first day he wore her. He remembers that tingling pain too well, even though it has been a couple of years that he has grown out of that 15-year-old drunk on adrenaline and passion.

I take my feet, now wrinkled and bland, out of the water. The sun has faded a little, and slowly grey clouds start to appear, demonstrating our lack remaining time.

"You must have really loved her."

"Love. . . I don't even know what that means. Everyone says it all the time. I love your shirt, I love that show, I love you. What does it matter anyway? Maybe when it's real you don't have to say it."

I smile at his words, and realize I have never been in love before and neither has he.

SPECIAL THANKS

25,000 DEDICATED TEACHERS for motivating their students to participate in The Scholastic Art & Writing Awards.

REGIONAL AFFILIATES for uniting communities to celebrate creative youth.

LOCAL AND NATIONAL JURORS for lending their time and energy to emerging artists and writers.

VIRGINIA PFAEHLER (ALUMNA, 2008) for selecting the authors featured in this year's anthology.

PHILIP PEARLSTEIN (ALUMNUS, 1941 AND 1942) for inspiring young artists to follow in his footsteps.

THANE ROSENBAUM (ALUMNUS, 1976) for his commitment to the development of creative teenagers and encouragement of their work.

TOM OTTERNESS (ALUMNUS, 1971) for sharing his time, talent, and experience with the next generation of young artists and writers.

STEVE DIAMOND (ALUMNUS, 1971) for his unwavering commitment to the Alliance for Young Artists & Writers.

ELIE WIESEL for offering words of advice and praise to young writers.

JESSE EISENBERG for contributing his talents to honoring young writers.

THE NATIONAL WRITING PROJECT and the **NATIONAL ART EDUCATION ASSOCIATION** for helping expand the reach of The Scholastic Writing Awards throughout the country.

OVATION TV for their creativity, dedication and commitment to our national award winners.

THE MAURICE R. ROBINSON FUND for having a vision and creating an opportunity to identify young artists and writers through The Scholastic Art & Writing Awards.

ABOUT THE AUTHORS

LANE BAKER couples his love of medieval and historical fiction with a desire to expose the emotions and humanity of the actual raid on Lindisfarne in 793 AD. With this piece, he wishes to convey the sense of gratitude that the main character, James, eventually gains. Currently a freshman, he aspires to become a full-time author after graduation.

CELIA BELL is a senior at Byrn Mawr School. She believes in the importance of firmly situating herself in an environment that inspires her. *The Impossible Fate of William Minnafee,* based largely on a South Carolina island, conveys the transition from childhood to adulthood and the loss of innocence that accompanies it. In the future, she wishes to travel and perhaps join a service corps.

THORNTON BLEASE is a home-schooled sophomore. His piece was inspired by the obstacles artists must overcome to pursue their dreams. In ten years he sees himself as not only a published novelist, but also as a socially conscious writer.

NOOR BRARA will be a senior at the American Embassy School in New Delhi, India. She believes that words in particular invite the eyes and minds of everyone to begin reading without a conscious consent. She hopes to pursue a career as a literary magazine editor in Manhattan.

BENJAMIN COPAN is a junior at Wellington Community High School in Wellington, Florida. Inspired by Robert Pinsky's work, Benjamin seeks to unmask the mistakes and ridiculousness that professionalism often conceals. In ten years, he plans to be a chemist, a physicist, an economist, a number theorist, a writer, or some exotic combination thereof.

EMILY CORWIN will be a freshman in college. Her poetry is heavily influenced by Francesca Lia Block. She credits Kenyon's Young Writers Workshop for encouraging her talent. Whether her future holds a demanding day working in a third-grade classroom or helping out in a college counseling office, she will always make time for poetry.

MARISSA DEARING will be a sophomore at Maret School. After spending six weeks in Morocco, she was inspired to recognize the shared humanity of the global community. Morocco's exotic appeal sparked her desire to increase the world's awareness of interconnectivity and to lessen the suffering in that region of the world.

WILL DODGE will be a freshman at the Charleston County School of the Arts. When people read his poem, he wants them to recognize the narrator in a person they know or in themselves. He hopes to work for a music and culture magazine in Portland, Oregon.

JARED DUMMITT will be a freshman at the University of Chicago. His portfolio was inspired by the everyday actions of his grandfather, sister, and twin brother, and how these actions shaped their relationships with the world. He is trying to leave his possibilities for the next ten years as open as possible.

KAILANA DURNAN will be a freshman at Bowdoin College in Maine. Her piece was inspired by her great aunt Sabra, an avid bird lover and vibrantly emotive person. In ten years, she hopes to build more subtle, complex stories into her poetry.

ANNA ENZWEILER will be a college freshman. She hopes that her readers can gain an appreciation for the beauty of the world around them and the people that populate it. In ten years, she hopes to be a freelance writer and a college English or creative writing professor.

ALEXANDRA FRANKLIN is a senior at Jackson Prepatory School. Her piece was inspired by conversations overheard while passing strangers on the sidewalk. She would like readers to plumb the depths of silence in order to better understand literature. In ten years, she will be living happily with a typewriter, a blender, and many books.

EMMA FUNK is a sophomore in Fairbanks, Alaska. She is inspired by the struggle between the desire for maturity and the lingering wistfulness for childhood. In ten years, she hopes that she will learn to relax, or at least to find more joy in failure.

MEGAN GLASCOCK will be a high school freshman in Whitefish, Montana. Her piece strives to convey the Montana scenery to people unfamiliar with the state's natural beauty. In ten years, she hopes to be a successfully published author.

MELINA GOTERA is a junior at Cedar Falls High School in Cedar Falls, Iowa. Her poem recounts historical events using lyrical images.

ABIGAIL HERTZLER graduated from Lancaster Mennonite High School in Marietta, PA. She will be attending Goshen College in Goshen, Indiana where she will be majoring in Environmental Studies and minoring in writing. Her interest in horses and horseracing led her to a group of likeminded equine aficionados and inspired this play, her first stab at dramatic writing.

PAULINE HOLDSWORTH will be a freshman at the University of Toronto. Places inspire her most: the places people speed by on the highway and the sign posts to places people will never go. Ten years from now, she plans to be traveling and writing. She hopes that somewhere in her words, readers will find something that reminds them of themselves.

FILIPA IOANNOU attends Hunter College High School in New York City. Her poem illustrates the simple objects in life from which individuals gain great meaning.

CLARE IRALU is an eighth-grader in Gallup, New Mexico. After studying ancient civilizations in school, she was intrigued by Ariadne's perspective. She aspires to be a middle-school art teacher.

AUBREY ISAACSON will be a freshman at Coastal Carolina University in South Carolina. In her piece, she took a traditional lifestyle and added mental instability to throw off the household balance. She wants the main character's reality to haunt the reader. Ten years from now, she hopes to continue examining the underlying truth within humans.

DONTE JEFFERSON attends Lusher Charter School in New Orleans, Louisiana. He writes about the difficulty of having a mixed family.

KAITLIN JENNRICH is a high school freshman in New Glarus, Wisconsin. Her piece was inspired by boring Algebra classes and seemingly useless fire drills. She believes that the best stories are ones in which the readers recognizes themselves. In ten years, she sees herself going on long walks under the guise of "looking for inspiration," when, really, she will just be procrastinating.

SARA KASSEL lives in Hinesburg, Vermont. Astrology and Wallace Stevens inspired her piece, which she hopes will lead readers to question the choices they make. In ten years, she hopes to be either traveling or part of an alternative satellite school teaching any number of subjects.

LORETTA LOPEZ attends the American School Foundation of Guadalajara in Mexico. Her piece was inspired by a conversation with a tattooed foreigner. In ten years, she sees herself as happy, proud, and writing every day for hours.

WILL MANTELL attends Horace Greeley High School in New York City. His piece comments on the monopoly a certain company lords over the standardized testing business.

ALICE MARKHAM-CANTOR attends the Writopia Lab in New York City. She utilizes an unique perspective—that of an elderly woman—in her short story.

LINDSEY MAXON will be a freshman in the University of Texas at Arlington Plan II Honors Program. Multiple flights above the Southwest inspired her to write about the desert from a different perspective. She hopes that readers will realize that there is always a new way to look at the world. In ten years, she sees herself working on a novel and living either in a big city or a small town in Arizona.

YONI NACHMANY attends Hunter College High School in New York City. He was inspired by a recent Passover Seder he celebrated with his Israeli relatives. His goal was to express the struggle between balancing his Israeli and American identities. He cannot see himself in any particular place in ten years, but knows he will continue learning.

EUNJU NAMKUNG will be a freshman at Yale University. Her piece delves into the father-daughter dynamic in a family with traditional values.

KAREN NIEWOEHNER will be a freshman at Minnesota State University-Moorhead. Her science fiction story is based on Bermuda Triangle theories. In ten years, she sees herself in either a writing or editing career.

MOLLY O'NEILL is a senior at Greenwich Academy in Connecticut. When she discovered that the strict form of a sonnet could keep her entertained in physics class, she enjoyed mixing traditional forms and modern themes. She hopes to live a thoughtful yet adventurous life that has a positive impact on the world.

ADRIAN PASKEY will be a junior at Boiling Springs High School in Pennsylvania. His grandfather's influence and his passion for music combined to produce his essay. If nothing else, he wants readers to be mindful of the gifts given to them by their families. He aspires to become a doctor.

AMERICA PEREZ attends Colorado Academy in Denver, Colorado. Her poetry incorporates elements of English and Spanish to convey her family's story.

CHELLI RIDDIOUGH deferred enrollment at Williams College to travel to El Salvador, New Zealand, and Holland. Each piece in her portfolio was inspired by a sense of discontent. She would like readers to realize that they are surrounded by people, each with their own problems, life, and perspective. In ten years, she sees herself living in a big city and wearing a lot of black.

AYESHA SENGUPTA is attending the University of Cambridge. She is inspired by her own imagination and the inability to reign in her emotions. She believes that writing feels like setting up a corridor of mirrors which reflect and distort, and that the real world is to be seen in each one of them. In ten years, she will speak of being a scientist, but think of herself as a writer.

HARI SRINIVASAN of Cupertino, California believes that people's differing abilities should not limit their ability to share experiences and inspiration. For most of his life he was trapped in a silent zone—then he learned to type. While he hopes to be contributing to the field of Autism research in ten years, he also plans to continue his exploration of language through creative writing.

AUSTYN SULLIVAN will be a freshman at Evergreen State College in Olympia, Washington. His memoir is a reflection on grief, suicide, and responsibility. He wants readers to realize that parts of a person are lost in the death of the ones they love, but that what is never taken away is their ability to love them. He hopes to help people with the knowledge of his own experiences.

NICOLE THOMASON is a high school freshman from Spring, Texas. She was inspired while helping her neighbors clean up their house after it caught fire. She hopes that readers will see how much a positive outlook can affect their lives. Ten years from now, she sees herself in medical school, training to be a doctor.

ALBA TOMASULA Y GARCIA will be a freshman at the University of Chicago working towards a Master's degree in Animal Studies. She was inspired by a trend she noticed in some people to ignore or deemphasize the harm that environmental degradation can cause. She wants readers to realize that humans are not immune to the changes in the world.

YADIRIS VALDEZ attends the DreamYard Program at Arturo Toscanini Junior/Senior High School. Her piece describes her ideal poem.

XUEYOU WANG will be a senior at Hillcrest High School in Utah. She would like readers to identify with Anja and meditate on the meaning of her choices. In ten years, she sees herself as a hopefully-published (yet possibly starving) screenwriter, novelist, or poet.

LAURA WEISS will be a freshman at Oberlin College. She hopes that after digesting her piece, readers will examine the often sexist content of the media with a shrewder eye. In ten years, she hopes to be a full-time writer in all forms of media.

ANNA WONG will be a freshman in Richmond, Virginia. Visiting her great aunt inspired her piece. She would like readers to realize that they should be the person they want to be every day that they can. Ten years from now, she will be in the midst of pursuing two things: publication and a husband.

LAUREN YOUNGSMITH lives in Denver, Colorado. She was inspired to construct a better sense of her personal history by examining the tragedies of her family. She would like to change the way people look at negativity and misfortune. In ten years, she hopes to be a published author, have art in galleries, and perhaps become a tattoo artist.

YVONNE YU lives in Hong Kong, China. Her portfolio was an attempt to acknowledge the captivating qualities of death, then lighten them up so as not to be consumed by them. She wants readers to be able to find the beauty in tragedy without making it their entire world. In ten years, she hopes to live near an aquarium, edit a literary arts magazine, and be happy.

ANDREW ZABELA, JR., lives in Chicago, Illinois. He was inspired by the beauty and nature of his town. The next ten years of his life will be spent improving as a writer.

KATHY ZHOU is a sophomore at Plainview High School in Ardmore, Oklahoma. Her short story describes a relationship that thrives in the hours when sleep is unavailable, and two people who are good for each other even when they are not at their best.

REGIONAL AFFILIATES

REGIONAL AFFILIATE NETWORK OF
THE ALLIANCE FOR YOUNG ARTISTS & WRITERS

The Alliance partners with Regional Affiliates nationwide that coordinate The Scholastic Art & Writing Awards at the local level. Public school systems, state education agencies, teacher organizations, art museums, arts councils, libraries, private foundations, businesses, and nonprofit organizations in the Network share a deep commitment to recognizing the creative achievement of young artists and writers in their areas. The Alliance is grateful to the following organizations and donors for their efforts to further the Alliance mission of motivating, validating and encouraging young artists and writers in their communities.

WRITING REGION-AT-LARGE

To provide opportunities for students in areas of the country without Regional Affiliates, the Alliance for Young Artists & Writers administers the Region-at-Large Scholastic Writing Awards. Students in the Region-at-Large submit work for preliminary level judging, and esteemed jurors from across the country evaluate the students' works. The most outstanding works receive Gold Keys and are forwarded to the national level of judging.

Regional Affiliate Organizations & Sponsors

The Alliance would like to thank the Regional Affiliates listed on the following pages and their donors for coordinating The Scholastic Art & Writing Awards in their areas.

California
San Francisco Unified School District
San Francisco Writing Region

___

Florida
Miami–Dade County Public Schools and The Miami–Dade County Fair & Exposition (The Fair)
Miami-Dade Writing Region

___

Indiana & Ohio
Fort Wayne Museum of Art
Northeast Indiana and Northwest Ohio Writing Region
Additional Sponsors: JP Morgan Chase and News-Sentinel

___

Kentucky
Department of English, Northern Kentucky University, College of Arts and Sciences
Northern Kentucky Writing Region
Additional Sponsors: Northern Kentucky University Department of English, Northern Kentucky University College of Arts and Sciences, Staples, Inc., and Thomas More College

___

Mississippi
Eudora Welty Foundation
Mississippi Writing Region

___

MISSOURI

Prairie Lands Writing Project at Missouri Western State University
Missouri Writing Region
Additional Sponsors: Missouri Writing Projects Network and Missouri
  Association of Teachers of English

———

NEVADA

Nevada Foundation for the Arts
Southern Nevada Writing Region
Additional Sponsors: College of Southern Nevada Image Gallery, Nevada State
College, Art Institutes of Las Vegas, CCSD School-Community Partnership
Office, Plaza Gallery, Lied Discovery Children's Museum, SouthwestUSA
Bank, Brand Inc. (see complete list at www.nevadafoundationarts.org)

———

NEW YORK

Alliance for Young Artists & Writers, Inc.
New York City Writing Region
Additional Sponsors: Scholastic Inc., The New York Times Company, and
Command Web Offset

———

NORTH CAROLINA

Public Library of Charlotte & Mecklenburg County
Mid-Carolina Writing Region

———

PENNSYLVANIA

Lancaster County Public Library
Lancaster County Writing Region

Waynesburg College
Southwestern Pennsylvania Writing Region
Additional Sponsors: CONSOL Energy, Pennsylvania Rural Arts Alliance,
Community Foundation of Greene County, Observer Reporter, and friends of the
arts in Greene, Fayette, and Washington Counties

TEXAS

Harris County Department of Education

Harris County Writing Region

Additional Sponsors: Texas Art Supply, Women in the Visual and Literary Arts, Indo-American Charity Foundation, Glassell Junior School of Art, Museum of Fine Art Houston, Houston Chronicle, and Barnes & Noble Booksellers

———

VERMONT

Great River Arts Institute

Vermont Writing Region

———

VIRGINIA

The Visual Arts Center of Richmond

Metro Area Richmond Writing Region

NEW WRITING AFFILIATES 2009-2010

The Alliance is pleased to announce a record number of new Writing Regional Affiliates in 2010. Thanks to these new partners, The Awards will affect the lives of thousands more students across the country:

CALIFORNIA

California Writing Project

California Writing Region

———

FLORIDA

Blue Planet Writers' Room

Palm Beach Writing Region

———

ILLINOIS
Chicago Area Writing Project
Chicago Writing Region
___

INDIANA
Clowes Memorial Hall of Butler University and Hoosier Writing Project
Central/Southern Indiana Writing Region
___

MASSACHUSETTS
New England Art Education Conference, Inc.
Massachusetts Writing Region
___

MAINE
Southern Maine Writing Project
Maine Writing Region
___

NEVADA
Sierra Arts Foundation
Northern Nevada Writing Region
___

NEW YORK
Casita Maria Center for Arts Education
New York City Writing Region
___

OKLAHOMA
Tulsa Community College
Oklahoma Writing Region
___

PENNSYLVANIA
Philadelphia Arts in Education Partnership (PAEP) at the
University of the Arts
Philadelphia Writing Region

WISCONSIN
Still Water's Collective
Milwaukee Writing Region

IOWA MUTLI STATE WRITING REGION
The Connie Belin & Jacqueline N. Bank International Center for Gifted Education and Talent Development
Serving the following states: *Arkansas, Colorado, Idaho, Iowa, Kansas, Michigan, Minnesota, Montana, North Dakota, South Dakota,* and *Wyoming.*
Serving parts of the following states: *Illinois, Kentucky, Nebraska,* and *Wisconsin.*

PARTNERSHIP OPPORTUNITIES

SUPPORT THE CREATIVE ACHIEVEMENT OF YOUNG WRITERS: JOIN THE REGIONAL AFFILIATE NETWORK OF THE ALLIANCE FOR YOUNG ARTISTS & WRITERS

By joining the Regional Affiliate Network, your organization can:
- Increase opportunities for teenagers to receive regional and national recognition for their creative talent, publish their works, and receive scholarships;
- Create connections among students, teachers, schools, and language arts organizations in your community;
- Enhance your organization's visibility as part of a longstanding national network that supports young writers.

For more information on becoming a Regional Affiliate of the Alliance for Young Artists & Writers, please contact Kat Hendrix at khendrix@artandwriting.org or 212.343.7774.

ALLIANCE SCHOLARSHIP PARTNERS

The Alliance would also like to thank the colleges and universities that provide scholarships to national Scholastic Art & Writing Awards recipients in writing categories. These include: Adelphi University, Bard College, Bennington College, Bruton Parker College, Chatham University, College of Mount. St. Joseph, University of Maine at Farmington, Kansas State University, Kenyon College, and Salem College. To learn more about the Alliance Scholarship Provider Network, please contact Alex Tapnio at atapnio@artandwriting.org or 212.343.7613.

ABOUT THE ALLIANCE FOR YOUNG ARTISTS & WRITERS

The Alliance for Young Artists & Writers, established in 1994, is a nonprofit organization that identifies America's most creative teens through the presentation of The Scholastic Art & Writing Awards. The Awards are the largest, most prestigious and longest-running scholarship and recognition program for teenage artists and writers. Presented annually since 1923, The Awards are credited with identifying the early promise of Andy Warhol, Truman Capote, Sylvia Plath, Joyce Carol Oates, Richard Avedon, Zac Posen and many others. Through partnerships with regional affiliates across the United States, the Alliance works with communities of scholars, artists and educators to administer the program locally. The most outstanding works are reviewed by notable alumni and experts, and winning students are provided with opportunities for recognition, exhibition, publication, professional development, and scholarships. The Alliance also collaborates with colleges across the country to leverage an additional $3.9 million in financial aid for award recipients who demonstrate exceptional promise. To learn more, visit us at **www.artandwriting.org.**

Special recognition opportunities include:

THE NATIONAL ART EXHIBITION OF THE SCHOLASTIC ART & WRITING AWARDS, an exhibition held in New York City each June of national award-winning work by America's most talented teenagers;

THE SCHOLASTIC ART & WRITING AWARDS NATIONAL CATALOG, an annual publication that showcases nationally-recognized work;

ONLINE EXHIBITIONS AND ANTHOLOGIES, selections of artwork and writing published online at **www.artandwriting.org.**

ALLIANCE BOARD OF DIRECTORS

ALLIANCE STAFF

Virginia McEnerney, *Executive Director*
Matthew Boyd, *Coordinator,* National Programs
Bryan Doerries, *Associate Executive Director,* Programs
Katherine Hendrix, *Senior Manager,* Regional Affiliates & Partnerships
Ariel Magnes, *Manager,* External Relations
Venas Matthews, *Senior Manager,* External Relations
Nicole McCann, *Project Administrator*
Grace McLean, *Assistant,* Affiliate Network & Outreach
Jessica Schein, *Bookkeeper*
Kerri Schlottman, *Director,* External Relations
Danniel Swatosh, *Manager,* Art & Design
Alex Tapnio, *Senior Manager,* National Programs

Lisa S. Feder-Feitel, Editorial Consultant, *The Best Teen Writing of 2009*

OPPORTUNITIES FOR CREATIVE TEENS

The Scholastic Art & Writing Awards offers early acclaim and scholarship opportunities for creative teenagers. Supported by their visual arts and writing teachers and other community mentors, participants create and submit their best works in any of the following categories:

VISUAL ARTS

Architecture, Comic Art, Ceramics & Glass, Digital Art, Design, Drawing, Fashion, Film & Animation, Jewelry, Mixed Media, Painting, Photography, Printmaking, Sculpture, Video Games, Art Portfolio, Photography Portfolio

WRITING

Dramatic Script, Humor, Journalism, Personal Essay/Memoir, Persuasive Writing, Poetry, Novel Writing, Science Fiction/Fantasy, Short Story, Short Short Story, General Writing Portfolio, Nonfiction Portfolio

NEW CATEGORY FOR 2010

Creativity & Citizenship Award, co-sponsored by the National Constitution Center

Each October, program materials are made available to students in grades 7–12. Fifteen $10,000 scholarships are presented to Portfolio Gold medal recipients and more than $3.9 million in scholarships is made available to National Gold medal winning students.

Visit our Web site at **www.artandwriting.org** to learn more about The Awards, for deadlines and entry information, and to view galleries of national award-winning art and writing.

HOW TO DONATE

SUPPORT THE ALLIANCE FOR YOUNG ARTISTS & WRITERS

Help us continue to celebrate and support our nation's most creative teens. The Alliance for Young Artists & Writers is a nonprofit organization, supported entirely by charitable contributions. Donations help underwrite national and local projects including exhibitions, readings, publications, and scholarship opportunities for young artists and writers in grades 7-12.

Please make a tax-deductible donation today:

By Credit Card
Visit www.artandwriting.org, and click "Support" to make a secure donation.

By Check
Checks should be made out to: Alliance for Young Artists & Writers, and mailed to:

Alliance for Young Artists & Writers
Attn: External Relations
557 Broadway
New York, NY 10012

Donations to the Alliance for Young Artists & Writers are tax-deductible to the fullest extent of the law.

For more information, contact Kerri Schlottman, Director, External Relations, by phone at 212.343.7773 or by email at kschlottman@artandwriting.org